STONEHAM PUBLIC LIBRARY
431 MAIN STREET
STONEHAM, MA 02180

Learning About . . .

The Civil War

Literature and Other Resources
for Young People

■   ■   ■

Elaine C. Stephens and Jean E. Brown

Professors of Teacher Education
Saginaw Valley State University

Linnet Professional Publications—1998

© 1998 Elaine C. Stephens and Jean E. Brown.
All rights reserved.
First published 1998 as a Linnet Professional Publication,
an imprint of The Shoe String Press, Inc.,
North Haven, Connecticut 06473.

The "Learning About . . ." series are annotated teaching resources for use by educators, librarians, and parents in selecting and using literature and other resources for school-age youth in significant areas of the curriculum.

The first book in this series is *Learning About . . . the Holocaust: Literature and Other Resources for Young People* by Elaine C. Stephens, Jean E. Brown, and Janet E. Rubin (1995).

Learning About . . . the Civil War: Literature and Other Resources for Young People is the second title.

Library of Congress Cataloging-in-Publication Data

Stephens, Elaine C.
    Learning about—the Civil War: literature and other resources
for young people / Elaine C. Stephens and Jean E. Brown.
      p.   cm.
    Includes index.
    ISBN 0-208-02449-2 (lib. bdg.: alk. paper)
    ISBN 0-208-02464-6 (trade pbk.: alk. paper)
    1. United States—History—Civil War, 1861–1865—Juvenile
literature—Bibliography.   2. United States—History—
Civil War, 1861–1865—Study and teaching (Primary)
3. United States—History—Civil War, 1861–1865—
Study and teaching (Secondary)
I. Brown, Jean E. II. Title.
Z1242.S74   1998
[E468]
016.9737—dc21   98-14569
                                     CIP

The paper in this publication meets the minimum requirements of American National Standard for Information Sciences—Permanence of Paper for Printed Library Materials. ANSI Z39.48–1984. ⊗

Printed in the United States of America

For my grandson, Mitchell Thomas Graham:
May your love of books and learning continue
to grow as you do. ECS

In remembrance of my great grandfathers
William L. Richardson and Joseph Coombs
who served in the Union Army from Maine,
and my great-great grandfather Loring C. Oliver
of the 19th Maine who died at Gettysburg. JEB

Contents

Acknowledgments

A book such as this reflects not only our vision and work, but also the encouragement, support, and inspiration of our many fine students and colleagues. Among the special people we wish to acknowledge are: Robert V. Anderson, Social Studies Coordinator for the Midland Public Schools, Midland, Michigan for his knowledge and insight; Dee Storey, Professor of Teacher Education at Saginaw Valley State University, Michigan for her generosity in lending us reading materials and recommending resources; Dallas Fischer, St. Vincent's School, for his assistance and historical insights; Nadine Burke, Delta College, for her steadfast support and interest; Connie Altimore and Randi Kawakita, teachers in the Midland Public Schools, Midland, Michigan for their perceptive review of an early draft; Ervin Sparapani and Melissa Hayden, colleagues at Saginaw Valley State University, for their interest and encouragement; and David Pugalee for being David.

We also acknowledge our fine editor and president of The Shoe String Press, Diantha Thorpe, whose friendship we value, whose sage advise we heed, and whose faith in us we appreciate; and Nancy McGrath, vice president of the company, who always reassures us with her humor, graciousness, and common sense.

Finally we acknowledge with heartfelt appreciation the steadfast love, support, and encouragement of our family members: Opal, Wes, Melinda, Tom, Griffin, Mary, Vesta, Elmer, Diane, and Frank.

Introduction

The Civil War is the thing that makes America different.
It was our most tremendous experience, and it is not quite
like anything that ever happened to anyone else. The story
of this war needs retelling . . . because it helped to shape
the future of the human race.

Bruce Catton (1988)

We have written this resource book to aid educators, librarians,
and parents in selecting and using literature and other resources
about the Civil War with school-age youth. There is no period of
our history that evokes more interest than the Civil War; no period
whose reverberations are still felt as strongly today. Each year numerous books, films, and videos appear that focus on some aspect
of the Civil War period. The study of the people, events, causes,
and consequences of this era, while concentrated in some areas of
the school curriculum, is also threaded throughout its entirety.

We have focused primarily on children's and young adult literature; adult books are cited in only a few instances. The selections
include fiction, biographies, informational books, picture books,
and poetry. We reviewed over 350 titles to select the more than 170
recommended in this resource guide. Our selection criteria included

literary quality, historical authenticity, effectiveness in fostering an intellectual and emotional connection with the subject, and age appropriateness. We concentrated primarily on newer books—ones that many teachers may be unaware of, but also included a few older books considered to be among the best of their genres. While no guide can be completely comprehensive, it is our hope that the titles and authors recommended in this book will serve as a useful starting point.

How to Use This Book

This resource book is the second in a series of guides. Based on valuable feedback we received from users of the initial volume, *Learning About . . . The Holocaust: Literature and Other Resources for Young People,* we have modified the format to make it easier to use. In chapter 1 we discuss the role of using literature to teach about the Civil War; we also provide information about how to use specific student activities with this literature, whether the curriculum is based on history and social studies, English language arts, or integrated content. Chapters 2 through 7 are organized thematically. These broad themes can be used as is or modified and adapted to meet curriculum objectives and outcomes. While each chapter has a special focus, it is not necessary to go through this guide, chapter by chapter, in sequential order. Material from each chapter can be used by itself or in combination with one or more other chapters. Chapter 8 provides a list of additional resources such as audio recordings, videos, and web sites.

Chapters 2 through 7 begin with an overview of the content of the theme, followed by a feature entitled "Prior to Reading: Think About. . . ." This feature provides questions for students to consider and discuss before reading any of the literature recommended in the chapter. Its purpose is to activate any prior knowledge the readers may possess and arouse their curiosity and interest in the topic. The next section, "Focus Books," alphabetized by author, provides the following information on each book:

1. Bibliographic citation.

2. Quote from the work that can be used to interest young people in reading the book or promote post-reading discussion.

3. "At a Glance"—a brief description of the book that includes a recommendation for the appropriate grade levels.

4. Summary of the book.

5. "Teaching Considerations."

6. "After Reading: Suggested Student Activities."

Following "Focus Books" is another section entitled "More Books" which provides abbreviated information on additional individual titles. Alphabetized by author, each entry consists of the bibliographic citation, summary, and grade level recommendation. The concluding feature of the book, the appendix, "National Standards for United States History," provides a chart showing how each focus book meets the standards. Finally, an author/title index makes it easy for readers to locate specific entries.

A word of caution regarding recommendations for grade level designations is in order. Grade designations should never be strictly adhered to when matching a particular book with a specific young person. A common error committed by adults when selecting books on complex subjects such as the Civil War is to provide students with materials that appear to be at their reading level, but actually require a higher level of intellectual sophistication and emotional maturity to truly grasp. We recommend, therefore, that students be given less complex material to begin with and then, as they acquire a conceptual base of understanding, be introduced to more difficult material. Additionally, there is a wide variation among students within any grade or age level. More important than the grade designation per se is the individual's background knowledge, interest, and maturity.

Throughout this resource guide, we frequently recommend that teachers at all levels read aloud short excerpts from a book to their classes. Such teacher read-alouds help to develop student interest, provoke curiosity, provide a common base of information, and create a shared learning experience. Moreover, picture books, which used to be written almost exclusively for young children, increasingly are written for older students, especially when addressing complex and sensitive subjects. These picture books can be used effectively as teacher read-alouds to promote interest and discussion.

While selecting and using literature is the primary focus of this guide, we have also provided information in chapter 8 about other resources that can be used effectively in conjunction with the literature described in the preceding chapters. The resources are organized into four major categories: media; web sites; selected museums and historical sites; and lesson plans, posters, photographs, and other teaching aids. Due to the enormous amount of resources related to the Civil War, this listing is meant only as a handy starting point for educators.

As expressed by Bruce Catton in the quote at the beginning of this introduction, "The story of this war needs retelling . . . because it helped to shape the future of the human race." It is our hope that this resource book helps you in your quest to make the history of the Civil War era and its continuing significance come alive through literature for your students.

I

Using Literature to Learn About the Civil War

The Civil War and Our National Identity

The Civil War is a source of fascination for Americans of all ages. The idea of a war that divided communities and turned members of families against each other continues to provoke interest and debate more than 130 years after its conclusion. We know many facts, the *Whos*, *Whats* and *Wheres*, but we are still trying to understand the *Whys* of the war and their ramifications.

Part of the mystique of the Civil War also seems to be that each side had a popular cause as a rallying call. For the South, its justification was preservation of states' rights and a decentralization of the federal government; whereas for many in the North, the rallying cry was "The Union Forever." These single issues focused on a wide philosophical gap between the regions and evoked strong emotions from both sides. Others in the North justified the Civil War as the means for eliminating the institution of slavery. While each of these positions represents popular opinion, the causes were far more complex and the divisions between the two regions much deeper.

While many people in the North and in the border states were opposed to slavery and even appalled by it, the official position of

1

the federal government was that the Civil War was being waged to reunite the country. The Civil War was not initially a war against slavery. In fact, President Abraham Lincoln was so eager to reunite the country that he initially agreed to allow the Southern states to retain their slaves. While many Northern politicians believed that slavery was an unfortunate political reality, the Abolitionists recognized the Civil War as an opportunity to bring the South to its knees and free the blacks held in slavery. The attitude of many Northern politicians changed in late 1862 when President Lincoln recognized the need to abolish slavery. On January 1, 1863, when President Lincoln issued the Emancipation Proclamation, the Civil War became a war about freedom and human dignity for black Americans. Significantly, blacks played an ever-increasing role in helping to secure their freedom as they served in the military forces.

Perhaps interest in the Civil War endures because it reflects all the human drama of a family in turmoil. In his Nobel Prize acceptance speech, author William Faulkner spoke about the need for literature to address those enduring qualities of the "human heart in conflict with itself." The Civil War certainly provides a venue to explore those concerns. What can be more painful than the conflict of values and emotions that makes a father and son choose different sides in an argument, or more inspirational than a parent leading his family out of oppression, or more hopeful than friendships that transcend social convention? These are among the types of issues that are played out in various ways in the literature of the Civil War.

The Role of Literature in Learning Content

While literature has long been the core of the English curriculum, many history and social studies teachers also have recognized the value of using trade books, fiction as well as nonfiction, in their classrooms to help students gain a broader perspective of the times they are studying. Recently, with curricular changes in many middle schools and high schools such as integrated teaching units, block scheduling, and team teaching, recognition of the value of literature in other disciplines has increased. Literature allows readers to enter unknown times and places through the lives and experiences of characters. For example, students may read a textbook chapter telling about the hardships of life in the Middle Ages, but reading the Newbery Honor Book *Catherine, Called Birdy* (Clarion, 1994), a historical novel by Karen Cushman, provides them with a heightened sense of what life was really like for a teenager during that time. The following is an entry from Birdy's diary.

> 14th Day of December, *Feast of Saint Hybald, abbot of our own Lincolnshire. I wonder if he is a relative.*
>
> I am in disgrace today. Grown quite weary with my embroidery, with my pricked finger and tired eyes and sore back, I kicked it down the stairs to the hall, where the dogs fought and slobbered over it, so I took the soggy mess and threw it to the pigs. (p. 53)

When Birdy describes the icicles along the inside walls of her room in winter, readers know it is cold even in the manor house. That observation provides a basis for speculating about just what life might have been like for the poor people. Because Birdy engages readers in her life and the challenges that it provides her, they learn about the world she lives in. For example, a textbook might state that members of the landed gentry arranged marriages for their young daughters (age twelve or thirteen) to secure more property or wealth. For today's students the concept of arranged marriages is an abstraction that probably just seems absurd; however, when they read about the repulsive cast of suitors that Birdy must drive off, the concept comes alive. The process of reading about the experiences of someone close to their own age who is living in such different conditions makes the time vital and believable for students.

Literature provides a door for readers to enter and when they choose to go through that door they avail themselves of new worlds. The role of teachers is to provide their students with opportunities to open that door and experience books. For example, when today's students read Graham Salisbury's *Under the Blood Red Sun* (Bantam Doubleday Dell, 1994) which received the Scott

O'Dell Award for historical fiction, they are reading about a time long before they were born. World War II might as well be ancient history for them, but as they read this book, they experience the bombing of Pearl Harbor on a personal level. They feel the grief it causes the main character, Tommy, a first generation Japanese-American, and the confusion it creates for his grandfather. Literature puts a human face on events, successes, and defeats.

Developing critical thinking skills is a significant goal of the curricula for both history and language arts classes. This goal is reflected in the National Standards for United States History and the IRA/NCTE Standards for the English Language Arts. Inherent also in the curricula are the development of problem-solving and decision-making skills, an appreciation of the wide diversity of human experiences, and respect for the values upon which this nation is based. Integrating a wide range of literature with subject topics provides students with learning experiences that help them fulfill these curricular goals.

Roles of Teachers

Teachers have an opportunity to help students to make significant connections with books. In order to accomplish this, teachers need insights about the strengths and interests of their students as well as knowledge of a variety of books. One way to help students become readers who will be life-long learners is to provide them with opportunities to read widely. Reading can be contagious; once students catch the reading bug, they are eager to share it. The recommendation of a friend or classmate will often create more interest in a book than anything a teacher might say. So it is up to the teacher to have a variety of books, fiction and nonfiction, for students to explore.

We encourage teachers to offer a range of materials at a variety of reading levels. Providing students with opportunities to select what they will read encourages their involvement with books. We also believe that students should be allowed to read books that may seem to be on a lower reading level than is typically used at a particular grade level or in a specific content or subject matter classroom. In order to experience and learn from literature associated with subject matter topics, students must be able to read it with ease and comfort. If a student is struggling just to comprehend the words and sentences of a selection, then the larger purpose of using it to connect with the concepts of the subject matter topic is hindered or lost. Students must be allowed to select materials that are readily accessible to them intellectually so that they will be able to think about the message and its implications. If students have to struggle with the difficulty of the reading level, they will have even more difficulty learning from the material.

Teachers need to create a rich learning environment in which students can select books that meet their needs and their interests. Certainly, an extensive classroom library and opportunities for students to share what they are reading with their classmates will contribute both to a lifelong love of reading and to an increased understanding of subject matter.

How to Use Literature to Teach about the Civil War

The purpose of this book is to provide teachers with a wealth of information about literature, student activities, and other resources about the Civil War appropriate for use in their classrooms. With few exceptions, we have not included the multitude of fine adult books about the Civil War, primarily because these books are far more accessible and well known than many of those written for younger readers and because our focus is on children's and young adult literature. The selections includes historical fiction, biographies, informational books, picture books, and poetry.

Many entries are works of nonfiction, but frequently authors use historical fiction as the vehicle for writing about the Civil War or any other historical period. Perhaps the most effective bridge between fiction and fact is, in fact, historical fiction. The basis of historical fiction is a factual framework upon which the author builds the story. We enumerated the characteristics that good historical fiction share in our book *Teaching Young Adult Literature: Sharing the Connection* (Wadsworth, 1995). These include:

- Authenticity of detail about the period, which reflects careful research

- Presentation of historical figures in a manner consistent with their documented actions and words

- Accuracy of chronology of events

- Characters who are believable

- Relevance of the story to current times, attitudes, and beliefs as well as to the historical period

- A vivid and accurate sense of history
  (p. 33)

Certainly the Civil War period produced some of the most memorable people in the history of our country. Many biographies tell the life stories of people like Lincoln, Lee, Douglass, Barton, Tubman, and others whose contributions and influence were significant forces during the period. An effective biography is meticulously researched from primary documents, including those written by the subject of the book. Additionally, a successful biography presents the subject within the context of the time period in which he or she lived. In this way, the reader learns about the conditions and times as well as the individual.

Some informational books are comprehensive, providing the reader with the "big picture." These books include the factual background for the period; more often, however, informational books focus on a particular aspect of an issue, event, or movement and present an in-depth look at it. For example, one of the nonfiction books we recommend is Jim Murphy's *The Boy's War*, which relates stories and facts about a number of young boys who served on both sides during the Civil War (see entry in chapter 5). Again, as with historical fiction and biographies, factual accuracy is an essential component of nonfiction.

Picture books, until recently, were primarily for younger readers. Picture books now are often more sophisticated in both content and illustrations and can be enjoyed by readers of all ages. Additionally, teachers can read picture books aloud to a class to introduce a topic or to focus on a particular event or individual.

We have also included some poetry in this resource book. The intensity and drama of war lends itself to poetic form. Certainly one of the closest observers of the Civil War was the poet Walt Whitman. His experiences in Washington, D.C., serving the wounded, had a profound impact on his work.

Creating Involved Readers: Literature Involvement Strategies

Within each chapter we have included suggested student activities to accompany the focus books. Addressed to students, these activities are intended to be flexible and to meet a wide range of needs, interests, and abilities. We have tried to suggest a balance of activities that provide opportunities for discussion, writing, critical thinking, and creative expression. While most of these activities are self-explanatory, there are several literature involvement strategies that we use in chapters 2 through 7 that need additional description for teachers to be able to implement them successfully.

Discussion Continuum

One "can't-miss" literature involvement strategy is the discussion continuum. The discussion continuum is a strategy for involving all students in a lively discussion. It works well when teachers are frustrated that only a few students contribute while the rest sit back apathetically during a whole class or small group discussion. The teacher draws a continuum on the board with opposing statements at either end point. The key to the success of this strategy is writing opposing position statements that represent the range of student opinion. Controversial issues should have enough relevance to students to evoke a response.

As the students enter the classroom, they write their initials somewhere along the continuum on the spot that best specifies their own position on the issue. During the discussion, students explain their positions, often using references from their reading to back up their points. The only rules are that everyone must have a chance to speak before anyone can speak for a second time and that all positions must be listened to respectfully. Initially, the teacher may structure the discussion so that students representing views at opposite ends of the continuum alternate speaking. It is our experience, however, that once students get involved, they take over the discussion themselves and are soon responding to each other rather than using the teacher to keep the discussion going. It is also our experience that some students decide to change their positions and thus their places on the continuum as a result of the discussion.

The discussion continuum works well as a springboard for writing or for further research on an issue or creative project. As students become familiar with this strategy, they can create their own opposing statements in small groups or with a learning partner. Having students create their own statements helps them to develop critical thinking skills and to internalize what they are reading at a deeper level. (p. 82)

Graphic Organizers: Mapping

Mapping is a strategy that provides students with opportunities to create graphic representations of elements of their reading. As an organizational tool, mapping helps students to see relationships among concepts and ideas. There are many ways that mapping can be used as a literature involvement strategy to help students make connections with literature. We describe four graphic organizers that are particularly appropriate to use with the historical fiction, biographies, and nonfiction of the Civil War period.

Ideals/Values Mapping.   The first of the mapping strategies is "ideals/values mapping." Christopher Collier in "Criteria for Historical Fiction" (*School Library Journal,* August 1982, pp. 32–33), acknowledged that he and his brother James Lincoln Collier write historical fiction "with a didactic purpose—to teach about the ideals and values that have been important in shaping the course of American history." Based upon that admission, one way to look at historical fiction is from the perspective of the ideals and values inherent in the work. Ideals/values mapping provides students with a strategy to explore the ideals or values in literature, especially in historical fiction. The process is for students to identify an ideal or value that is significantly explored in the work and place it in a circle at the center of the map. Supporting evidence is then placed in circles and attached to the center (see figure 1.1). (pp. 248–50)

Figure 1.1. Ideals/Values Map

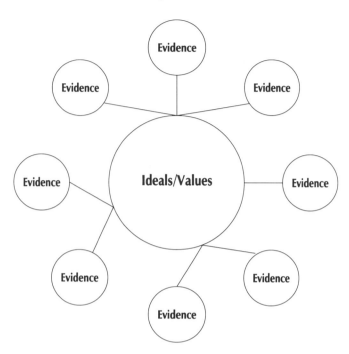

VIP Map. The second mapping activity, a "VIP map," is a graphic representation of key facts about an individual that the reader learns in a biography or autobiography. This mapping strategy both allows students to record what they have learned and to indicate areas about which they need more information. The categories can be adapted and new categories added as is appropriate to the life of the subject of the biography. For a model of the VIP map, see figure 1.2.

Idea Map. The third approach to mapping is the "idea map" designed to be used with informational books (see figure 1.3). The idea map focuses around the major topic of the reading. Readers then identify significant information, either specific facts or broader categories of information. It is helpful for students if they create a visual of some type that represents the major topic and that accompanies the words.

Figure 1.2. VIP Map (Biography)

Book Title: _____   Other Sources: _____

Subject: _____

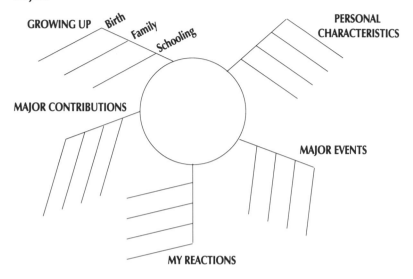

I want to know more about:

Figure 1.3. Idea Map

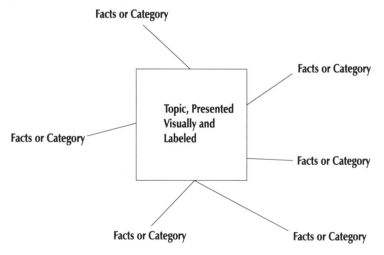

Venn Diagram or Comparison/Contrast Chart. A graphic organizer that is useful in conceptualizing similarities and differences between people, settings, events, themes, or any other predominant element is the Venn diagram or comparison/contrast chart (see figure 1.4). The diagram uses two or more overlapping circles where

Figure 1.4. Venn Diagram

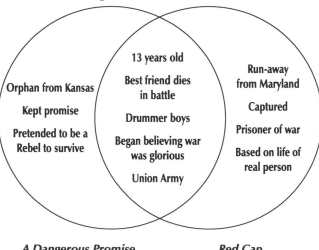

A Dangerous Promise   *Red Cap*

each circle represents one of the elements being compared and contrasted with the other. The overlapping oval area in the center represents the characteristics that the elements have in common. In the above example, we use two focus books from chapter 5, *A Dangerous Promise* by Joan Lowry Nixon and *Red Cap* by G. Clifton Wisler.

"What Would It Have Been Like to Live in _____?"

Another literature involvement strategy designed to be used with both nonfiction and fiction, especially historical fiction, is "What Would It Have Been Like to Live in _____?" This strategy helps students to immerse themselves in a historical setting. First students individually brainstorm the information that they have learned about life as it is portrayed in the book. The following questions may be used as springboards for student thinking and also to help structure the categorization that occurs after the brainstorming and sharing.

1. Do the characters talk differently from the way people talk today?

2. How do they dress? Does their mode of dress reflect the times?

3. What is the housing like at the time?

4. What conditions are most different from your life?

5. Would you like to have lived during this time? Why or why not?

Students share their lists and develop a master list of information on the board or overhead. It is then compiled and categorized to be used as a springboard for either discussion or writing.

Character Portraits

"Character portraits" is a literature involvement strategy designed to help students understand character development by examining the changes, development, and progression of major characters. To implement this strategy, teachers organize students into small groups. Each group examines a part or section of the book. (Usually it is preferable to divide the book into thirds.) Each group member reads the assigned section and individually writes three lists of words or phrases that describe the character's appearance, personality, and actions. Each student should have at least five descriptors in each category.

Composite lists are then made in each group. These lists will be the basis for describing the character in each section of the book. Groups may also decide to use a graphic organizer such as mapping. Each group will present its findings to the class so that the evolution of the character can be examined and discussed. Figure 1.5 shows how the composite information can be charted to help demonstrate character development.

Figure 1.5. Character Portraits

Character	Appearance	Personality	Actions
1st third			
2nd third			
Last third			

A Profile

While character portraits can be used with fiction to look at character development, the biographical presentation of historical figures is not always structured in such an evolutionary way. Biographies generally focus on the individual's accomplishments. It is those accomplishments that make the person memorable because they have had a far-ranging impact on others and on the society in which the individual lived. A "profile" is a literature involvement strategy that focuses on the lives of real people. In this strategy students focus on the accomplishments and characteristics or personal qualities of the individual that contributed to these accomplishments. For example, in doing a profile of Robert E. Lee, his battlefield successes would be among his major accomplishments. Thus the reader would look for qualities such as his leadership ability and his intellectual skill for planning and applying military strategy to his battle plan. Students are also asked for examples of other accomplishments that resulted from a particular characteristic or quality. While these data may be collected and developed in several ways, the following chart provides one format (see figure 1.6). The information from this chart or other formats can be used as a springboard for writing assignments or for class presentations.

Figure 1.6.   Profile of _____

Accomplishment	Characteristic/Quality	Other Examples

"Did You Know . . . ?"

We have found that when students are truly involved in reading nonfiction that they enjoy sharing what they are learning with others. This literature involvement strategy, "Did You Know . . . ?," has students chart their discoveries and then select one to explore further (see figure 1.7).

Figure 1.7.   "Did You Know . . . ?"

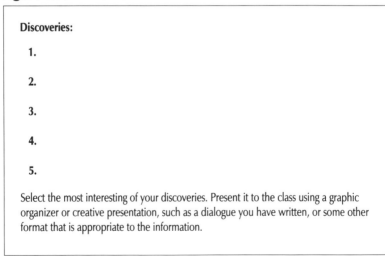

Discoveries:

1.

2.

3.

4.

5.

Select the most interesting of your discoveries. Present it to the class using a graphic organizer or creative presentation, such as a dialogue you have written, or some other format that is appropriate to the information.

Additional Research about a Topic

We often suggest that students do additional research about a topic that they have discovered in one of the books. While teachers frequently have guidelines for research projects, the following is one that we have found works well with students. Students are given the following questions as a basis for their exploration:

Prior to reading:

What do you need (want) to find out?

How will you get this information?

After reading:

What did you find out?

What are your reactions?

Students can use the answers to these questions as the basis for their in-depth examination. They begin their research by posing those questions that they wish to examine. The following chart helps them to organize their information. (See figure 1.8).

Creative Projects

Throughout this book, we frequently suggest that students respond to their reading in original and creative ways. While we do not always propose a specific activity for creative projects, we do list below some suggestions for involving students. Teachers frequently limit their post-reading instructional strategies with literature to discussion and writing activities. While these are valuable avenues for exploring literature and learning about it, other activities that allow more options to meet diverse learning styles and to encourage greater creativity should be developed, also. By using creative projects, teachers enhance ongoing student involvement with reading. Providing students with opportunities to stretch their imaginations by doing creative projects also provides them with opportunities for authentic interactions with books. Such creative projects lend themselves well to small groups, learning partners, and individual work, and usually create a depth of involvement, understanding, and aesthetic pleasure that is contagious and highly gratifying. Literature connections can be expressed through art, drama, music, media, and even in other content areas. These projects also offer a tangible way for teachers from several disciplines to work together

Figure 1.8. Additional Research about a Topic

Questions:	
Sources:	
Findings:	
Reactions:	
Ideas for reporting or presenting:	

and for students to see the interrelationships among their school subjects and their relationship to "real life."

The following are a few ideas for creative projects that have been used successfully by teachers:

1. Create a collage that illustrates the book as a whole or one of the characters in the book.

2. Create a script dramatizing a scene from the book; then prepare the production.

3. Create a publicity campaign for a book or an author. Consider posters, videos, newspaper/magazine reviews, and radio or print ads.

4. Design a cover or a jacket for a book.

5. Compose a song based on the conflict in the book or on one of the characters.

6. Design a mural based on the action in the book.

7. Prepare and conduct a talk show based on the issues in one or more books.

8. Make artistic representations of the characters, setting, or action as you think they look.

9. Create a picture book, pop-up book, wordless picture book, or comic strip series based on the book. (pp. 255–56)

10. Create a newspaper in the style of the times, reflecting an event or day in the Civil War.

11. Using photographic collections from the time (from reprints in books), create a photo essay about some aspect of the Civil War.

12. Write a poem on any aspect of the Civil War, such as an individual, a battle, an event, or a movement.

Guidelines for Using Fiction and Nonfiction in Learning Content

Using literature, both fiction and nonfiction, to learn more about a topic in the content area classroom should not be approached in the same manner as reading assignments in a textbook. Using literature like a textbook defeats its value and purpose. Rather, teachers should use literature in a different way if their students are to be successful in broadening subject knowledge and understanding through this type of reading experience. In this way, teachers build upon the inherent quality of literature in order to help their students learn and enjoy learning. The following guidelines are designed to assist content teachers to incorporate literature into their classes.

Guidelines

1. Familiarize students with different literary genres. Help them to understand the differences between fiction and nonfiction.

2. Create a rich environment for learning, providing students with a variety of fiction and nonfiction at a wide range of reading and interest levels.

3. Be flexible in making assignments. Giving students options is a positive way to encourage their involvement.

4. Also be flexible in allowing students some choice in selecting their own reading selections. While some students may seem to be reading "easy" materials, they may in fact be building the essential background that they need to read more difficult books.

5. Keep current with the variety of recently published trade books that are related to the topics your students are studying. A current trend in nonfiction publishing focuses on books that do an in-depth examination of issues or topics rather than the broad overview books that present a more encyclopedic approach.

6. Provide a variety of activities designed to promote active student involvement with their reading.

2

A Troubled Land

In the history of any nation, there are difficult and even painful chapters, but perhaps none is as painful as a civil war. This was certainly the case in our history. While the Revolutionary War had freed us from foreign control, the Declaration of Independence, the Constitution, and the Bill of Rights had enough ambiguity to allow for different shades of interpretation. Those interpretations were colored by regionalism and the differing needs of the citizens in the two major regions.

The North was the industrial center of the country, while the South was primarily agrarian. While those differences created a different philosophy between the regions, the greatest difference was based on the attitudes and perceptions of people in each region about the nature and role of government. The roles and responsibilities of the federal government were established by the Constitution. However, there were differing interpretations of the meaning of the words. Many Northerners belonged to the Federalist party, which ascribed to a strong federal government. The opposing political party, the Democrat-Republicans, which supported states rights and objected to active involvement of the central government, reflected the popular sentiment of the Southern states. This political difference increased because the South felt that the federal government passed laws that would benefit the industrial North at its expense. For example, the government passed the Tariff of 1828, which taxed imported goods, thus protecting the goods that were being manufactured in the North. The South felt that this law was punitive because it preferred to purchase the less expensive European goods. There was also a growing debate about slavery in the country, and the South believed that the government was interfering in the lives of its people.

The political and economic issues were seriously compounded by social differences. The largely agrarian South was established on an aristocratic model of a gentry who controlled huge tracts of land and the wealth they yielded, primarily from cotton. They also controlled the people who depended on them for their livelihood, whether they were poorly paid white overseers or tenant farmers, or blacks who were slaves for life without pay or freedom, and often without humane treatment. The North, on the other hand, was more highly industrialized. Many people lived in towns where they were shopkeepers or tradesmen.

By the nineteenth century there was a strong anti-slavery sentiment in the North. In 1808 Congress passed laws prohibiting the importation of additional slaves to this country. Most Northern states abolished slavery, and blacks lived as freemen in many Northern states. In the South, education was a luxury of the wealthy who hired tutors for their children. These children were educated to take their place in the society of the antebellum South. In the North, some wealthy families had their children tutored too, but there were also opportunities for others to attend schools. While the twentieth-century concept of universal education did not yet exist, the North provided greater opportunities for young people to improve their station in life by learning to read, write, and do mathematical calculations. The class distinctions in the South were absolute, with the wealth and power held by the large landowners; whereas, in the North there was a far more clearly defined middle class of merchants, attorneys, teachers, physicians, and nurses. Many of the wealthy and powerful men of the North were industrialists who had the foresight to see the manufacturing or transportation needs of a growing country and had amassed great wealth. This was enhanced by the business opportunities of the Civil War and continued after the war as the Industrial Revolution flourished in the late 1800s.

While we were one nation united by the common heritage of the battle for independence from England and by the legal and philosophical tenets of the Declaration of Independence, the Constitution, and the Bill of Rights, the issues of states' right and the boundaries of governmental power were never resolved. Throughout the early decades of this country, the economic, political, and social differences became increasingly pronounced. They divided the sentiment of the country and made the Civil War inevitable.

Certainly, if there was one issue that philosophically, ethically, and emotionally divided the country more than any other, it was slavery. Through the first decades of our country slavery was a reality. It was also considered to be an economic necessity for the large landowners in the South who needed large numbers of inexpensive workers. Northern states slowly began to abolish slavery. As slaves escaped to free states, their stories were widely retold. Northerners were appalled by the treatment that many slaves had experienced; thus the emotional battle between the regions began.

In this chapter, we explore the events and practices that led to the economic, political, and social conditions that contributed to the national unrest. This chapter is designed to present the "big picture" of the Civil War period. Some of the books that we discuss here are nonfiction because they effectively frame the issues that contributed to the Civil War. Other books give readers a perspective on the whole scope of the war.

We have also included books that focus on the early slave trade or other specific events that contributed to the national dilemma that ignited in 1861. A number of the books, replete with drawings, maps, photographs, and paintings, provide readers with as vivid a visual experience as possible. Perhaps the relative newness of the art of photography at that time contributed to the amount of attention that was paid to capturing the period in pictures. This chapter, as an overview of the antebellum events, the war, and the conditions that followed it, also introduces figures and events that will be examined more specifically in books selected in later chapters. We are providing a framework for the war and for this book by introducing many of the ideas, the people, and the events that shaped the period and reverbrate throughout the history of the United States.

Prior to Reading: Think About . . .

Young people need to do some preliminary thinking and talking to help them understand what they read or what is read to them about the Civil War. They need opportunities to ask questions and to raise issues and concerns. The following questions can be used to prompt this discussion:

- What do you already know about the Civil War? Make a list.

- What do you already know about how slavery came to be in our country?

- What do you think the different attitudes about slavery were prior to the war?

- What do you already know about the events leading up to the actual declaration of war?

- What things are you interested in learning about the Civil War? Make a list.

- The Civil War happened almost 150 years ago. Why do you think people are still so interested in it? Why do we need to learn about it now?

- What are all the different ways we can learn about the Civil War? Make a list.

- Choose a quotation taken from one of the books described in this chapter. What do you think it means? What does it make you curious about in the book?

Focus Books

**Catton, Bruce. *The Picture History of the Civil War.*
American Heritage/Wings Books, 1960, 1988. 630 pages.**

The American people in 1860 believed that they were the happiest and luckiest people in all the world, and in a way they were right. Most of them lived on farms or in very small towns, they lived better than their fathers had lived, and they knew that their children would do still better. . . .

This may or may not have been the end of America's golden age, but it was at least the final, haunted moment of its age of innocence. (p. 9)

At a Glance ▪ This nonfiction account, authored by one of the major historians of the Civil War, provides an excellent overview of major events. This is a valuable resource for every secondary school class because it introduces significant topics.

Summary ▪ The names of events preceding and during the Civil War are familiar to many Americans, but the details are often less clear. This volume will provide students with many of those details by presenting an overview of many of the major occurrences and figures involved in the war. The book also includes reprints of newspapers from the times, posters, drawings, political cartoons, maps, sketches, photographs, and paintings. The book is designed to show the war as well as discuss it. In addition to the wonderful variety of illustrations, the accounts are measured and reflect the balance that is typical of Catton's work. He frames the events of the war within the broader context of American life, reflecting how it consumed all of American society. Catton demonstrates that war is as much political as it is military.

Teaching Considerations ▪ While this book does not address any one topic in great depth, it does an excellent job of illustrating the breadth of the Civil War and the social and political issues surrounding it. Certainly, the illustrations provide readers with insights about the time.

After Reading: Suggested Student Activities

1. Review the visual portrayal of Lincoln throughout this book. Examine how he is presented in different sources such as political cartoons and caricatures. Then compare and contrast that depiction with the image of him in the photographs taken throughout the period.

2. Select one person from the period and write a profile of him or her.

3. Prepare a "Did You Know . . . ?" chart as you focus on one of the topics from this book. (Teacher's Note: See the guidelines in chapter 1 for this strategy.)

4. As you preview this book, find a topic that you want to learn more about. Find at least three additional sources to expand your background. Write an informational paper about it.

**Frank, Andrew K. *The Birth of Black America:
The Age of Discovery and the Slave Trade.*
Chelsea House Publishers, 1996. 112 pages.**

The first African captives to reach the North American colonies arrived in August 1619, a year before the Pilgrims' celebrated Massachusetts landing in the *Mayflower.* These Africans, 20 in all, had already been given Spanish names but were brought on a Dutch ship, giving rise to the speculation that they were taken in a raid on a Spanish slaver (the name of the Dutch ship was never recorded). The ship landed at the settlement of Jamestown, Virginia, where its crew traded the captives for supplies and sailed away again. (p. 50)

At a Glance ▪ This well-written informational book tells the story of the development of the African slave trade in the Americas from the fifteenth century through 1865. Appropriate for junior high/middle school students, it could also be useful for secondary school students.

Summary ▪ Part of the sixteen-volume Milestones in Black American History series, this book provides details about the European Age of Discovery as it pertains to the development of the African slave trade in the Americas. Slave trade in Africa and the differences between how slavery was practiced in Africa and in the Americas are examined. Chapters are devoted to the Middle Passage, that torturous and often fatal ocean voyage of the slave ships across the Atlantic Ocean, and the selection and "seasoning" processes for those captives who did survive. Other sections include the economic, social, and religious reasons for slavery as well as instances of mutiny and revolt.

Teaching Considerations ▪ Accompanied by illustrations, photographs, and a chronology of significant dates, *The Birth of Black America* is an excellent resource for students and educators. Most students know very little about how slavery came to the Americas and need help to place the practice of slavery in the United States within the larger context of European explorations and discoveries.

After Reading: Suggested Student Activities

1. Select five new things you learned from this book. Create a "Did You Know . . . ?" chart and a visual representation of this information. (Teacher's Note: See the guidelines in chapter 1 for this strategy.)

2. Discuss with your class the economic, social, and religious reasons given for slavery.

3. Discuss with your class the differences between slave practices in Africa and in the Americas and how cultural differences contributed to these differences.

Hansen, Joyce. *The Captive.*
Scholastic Books, 1996. 195 pages.

When we reached the beach, men, women, and even a few young children filed into the fort. The white men examined the people in chains the same way that I've seen men examine a goat or a cow before purchasing it—squeezing a man's arms, his legs, then peering inside his mouth and ears—pulling his eyes open. One man shouted something at his examiner in a strange language, but the white man slapped him sharply and yelled back. Even though the prisoner was strong and healthy, there was nothing that he could do because his hands and feet were bound.

One moment became more horrifying than the next

as I saw another white man pick up a glowing hot iron
and press it between the prisoner's shoulder blades. He
shrieked in pain as one of the blacks dressed in white
man's dress rubbed palm oil on the mark the iron had
made. (p. 72)

At a Glance ▪ In this gripping novel, Hansen relates the experience
of a young African who is stolen from his family to be sold into
slavery. This book is appropriate for junior high/middle school
students. Because of its exciting action, older readers might also
enjoy it.

Summary ▪ Twelve-year-old Kofi is the youngest and favorite son
of an important chief. His father gives him a flute and a gold orna-
ment as a special treat at the annual ceremony honoring the past
and present Ashanti kings. But Kofi's family is betrayed by their
trusted family slave, Oppong, the celebration disrupted, his father
murdered, and Kofi taken into captivity. So begins a challenging
and painful time for Kofi. He struggles and briefly escapes from his
captors before being taken to the coast to be sent to the New World
as a slave. Although conditions are basically unspeakable on the
slave ship, Kofi makes two friends, Tim and Joseph, who help him
and provide him with a sense of support. Once the ship is docked
in Boston, they (Kofi, Tim, and Joseph) are sold and they go
through even more difficult times until they finally are able to escape.

Teaching Considerations ▪ This book will help to dispel the belief
held by many students that slavery was only a Southern institution.
The scenes in Massachusetts provide students with a realistic view
of the late eighteenth century in this country. The book is fast-paced
and filled with exciting events.

After Reading: Suggested Student Activities

1. Discuss the irony of Oppong's betrayal of Kofi and his family.

2. If you were Kofi, would you have returned to your village? Why
   or why not? (Teacher's Note: This activity also could be used

with a whole class by implementing it as a discussion continuum. See the guidelines in chapter 1 for this strategy.)

3. Examine the history of slavery in the Northern states. Discuss why it was outlawed in these states and retained in the South.

4. Research slave traffic. Prepare a report to share with the members of your class.

Haskins, Jim. *The Day Fort Sumter Was Fired On:*
A Photo History of the Civil War.
Scholastic, 1995. 96 pages.

Two events galvanized the opposite sides in the fight over slavery almost as radically as the battles in Kansas. One was the publication in 1852 of the book *Uncle Tom's Cabin* by Harriet Beecher Stowe. A work of fiction, it dramatized the evils of slavery and the destruction of families by slavery. . . . The other was the U.S. Supreme Court's decision in the case of *Scott* v. *Sandford*. Dred Scott was a Missouri slave whose master had taken him to live first in free Illinois and then in the Wisconsin Territory, where slavery had been excluded under the Missouri Compromise of 1820. (p. 12)

At a Glance ▪ This nonfiction account frames the events that led to, occurred during, and followed the Civil War, presenting issues in a clear and concise manner. This text could be read by upper elementary and junior high/middle school students.

Summary ▪ The short chapters of this volume cover major topics, from the "seeds" of disharmony between the North and South to political issues that contributed to the troubles. Haskins also devotes chapters to looking at the roles that were played during the war by young people, women, photographers and the press, and African Americans. Other chapters are devoted to battles and the military.

Teaching Considerations ▪ Haskins presents a perspective of the social and political, as well as military, conditions of the times.

Each chapter is brief and tightly focused, with the text complemented by vintage photographs, sketches, paintings, or maps. Each chapter could also be used alone to add background information for students.

After Reading: Suggested Student Activities

1. Select one of the historical figures discussed in this book and do research to find out more about the person in preparation for writing an "interview" with the figure. Work with your learning partner to do the initial research. Imagine that you are a newspaper reporter covering the war. One of you should assume that you are working for a newspaper in a Northern or border state while the other is working for a Southern newspaper.

2. Imagine that you are living during the time of the firing on Fort Sumter. Hold a town meeting to discuss public reactions and concerns about this action. Assume that you are living in a border state where the sentiments of the community would reflect both sides of the issue and a number of variations on those positions. Once you have established your "identity" for the town meeting, research the issues and their impact to establish your point of view.

3. Research the early use of photography. What do the photographs add to a nonfiction account such as this book? Prepare an oral report to demonstrate your findings to your classmates.

Myers, Walter Dean. *Now Is Your Time! The African-American Struggle for Freedom.* Scholastic, 1991. 292 pages.

Before his marriage, Washington had not been a wealthy man. Martha, who had inherited her first husband's money, lands, and Africans, changed that. When Washington's brother Lawrence died in 1761, George also inherited the large estate in Virginia called Mount Vernon. It was here that the Washingtons lived, using many of the Africans as house and personal "servants," as was the custom.

Washington, a Virginian by birth, represented a study

in contrasts typical of his time. On the one hand he considered slavery an evil practice and against the best interests of the country. On the other hand there were over three hundred Africans on his plantations. (p. 50)

At a Glance ▪ A well-written and engaging book, *Now Is Your Time! The African-American Struggle for Freedom* provides an overview of the African-American experience from the arrival of the first captives in 1619 through the Civil Rights movements of the 1960s. Appropriate for upper elementary and junior high/middle school students, this book will also interest high school students. Excerpts can be used effectively as a teacher read-aloud for all but very young children.

Summary ▪ In the introduction, Myers states, "The African-American experience cannot be told in one story, or even a hundred, for it is a living experience, ever changing, ever growing, ever becoming richer. Events of the past cannot change, but they can change in our perception of them, and in our understanding of what they mean to us today. What we understand of our history is what we understand of ourselves" (p. ix). The reader then embarks upon a fascinating journey as Myers begins his book with a chapter entitled "The Land" that describes the exploration and settlement of North America, where people who had been poor could become rich if they had enough land and enough cheap labor. The next few chapters describe the Africans who were brought to this country and the role religion, the destruction of the family unit, language, and other cultural symbols had in making captives into slaves. Next, the role African-Americans played in the American struggle for independence from Britain and why the Declaration of Independence and the Constitution did not apply to everyone is discussed. Subsequent chapters present other important events and significant people in the African-American struggle to be free and to have all the rights and privileges guaranteed to everyone in a democracy.

Teaching Considerations ▪ Walter Dean Myers, an award-winning author of young adult literature, has written a highly readable and engrossing account of events, issues, and personalities related to the African-American experience. Photographs, illustrations, posters, plantation records, and quotes add to its effectiveness. Myers's introduction, afterword, and author's note merit student attention for their insights and reflections on his own personal historical search. This book was the 1992 Coretta Scott King Award winner.

After Reading: Suggested Student Activities

1. African American history has been a neglected area of study for many years. Discuss with your class why it is important to learn about this aspect of our nation's history.

2. Develop an annotated timeline of significant events leading to the Civil War presented in this book.

3. Select a chapter from this book to teach to someone who has not read it. Develop three ways to present the pertinent information, at least one of which must be visual.

4. Choose an event, person, or issue from the Civil War era presented in this book that you want to know more about. Research it and present the information to your class in an interesting format.

Robertson, Jr., James I. *Civil War!: America Becomes One Nation.* Alfred A. Knopf, 1992. 184 pages.

"Civil War! Civil War! We're going to war!" screamed American newspapers in the spring of 1861.

Everyone seemed excited and joyful. Men rushed to join the armies: they were afraid the war might end before they could be part of it. Women tearfully watched them go. Many of them secretly wished that they too could be soldiers. "God is on our side!" Northerners and Southerners alike shouted. Each side agreed: this was going to be a short, clean, nice war—a quick contest in which there would be much chance for glory and little chance of being killed or wounded.

As a matter of fact, the Civil War became the most important event in the history of the United States. It lasted four long years. It began with old-fashioned infantry charges and cavalry attacks. It ended with massed firepower and the greatest slaughter of soldiers the world had seen up to that time. No war in world history between 1815 and 1914 was as large or as far-reaching in its results. (p. vii)

At a Glance ▪ Robertson's concise history of the Civil War begins with a chapter on King Cotton and ends with an explanation of why the Civil War still has such an impact on people today. Upper elementary school students and junior high/middle school students will be able to read this text easily.

Summary ▪ Throughout this account of the Civil War, Robertson attempts to present issues and events from the perspective of both the South and the North. The book begins with an analysis of the differing beliefs systems about slavery and the contrast between the agricultural South and the industrial North. Among the other topics discussed are the role of the abolitionists, resources in the South and North, the two presidents, major battles and commanders, disease and medical practices, and life on the homefront. The book contains many illustrations, photographs, an extensive chronology of significant dates, a glossary, and recommendations for additional reading.

Teaching Considerations ▪ Labeled "An Illustrated History for Young Readers," this introduction to the Civil War was written by James Robertson, Jr., an authority on the Civil War. His great-grandfather was a Confederate soldier who, according to family history, served as Lee's personal cook. Some readers may find some of his interpretations controversial, while others may view them as presenting a more balanced perspective.

After Reading: Suggested Student Activities

1. Make a list of the major issues and causes of the Civil War as described by James Robertson, Jr. Use them to prepare for a small group or class discussion on the same topic. Be prepared to discuss how they compare with other views you have heard or read.

2. Create a visual representation illustrating the major differences between the North and South.

3. Prepare a graph or some other form of mathematical chart that demonstrates the role that sickness, disease, and poor medical practices played in the deaths of many Civil War soldiers.

4. Find additional information about the role women played in the Civil War and how it changed their lives. Based on this information, create a fictionalized character who lived during this era. Write a biographical sketch of her life.

Ruby, Lois. *Steal Away Home.* Simon & Schuster, 1994. 192 pages.

> Will asked, "What you in town for, Marshal Fain?"
>
> "Looking for slave stealers."
>
> "You ain't gonna find none here," Jeremy said. "We're every one of us law-abiding citizens. James Weaver's pa, he's even a lawyer."
>
> But Marshal Fain wasn't about to be put off by a mangy flock of boys. "There's people been stealing the Nigras, and there's people been hiding 'em out."
>
> James's chest tightened. Should he run for home? But what if the marshal got suspicious and followed him home and went after Ma? What if he asked had they seen any runaway slaves, and Rebecca blabbed it all out about the ones that been sleeping in their bedrooms and attic, sometimes so many of them that they put bedrolls all over the floor and had to eat in shifts. Too risky. So James stayed put. (p. 48)

At a Glance ▪ The year 1856 was a turbulent and significant time, as antislavery and proslavery factions battled for control of Kansas and Missouri. *Steal Away Home* tells the parallel stories of twelve-year-old James Weaver and his Quaker family living in Lawrence, Kansas, during that time and twelve-year-old Dana Shannon and her family, 135 years later, who discover a skeleton in a secret room in the old Weaver house. This intriguing approach to historical fiction will capture the interest and attention of upper elementary and junior high/middle school students.

Summary ▪ Dana Shannon is peeling layers of wallpaper off a bedroom wall in an old house in Lawrence, Kansas, that her parents have purchased to turn into a bed-and-breakfast when she discovers a small secret room and an old skeleton. She also finds a diary written by Millicent Weaver in 1856, which helps her as she tries to learn the truth about the skeleton and what happened in the house over 135 years before. The author alternates chapters between Dana's experiences investigating the past and James Weaver's life during 1856. James and his family are Quakers who moved to the territory of Kansas and are committed to opposing slavery. His parents, however, are divided as to the proper approach—his father, a lawyer, believes in legal remedies; his mother, a devout Quaker and independent-minded woman, harbors runaway slaves without the knowledge and permission of her husband. James feels caught in between and struggles to understand the confusing issues and events and what his own response to them should be.

Teaching Considerations ▪ *Steal Away Home* provides an excellent device for making connections between historical events of the past and life today. Ruby ends each chapter leaving the reader wanting to know more as the answers to the mysterious past are gradually discovered. The pre-Civil War conditions, issues, and events in Kansas and Missouri are a significant part of the historical study of the Civil War, but they often are confusing and difficult for students to understand. *Steal Away Home* is an effective tool for personalizing this time period in a way that students can relate to, and it would make an excellent companion piece to an informational selection on the topic. Also, James and Dana are both faced with ethical issues that they must struggle to resolve and with which today's readers can identify. Providing students with additional background information about the Quakers' beliefs and the pre-Civil War conditions in Kansas and Missouri will enhance their understanding of the significance of the events portrayed in this book.

After Reading: Suggested Student Activities

1. Compare and contrast the similarities and differences between Dana and James, their families, and the times. Develop a Venn diagram using specific examples from the book. (Teacher Note: See the guidelines in chapter 1 for this literature involvement strategy.)

2. Identify a significant ethical dilemma that James faced and one that Dana encountered. In a small group or classroom discussion, describe how they each resolved their problem and what you might have done if faced with a similar situation.

3. Lizbert Charles plays a significant role in the lives of both the Weavers and the Shannons. Find a creative way to portray her for someone who has not yet read this book. For example, you might write a character sketch, draw an illustration, develop a collage, or write a script for a monologue delivered by her.

4. Find out more about an event or person or issue described in *Steal Away Home*, such as the sacking of Lawrence or John Brown or Beecher's bibles. Write a report and prepare an accompanying visual demonstrating the connection to this book.

Sandler, Martin W. *Civil War: A Library of Congress Book.* HarperCollins Publishers, 1996. 91 pages.

> Upon news of Lincoln's election, seven Southern states secede from the United States and form the Confederate States of America. On April 12, 1861, forces of the newly forming Confederate army fire upon and capture the federal garrison at Fort Sumter, South Carolina. Four more Southern states then secede. The nation splits apart, and the North and South are at war. (p. 15)

At a Glance ▪ This nonfiction account provides readers with an overview of the Civil War. The simple, direct text of this book makes it a useful classroom tool for the elementary grades; however, the rich variety and selection of photographs and illustrations make the book a valuable addition to any classroom through middle school and high school.

Summary ▪ Sandler begins in 1860 with the roots of conflict between the North and the South based on their differing economic systems and traces the antecedents of the war to the conflicting attitudes about slavery. He highlights major characters and events of the time and follows the chronological path of the war to its conclusion. The text provides valuable perspectives on the differences between the Civil War and earlier wars. It characterizes the Civil War as a modern war because of the type of armaments that were used both on land and sea. And it was also the first war to be photographed, as Mathew B. Brady sent teams of photographers to cover both sides of the conflict. This book provides an overview of all aspects of life for the soldiers, from the tedium of camp life to face-to-face combat.

Teaching Considerations ▪ The book gives an overview that will be a useful springboard for further in-depth study. While this is a valuable classroom addition, teachers should take the opportunity to teach students how to look at the photographs and illustrations because they tell as much of the story as the text does. Additionally, a number of boxed quotes appear throughout the text offering good insights into the participants' experiences using their own words.

After Reading: Suggested Student Activities

1. Discuss with your classmates the role of photography in covering the Civil War. What was its impact?

2. Each of the short chapters in this book provides a topic for further study. Select one chapter and research it more fully. Share your findings with your class.

3. Take the position of either a Southerner or a Northerner and assume that you are living in 1860, with war looming in the future. Write a position paper either advocating going to war or not. Be sure to support your position with factual information.

4. Select one of the figures discussed in the book and write a profile of him or her, after you have done further research.

Smith, Carter, editor. *Prelude to War: A Sourcebook on the Civil War*. The Millbrook Press, 1993. 96 pages.

People everywhere rejoiced at the news, believing that the [Missouri] Compromise had permanently solved the problem of the expansion of slavery.

Others weren't so sure. Thomas Jefferson felt that the new law signaled the beginning, not the end of conflict. "I consider it the knell of the Union," he wrote. In the North, another aged statesman, John Adams, feared that the Compromise might be the title page "to a great, tragic volume." (p. 26)

At a Glance ▪ This book, one of the American Albums from the Collections of the Library of Congress, is the first of six excellent sourcebooks on the Civil War. This volume identifies and briefly discusses many of the events from 1820 to 1859. Due to its versatility and wealth of visual aids, it will serve as a valuable background reference for teachers and students at all levels.

Summary ▪ As is true of all the books in this series, this volume is replete with photographs, drawings, and paintings. It begins with introductory material and a map that shows the United States and its acquired territories in 1853. This is followed by a three-tiered timeline presenting events in world history, American history and culture, and in slavery from 1820 to the beginning of the Civil War. This chronology helps readers to understand the events leading up to the Civil War within the national and international context. The book is divided into two parts: "Conflict and Compromise" and "A House Divided." Part 1 presents such topics as the Missouri Compromise, descriptions of the Southern cotton economy and the Northern industrialized economy, the admission of new states to the Union, and support for slavery and the beliefs of the Abolitionists and others. Among the topics presented in part II are the Underground Railroad, John Brown, the Dred Scott case, initial secession of states from the Union, and the problems at Fort Sumter.

Teaching Considerations ▪ This book is suitable for teachers and students alike who are looking for a framework for the times; however, it is an overview rather than an in-depth examination. While it introduces numerous aspects of the times, students may need more context to understand the events. Consistent with the other volumes in this series, each section of the book is accompanied by photographs, sketches, or paintings. Of particular interest are photographs of documents and announcements from the times. As with subsequent volumes in this series, each section of this book is brief and could easily be read by a wide range of students. Advanced students looking for a succinct introduction to numerous topics related to the events leading up to the Civil War might also find this book useful.

After Reading: Suggested Student Activities

1. Write an essay either supporting or rejecting the following statement, imagining that you are responding in 1860: "Although we are one nation, the conditions that divide us are greater than our common heritage."

2. In cooperative learning groups, select an event from the book as the basis for an in-depth study. Building on the information that the group has developed, formulate a debate question on the issue and have members of the group take either a pro or con position. Present your debate before the rest of the class.

3. Make a list of ideas that you had about this period prior to reading this book. Parallel to each item on the list record the new information that you have learned.

4. Select a key political or social decision that was made during this period. Illustrate the short-term and long-term effects and implications through a series of drawings or cartoons that specifically reflect the decision's impact.

5. With your learning partner, create a timeline of what you believe to be the major events leading to the Civil War. Create a rationale for your choices. For each event, trace immediate and long-term consequences.

Turner, Ann. Illustrated by Ronald Himler. *Nettie's Trip South*. Macmillan, 1987. 27 pages, unnumbered.

> Addie, I can't get this out of my thoughts:
> If we slipped into a black skin

like a tight coat,
everything would change.
No one would call us by our last names,
for we would not have them.
Addie and Nettie we'd be,
Until we were worn out and died.
When someone called, we'd jump!

(p. 21, unnumbered)

At a Glance ▪ Deceptively simple, this powerful picture book describes the trip a young girl takes from Albany, New York, to Richmond, Virginia, in 1859 as she encounters slavery for the first time. Based on an actual diary, it would make an effective teacher read-aloud and is appropriate for all ages.

Summary ▪ Written in the form of a letter to her best friend, this book describes ten-year-old Nettie's experiences and reactions to slavery as she and her older sister and brother travel to the South prior to the outbreak of the Civil War. From a child's perspective, she questions what it means to be "three-fifths of a person" when her sister tells her that's how slaves are described in the Constitution. Increasingly horrified by what she sees, Nettie becomes sick to her stomach when they attend a slave auction and witness two children her own age being separated from each other after being sold to different men. Returning home she reflects upon her experiences and realizes that everything in her life would change if her skin color were black.

Teaching Considerations ▪ Ann Turner was inspired to write this story based on her great-grandmother's dairy of a trip she took South when she was a young woman. According to Turner, her great-grandmother returned a committed abolitionist. Ronald Himler's pencil drawings are effectively understated and enhance rather than dominant the poetic nature of the text. Seeing the cruel realities of slavery through the eyes of a child makes *Nettie's Trip South* a compelling experience on many different levels. Younger readers can be helped to understand Nettie's feelings, while older readers can analyze why the author chose to tell the story from the perspective of a ten-year-old girl rather than that of an adult.

After Reading: Suggested Student Activities

1. Nettie's brother is a newspaper reporter, and the trip South is to be the basis for his first story. Write that story from his perspective, selecting the type of coverage you consider appropriate.

2. In an introduction to this picture book, the author states that it was inspired by the diary of her great-grandmother, who became a committed abolitionist after her trip South. Imagine that you are Turner's great-grandmother. Write a persuasive speech against slavery to be delivered at a rally held by abolitionists.

3. Although it was against the law to teach slaves to read and write, some learned anyway. Imagine that you are Tabitha, the slave Nettie meets in the hotel. Write an account of their meeting from Tabitha's perspective.

4. *Nettie's Trip South* lends itself well to dramatization. Develop a script elaborating upon one or several of the experiences described by Turner. Perform it with other members of your class.

Walter, Mildred Pitts. *Second Daughter: The Story of a Slave Girl.* Scholastic, 1996. 214 pages.

"John, dear," the mistress asked, "tell me what is all this whining about slavery? All I hear is talk about freeing slaves."

"It's nothing for you to worry about," he answered matter-of-factly.

"It's part of our investment, so it *is* something for us to worry about. What would happen if we freed the darkies? How could they take care of themselves? They're like children and they're lazy, stupid, raucous, and loud." (pp. 103–4)

Sheffield [Massachusetts] was among the first counties to have a meeting on ending slavery and on declaring in favor of independence from the king. The general court acting on the will of the people agreed that there should be an end to slavery and sent the bill to Governor Gage to have the king turn their wish into law.

This time the mistress, feeling threatened, pleaded with the master to send a petition to the governor to forward to the king, asking that the wishes of ruffians and backwoodsmen not be heeded. Men of property did not wish this to happen. It was those who had nothing and wanted nothing that wished to destroy the colonies and the king's rule. (p. 109)

At a Glance ▪ Set immediately before and during the Revolutionary War, this intriguing historical novel is based on the 1781 case of Mum Bett, a slave who sued her owner for freedom under the new Massachusetts constitution and won. Appropriate for upper elementary and junior high/middle school students, this book tells a little known but important story in the early struggle to end slavery.

Summary ▪ Aissa and her older sister, Bett, are slaves to Judge Ashley and his family in Sheffield, Massachusetts. Aissa, rebellious and outspoken, adores her older sister and tells the story of how Bett secured their freedom. Bett, who holds important responsibilities in the household, is allowed to marry Josiah, a freedman; but according to the law, their children will be slaves because their mother is. Bett frequently overhears the conversations of the lawyers and other men writing the new Massachusetts constitution and wonders if the words about equality, freedom, and independence apply to slaves also. Josiah and another freedman, Agrippa, petition for the freedom of the slaves in Massachusetts, but are refused. When the Continental Army, losing the war and desperate for men, promises money and land to blacks who enlist, Josiah joins to earn money to buy Bett's freedom. Judge Ashley refuses to help Bett get the soldier's stipend due her as Josiah's wife because she is a slave and therefore, not legally married, but a frequent visitor to the Ashley household, Lawyer Tapping Reeve, intervenes for her. When Josiah is killed in battle and conditions become even more inhumane for Bett and her family in the Ashley household, she decides she will no longer endure it and leaves, refusing to return. She then requests Reeve's help in securing their freedom under the state's constitution.

Teaching Considerations ▪ Most students have limited awareness of the efforts to abolish slavery prior to the Civil War and the role blacks played in this struggle. Many slaves viewed the conflict between the colonies and England as an opportunity to secure their own freedom. Did not the Declaration of Independence apply to them, also? During the Revolutionary War, blacks fought for both the Continental Army and the Redcoats because at one time or another each side promised them freedom, but at other times, each refused to enlist blacks. A few became free when their Tory masters fled, while others petitioned for their freedom. The court case (Brom & Bett v. Ashley) upon which *Second Daughter* is based was a significant landmark in ending slavery in Massachusetts.

After Reading: Suggested Student Activities

1. Imagine that you lived during the time period in which *Second Daughter* is set. You are convinced you must take some personal action against slavery and decide to give a speech at a town meeting to persuade people to abolish slavery. Prepare and practice your speech; then give it at a simulated town meeting held by your class.

2. Bett and Aissa are vivid characters who grow and change throughout this story. Choose a creative medium to express their characteristics and changes.

3. There are many dramatic scenes in this book. Select one to perform with several of your classmates. Prepare a script and then act it out for the rest of the class.

4. Do more research to find out how and when each Northern state abolished slavery. Share this information with your classmates by developing an annotated timeline.

Zeinert, Karen. The *Amistad* Slave Revolt and American Abolition. Linnet Books, 1997. 101 pages.

Clearly the *Amistad* revolt had far-reaching effects on many lives, effects that Cinque and the other captives could not possibly have imagined as they fought for their freedom on that hot summer night in 1839 aboard the *Amistad*. (p. 89)

At a Glance ▪ Presented within the larger context of the abolitionist movement, this informational book tells the fascinating story of the African slave revolt aboard the ship *La Amistad* and the resulting effects of that action. Clearly written, this book is appropriate for junior high/middle school students and able upper elementary school students. Secondary school students also would enjoy this succinct account.

Summary ▪ Author Karen Zeinert, a former history teacher, tells the compelling story of the fifty-three enslaved West Africans aboard the ship *La Amistad,* who in 1839 revolted in an attempt to regain their freedom and return home. Tricked by the two Spaniards who promised to sail them back to Africa, their leader Cinque and the other brave Mende adults and children were arrested when the ship was seized off Long Island and taken to Connecticut. Thus began a two-year long series of legal and political maneuvers to free them. Prominent American abolitionists formed a committee to publicize the plight of the Africans and to galvanize public opinion against slavery; they also raised money for their legal defense. Eventually the case went to the U.S. Supreme Court where former president John Quincy Adams argued in their defense and won their release.

Teaching Considerations ▪ Teachers can capitalize upon the current interest created by the movie *Amistad* to help students begin to understand the many complex legal, social, economic, and political issues surrounding slavery in the United States prior to the Civil War. Other recommended books that also tell the story of the *Amistad* revolt are:

Jurmain, Suzanne. *Freedom's Sons: The True Story of the Amistad Mutiny.* Lothrop, Lee & Shepard, 1998.

Myers, Walter Dean. *Amistad: A Long Road to Freedom.* Dutton, 1998.

After Reading: Suggested Student Activities

1. The *Amistad* case was the media event of the day. Discuss how the abolitionists got the public's attention and how the public

responded. Compare the strategies and techniques for informing and persuading the public about an issue during this pre-Civil War period with those used today.

2. Imagine you are a reporter covering some aspect of the *Amistad* case. Using the same basic facts, write two newspaper articles, each from a different perspective, reflecting the attitudes and opinions of the day.

3. Prepare a chart that lists the major reasons given in 1839 for abolishing slavery and for preserving slavery.

4. Select one or more of the principal figures in the *Amistad* episode. Write a tribute or use another creative medium of expression to honor them.

More Books

Barrette, Tracy. *Harper's Ferry: The Story of John Brown's Raid.* The Millbrook Press, 1993. 64 pages.

This illustrated, nonfiction account presents an overview of John Brown's life and his fight for the abolition of slavery. Additionally, the account provides readers with a perspective on slavery in the United States. For John Brown, the freeing of slaves was a life-long obsession. Brown developed a plan to seize the arsenal at Harper's Ferry, Virginia. He believed that his action would be the symbolic rallying point for the antislavery forces; however, his siege at Harper's Ferry failed and only Brown and a handful of his followers survived to be tried for treason and sentenced to death. John Brown was a martyr for the opponents of slavery and his name was used to evoke antislavery sentiment. This basic book could be read by upper elementary students or used as a teacher read-aloud for all elementary grades. (See also chapter 4).

Charbonneau, Eileen. *Honor to the Hills.* A Tor Book, 1996. 192 pages.

Honor to the Hills is the third book in the critically acclaimed Woods family saga. Set in 1851, this historical novel explores the impact of the issues tearing the nation apart on the Woods family and their close-knit community in the Catskill Mountains of New York State. Fifteen-year-old Lily Woods struggles with how to respond when terror, betrayal, hatred, and danger shatter their once peaceful community. But she must take action when her sister is almost killed in an attack on the school for young Negro children where she teaches and when slave catchers kidnap family friends, members of a freedman family. Appropriate for high school students and able junior high/middle school students, this book combines an exciting story with insight into how major national issues affect ordinary people in more remote areas.

Fox, Paula. *The Slave Dancer.* Dell Publishing, 1973. 152 pages.

A Newbery Medal winner and perennial favorite, this powerful story is told through the eyes of thirteen-year-old Jessie, who is snatched off the streets of New Orleans in 1840 and thrown aboard the slave ship, *The Moonlight,* to work. Wanting to exercise the slaves so they will stay in good physical condition and command high prices, the captain orders Jessie to play his fife, and the slaves are forced to "dance" to his music. *The Slave Dancer* describes the horrors of the slave trade and the inhuman conditions aboard the slave ships. Although some of the vocabulary may be unfamiliar to some junior high/middle school students, this book could be used at that level and also with high school students.

Gay, Kathlyn, and Martin Gay. *Civil War.* Henry Holt & Co., 1995. 64 pages.

One of the titles in the Voices from the Past series, this book provides a concise overview of the issues and causes of the Civil War, major military actions, and social conditions during the war. Accompanied by maps, illustrations, vintage photographs, and quotes from primary sources, the text also provides fascinating bits of information about lesser known figures such as Kady Brownell and Emma Edmonds. Appropriate for junior high/middle school students, this book may also be useful to some high school students.

Hakim, Joy. *A History of US: War, Terrible War.* Oxford University Press, 1994. 160 pages.

Labeled "a storyteller's history of our nation written for young people from 9 to 99," this book, part of the ten-volume History of US series, provides an overview of the Civil War era. Written in a simple, conversational style, each page contains some form of visual aid, such as vintage photographs, cartoons, posters, and maps. The book also includes: quotes from primary sources, inserts with interesting pieces of information, definitions of specialized words, parenthetical explanations within the text, a chronology of events from 1820 through May 1865, Civil War songs, and a short annotated bibliography. While a wealth of information is available, it may be confusing to some readers if the book is read sequentially because the author does not appear to follow strictly either a chronological or a thematic format. Intended for upper elementary and junior high/middle school students, this book may also be useful to some high school students.

Kent, Zachary. *The Story of John Brown's Raid on Harper's Ferry.* Children's Press, 1988. 32 pages

This nonfiction account focuses on the efforts of John Brown and his followers to achieve a major antislavery uprising by capturing the federal arsenal at Harper's Ferry, Virginia (now West Virginia). While his efforts at Harper's Ferry failed and Brown was executed, he did gain widespread attention for the antislavery movement. This book is illustrated with both photographs and drawings. This basic book could be read by upper elementary students or used as a teacher read-aloud for all elementary grades. (See also chapter 4).

McPherson, James M. *What They Fought For: 1861–1865.* An Anchor Book, 1994. 88 pages.

In this short, critical essay appropriate for secondary students, especially those in college preparatory classes, McPherson analyzes this pivotal question: "Why did Americans fight against each other?" Based on the personal letters and diaries of almost one thousand Union and Confederate soldiers, McPherson argues against a commonly held belief that ordinary soldiers had very little awareness of the issues and no idea of what they were fighting for. Instead, he asserts that "not all, of course, but a large number of those men in blue and gray were intensely aware of the issues at stake and passionately concerned about them" (p. 4). McPherson, a noted scholar and historian, prepared this book for the Walter Lynwood Fleming Lectures in Southern History at Louisiana State University.

In it he describes the beliefs and motivations of soldiers on both sides.

Meltzer, Milton. *Voices from the Civil War: A Documentary History of the Great American Conflict.* Crowell, 1989. 203 pages.

Noted author Milton Meltzer has compiled a fascinating collection of documents, including personal letters, diary entries, newspaper clippings, songs, speeches, and memoirs from people who were on both sides of the Civil War conflict. The selections include the well known as well as ordinary people from all walks of life. Meltzer provides a brief introduction to each selection that puts them into context. This documentary history gives readers an inside perspective on the Civil War, from its origins through the conclusion. Appropriate for a wide range of reading levels, excerpts could also be used effectively as a teacher read-aloud.

Ward, Geoffrey C., with Ric Burns and Ken Burns. *The Civil War: An Illustrated History.* American Documentaries, Inc., 1990. 425 pages.

This richly illustrated companion volume to the PBS television series is a comprehensive and valuable resource. More than an account of the battles and political events, it provides a fascinating portrait of the people and the times, both North and South, rich and poor. A well-researched book, it includes essays by four prominent Civil War historians, in addition to the more than 500 illustrations, many of them never before published, and rare photographs. Teachers, secondary students, and interested junior high/middle school students will turn to this book over and over again.

Wisler, C. Clifton. *Caleb's Choice.* Lodestar Books, 1996. 154 pages.

Set in Texas in 1858, this novel tells the story of Caleb Dulaney, sent to live with his grandmother in northern Texas when his own family falls upon hard times. While traveling there, he encounters a slave auction and becomes aware of other cruelties that he had previously ignored. Life at his grandmother's is quite different from the privileged, city life Caleb is used to living. Furthermore, people are violently divided over the new Fugitive Slave Law, slave hunters roam the countryside, and rumors abound about something called the Underground Railroad. Caleb is confused and unsure whether fleeing slaves should be turned in or helped. But when a runaway slave rescues him from drowning, he begins to see things differently. This book is appropriate for upper elementary and junior high/middle school students.

Yates, Elizabeth. *Prudence Crandall*. E.P. Dutton Co., 1955; Boyds Mills Press, 1996. 238 pages.

Originally published in 1955, and written by Newbery Award-winner Elizabeth Yates, the historical novel, *Prudence Crandall*, has stood the test of time and was reissued in 1996. Based on the actual life of the young Quaker teacher Prudence Crandall, the book tells the dramatic story of her efforts to provide schooling for "young ladies of color." In 1833 opening a school for young white girls in Canterbury, Connecticut, is considered a daring move; a school for young black girls is an outrage. Prudence is subjected to hostility and attacks by the angry townspeople. Laws are passed, and she is forced to endure long trials and even imprisonment. Throughout it all, Prudence is steadfast and courageous. This book tells an important story and is appropriate for upper elementary and junior high/middle school students.

3

Struggling to Be Free

It is a reality of human nature that virtually every nation in the world has one or more tragic chapters of human rights abuses in its history. Often these abuses involve the enslavement of others. The reasons for servitude are initially economic: What better way to get a job done and done quickly than by people who do not have the right to refuse to work nor have any control over the working conditions? Beyond those "advantages" for the owners are the financial ones: What system has lower overhead? The usually deplorable working conditions of slaves are often mirrored by equally inhumane living conditions.

Frederick Douglass in *Escape from Slavery* describes his own experiences, which were relatively representative:

> Men and women slaves received, as their monthly allowance of food, eight pounds of pork, or its equivalent in fish, and one bushel of corn meal. Their yearly clothing consisted of two coarse linen shirts, one pair of linen trousers, like the shirts, one jacket, one pair of trousers for winter, made of coarse negro cloth, one pair of stockings, and one pair of shoes; the whole of which could not have cost more than seven dollars.
>
> The children unable to work in the field had neither shoes, stockings, jackets, nor trousers, given to them;

their clothing consisted of two coarse linen shirts per year. When these failed them, they went naked. Children from seven to ten years old, of both sexes, almost naked, might be seen at all seasons of the year. (p. 5)

Apologists for the Old South might argue that this is only one scenario and that there were benevolent slave owners who looked at their slaves "like family," allowing them to live in "good" conditions, being well clothed and well fed. This type of reasoning denies all that we know about human needs and fulfillment. While it is vital not to be hungry or cold, human beings cannot feel safe when their humanity is denied and they are treated like objects. By its definition and practice, slavery is inhumane because it robs its victims of the right to choose freely.

The history of slavery is intertwined with our early years. The first slaves arrived in Jamestown in 1619, the year before the Pilgrims landed at Plymouth. In the period between 1650 and 1850, it is estimated that twelve million Africans were taken from their homes to be enslaved in Europe or the Americas; however, as many as one third died en route on slave ships. The Middle Passage, the sea voyage, lasted between two and three months, during which the captives were packed in racks under the decks. Slavery was banned in most European countries in the seventeenth century and by 1808 the United States had outlawed the importation of slaves from Africa. The illegal transportation of slaves flourished, however, and as late as 1860 U.S. officials captured twelve slave ships with 3,119 potential slaves aboard. One third of all Southern households had slaves, and one half of those had five or fewer slaves. There were more people held as slaves in the Southern states than anywhere else in the world.

It is a common misconception that slaves passively accepted their servitude. There were cases of mutinies on slavers that led to even more brutal restrictions during the Middle Passage. From the earliest days, there are documented cases of rebellions and revolts by slaves. Nat Turner, a slave from Virginia, lead an uprising in 1831 in which over fifty whites were killed. Turner and many other blacks were then executed in response. Denmark Vesey, a freed slave in South Carolina, planned a major uprising, but his plans were discovered and he was executed in 1822 along with thirty-three others.

Slave-owning was a tradition and a way of life in the South for many members of the landed gentry. Large plantations often had several hundred slaves, and within the slave community, there emerged a social structure where the field hands were at the lowest level and the house slaves held the highest. Maintaining a large plantation was like running a small town. Skilled trades such as carpentry, harness and saddle-making, and sewing created opportunities for able young slaves that paralleled the apprenticeship system among whites. The primary difference was that once slaves mastered a trade, they, and the use of their trade, were still under the control of the master. Even the best skilled and most able slaves could not seek better situations in life unless they managed to do extra work and earn enough money to buy their own freedom. And this presupposes that their owners were willing to let them "buy themselves." Often the owners would not grant freedom at any cost because they felt that the slaves were their property, like a chair or table. Many slave owners believed that slaves were not truly human beings or at least, that they were not equal to them in their humanness.

The work was grueling, the days long, and the restrictions severe, but in the face of all of these difficulties, there were slaves who found a way out, who managed to make new lives for themselves and often their families. The constraints of bondage do not only contain a person physically. A person enslaved may be robbed of some of those qualities that help to give meaning to human beings: the power to think freely, the opportunity to learn widely, the promise to dream wildly, and the will to hope reasonably. It is these qualities that helped many slaves to achieve freedom, whether through escaping or by transcending their daily reality through their own acts of kindness to others or their own sense of religious faith.

While accurate records were never kept, it is estimated that by 1850 more than 100,000 slaves had escaped and fled to the North and on to Canada on the Underground Railroad. These escaped slaves were valued at over $30 million. The Fugitive Slave Laws of 1850 allowed slave catchers to enter free states and recapture slaves who had run away. These laws also fueled antislavery sentiment in the North. Canada was the closest and safest refuge for the escapees. The majority of escapees found their way or were taken to stations on the Underground Railroad to make their way North. The Underground Railroad was a group of free blacks, former slaves, and abolitionists who provided guides, "conductors," routes, safe houses, transportation, and supplies for those seeking freedom.

Among the most revealing prohibitions of slavery were the legal restrictions against allowing slaves to learn to read and write. The inherent power of the written word was threatening to the slave owners, who recognized that if slaves could read, they could gain access to the world. If they had the ability to read, they might run; they might encourage insubordination among other slaves; they might forge travel passes; and even more significantly, they might challenge the whole institution of slavery.

In this chapter we examine the experiences of blacks in America during the time of slavery. We include books that tell of life in the slave quarters and life on the run, recounting the stories of slaves fleeing to freedom. While we look at experiences with the Underground Railroad and the abolition movement in this chapter, the leaders of this movement—such as Harriet Tubman, Sojourner Truth, and Frederick Douglass—are presented in the next chapter, "Those Who Made a Difference."

Prior to Reading: Think About . . .

Young people need to do some preliminary thinking and talking to prepare them to understand what they read or what is read to them about the Civil War. They need opportunities to ask questions and to raise issues and concerns. The following questions can be used to prompt this discussion:

- What do you already know about the conditions of slavery in this country prior to Emancipation?

- What things are you interested in learning about in the struggle to be free?

- What do you already know about the Underground Railroad? What other things are you interested in learning about it?

- What do you already know about the legal restrictions runaways and those who attempted to help them faced?

- What are all the different ways we can learn about how Americans of African descent struggled to be free? Make a list.

- Choose a quotation taken from one of the books described in this chapter. What do you think it means? What does it make you curious about in the book?

Focus Books

Feelings, Tom, with an Introduction by Dr. John Henrik Clarke.
The Middle Passage: White Ships/Black Cargo.
Dial Books, 1995. 76 pages, unnumbered.

Nowhere in the annals of history has a people experienced such a long and traumatic ordeal as Africans during the Atlantic slave trade. Over nearly four centuries of the slave trade—which continued until the end of the Civil War—millions of African men, women, and children were savagely torn from their homeland, herded onto ships, and dispersed all over the so-called New World. Although there is no way to compute exactly how many people perished, it has been estimated that between thirty and sixty million Africans were subjected to this horrendous triangular trade system and that only one third—if that—of those people survived. (p. 8, Dr. John Henrik Clarke)

At a Glance ▪ In sixty-four paintings, award-winning illustrator Tom Feelings creates a visual narrative of capturing of African men and women from their homes and transporting them in slave ships to the New World. Appropriate for secondary school students.

Summary ▪ This book creates a sense of the horror of "forced migration." This is a wordless book, with the exception of initial moving comments by Tom Feelings and a powerful introduction by Dr. John Henrik Clarke. The book tells the story of the capture, torture, abuse, and killing of the captives, but it is also the story of those who survived the unspeakable.

The images in this book are powerful. Feelings shows the torture of black men and the taking of black women; human beings piled and stacked in cubby holes below deck; men, women, and children shackled, tied, and harnessed. Controlled by white men with guns, whips, swords, and ropes, these enslaved people endured too little space, horrible food, debilitating diseases, abuse from crew members, and death.

Teaching Considerations • This book is appropriate for the secondary schools because the paintings are so powerful that students should be mature to react to this book. The paintings evoke strong emotions and teachers need to talk with students about the illustrations and the circumstances that inspired them. The book received the Coretta Scott King Illustrator Award. Another title that could be used with it is *From Slave Ship to Freedom Road* by Julius Lester, with illustrations by Rod Brown (Dial, 1998).

After Reading: Suggested Student Activities

1. Put a face on the Middle Passage experience by creating and naming a captive. Do a character portrait of the captive. (Teacher Note: See the guidelines in chapter 1 for this story.)

2. Select one of the illustrations that had a significant impact on you. Explain, in a short journal entry, how you felt and why.

3. After viewing the pictures and reading Tom Feelings's introductory remarks, explain in a class discussion what you think he meant when he said he has finished a "psychological and spiritual journey back in order to move forward."

4. Do research about the Middle Passage and share your findings with members of your class.

Freedman, Florence B. *Two Tickets to Freedom.* Scholastic, 1971. 96 pages.

No sooner had they left the station than Ellen, who had concealed her fears and played her part with so much courage and wit throughout the journey, grasped William's hand and said, "Thank God we are safe!" She burst into tears, and wept like a child. (p. 48)

At a Glance ▪ This is the true story of William and Ellen Craft, a slave couple who devised a daring plan to escape to freedom. This book could be read by most upper elementary and junior high/middle school students.

Summary ▪ William and Ellen Craft lived on a Southern plantation. William had been allowed to learn a trade, and his wife Ellen was the personal maid to her mistress and an accomplished seamstress. They were permitted to live together as man and wife. But no matter how well they were treated, they were not free; they still "belonged" to their owners. Many slaves who tried to escape to freedom were recaptured and punished severely or even killed. William and Ellen decided that they needed to plan a way to go North. Ellen was so fair that she could pass for white, so they decided to disguise her as a frail young white man. William would travel with her as her slave. Getting permission to visit relatives over Christmas, Ellen, as "Mr. Johnson," purchased railroad tickets for William and herself. After a series of trying experiences and potential problems, Ellen and William arrived in Philadelphia to begin their life in freedom. Their troubles were not over: they joined the abolitionist cause to help others, and their safety was in question. They spent time working for the cause in Boston, but when the Fugitive Slave Act was signed by President Millard Fillmore in 1850, they were in even greater danger, so they fled again. The Crafts went to Canada on their way to England, where they stayed until the Civil War ended.

Teaching Considerations ▪ The book is filled with action and will keep readers' attention as it provides an exciting story of courage and adventure. Teachers should be alerted that the accounts of the prejudice and bigotry that the Crafts experienced include racial epithets that are an appropriate reflection of attitudes of the times and do not detract from the book. Teachers will need to frame this offensive language in context for their students.

After Reading: Suggested Student Activities

1. Imagine that you are escaping from slavery on the train heading to freedom. Write a journal entry reflecting on what you experience and feel that day.

2. Examine the Fugitive Slave Bill of 1850. What were the provisions of this bill and its implication? Make sure to reflect historical accuracy in your response.

3. The Crafts encountered a number of influential people in the fight for freedom for slaves. Select one of these people and prepare a report about that person and his or her role in the battle against slavery.

4. Historically during this period, there were attitudes that supported the belief that only white men were capable of making significant decisions. Many people believed that along with slaves, women and children were types of property and should be under the control and protection of men. Using this social and political perspective as a framework, plan and hold a town meeting to discuss the presence of escaped slaves and slave hunters in your community.

Hamilton, Virginia. Illustrated by Leo and Diane Dillon.
Many Thousand Gone: African-Americans from Slavery to Freedom.
Alfred A. Knopf, 1993. 151 pages.

Running-aways considered themselves free once they had crossed the north shore of the Ohio River. They understood they were free, but not safe. There were still dangers—bounty hunters and proslavery settlers, who might capture a fugitive for the reward posted by the slave owner.

Southerners called the running-aways maroons, wild ones, or desperadoes. Every day they were free was a reminder to other slaves that escape was possible. Nothing except a slave uprising upset the slaveholder more than the thought of a maroon stalking his plantation, bent on leading others to freedom. (p. 35)

At a Glance ▪ Award-winning author Virginia Hamilton has written a series of short accounts and vignettes describing slavery in this country and the experiences of those who struggled to be free, both well known and little known. Clearly written, this book is appropriate for elementary school students and would be easy but interesting reading for junior high/middle school students. It could also be used effectively for teacher read-alouds.

Summary ▪ *Many Thousand Gone: African-Americans from Slavery to Freedom* is divided into three parts: "Slavery in America"; "Running-Aways"; and "Exodus to Freedom." Each part consists of short chapters describing conditions, events, and the experiences of specific people. Part two is the longest section and includes information on the Gabriel Prosser uprising, the Nat Turner rebellion, Sojourner Truth, and Frederick Douglass, among others.

Teaching Considerations ▪ This book has received numerous awards, including ALA Notable Children's Book, ALA *Booklist* Editors' Choice, Bank Street/Child Study Association Best Book, and *The Bulletin of the Center for Children's Books* Blue Ribbon. It could be used as a companion to Hamilton's earlier book, *The People Could Fly.*

After Reading: Suggested Student Activities

1. Select an event or person from this book that you found particularly interesting. Depict the important points in a chart or collage or some other visual representation.

2. Imagine you are a newspaper reporter living during the time described in one of the chapters. Write a newspaper article about what occurred.

3. As a class project, develop a mural that tells the story of the African American struggle to be free using information you learned from this book.

4. Choose an event or person from this book that you want to know more about. Do research and present the information to your class in a creative format.

Hansen, Joyce. *Which Way Freedom?*
Avon Books, 1986. 120 pages.

"Where you from?" a familiar voice called out. "Who your master?" Obi hadn't seen Daniel sit down with a group of men under a nearby tree.

"Ain't got none," Obi mumbled, his eyes avoiding Daniel's. He was too upset to talk to a stranger—even one who had helped him.

"You free?" Daniel asked, finishing off his food. (p. 71)

At a Glance ▪ Joyce Hansen creates a compelling story of two young slaves seeking freedom. This book presents a fictionalized account of actual circumstances that slaves faced in the South. It is appropriate for junior high/middle school and secondary students.

Summary ▪ For Obi, Easter, and Jason, life is difficult on their owner's small plantation. As the Civil War begins, Obi and Easter realize that they will be sold. Although they are the only "family" each other has, Obi longs to be reunited with his mother who had been sold away. Obi and Easter are able to escape when they are hired out to work for some neighbors, but they are separated from Jason. Once they are free from the plantation, they are captured by the Confederate Army. The army wants to use them as laborers. Easter poses as a young boy, cooking for the officers, but Obi works digging trenches. He secretly also works on a boat to escape to the island where the Union forces are. When he escapes, Easter chooses to stay behind because she hopes to be able to go back to rescue Jason. Obi works for the Union Army until blacks are allowed to serve.

Teaching Considerations ▪ This book is a powerful endorsement of the connection between people and a sense of "family." Hansen provides valuable information about frequently ignored historical facts. This highly acclaimed book has been named a Coretta Scott King Honor Book, an ALA Notable Book, an NCSS-CBS Notable Children's Book in the Field of Social Studies, and a CCBS Choice.

After Reading: Suggested Student Activities

1. In good historical fiction, authors present actual events within the context of the story that they are telling. Research the massacre at Fort Pillow to determine how Hansen has used historical fact in this book. Write a short paper discussing the historical accuracy of the account in this book.

2. Create a chart listing new insights or information that you gained about the role of African Americans during this time.

3. Obi seeks to uphold a number of significant social values. Identify three of these values and then use them as the basis for a collage or series of drawings. These illustrations should demonstrate the enduring nature of these values.

4. Examine the choices that Obi and Easter made. In whole class discussion, be prepared to examine what these choices tell us about their character.

Haskins, Jim. *Get on Board: The Story of the Underground Railroad.* Scholastic, 1993. 152 pages.

Free blacks were an important source of help for escaped slaves. In fact, in the early days before whites in significant numbers began to help runaways, free blacks were more likely to help than were whites, whom escaped slaves would not have trusted to aid them. Even after whites began to help in an organized fashion, blacks who had already escaped reached back to help those who were still enslaved. In fact, the story of the Underground Railroad that has come down through history tends to understate the role of free blacks. (pp. 21–22)

At a Glance ▪ Award-winning author Jim Haskins has written an engaging and readable history of slave escapes, the courageous people involved, and the Underground Railroad. Appropriate for upper elementary and junior high/middle school students; however, secondary students will also find this book interesting and informative.

Summary ▪ Haskins begins his narrative by describing the possible origins of the name "Underground Railroad," and a brief summary of the history of slave escapes and fugitive slave laws. He then provides a more detailed account of the loosely organized Underground Railroad, beginning in the 1830s to the end of the Civil War. Numerous stories of harrowing escapes and courageous actions by various "stationmasters" and "conductors", such as Harriet Tubman and other lesser-known individuals, add to the richness of this account. Both proslavery and antislavery proponents publicized the Underground Railroad to serve their own purposes. The legend of the Underground Railroad grew after the Civil War ended, when many agents wrote their memoirs and some former stations became landmarks.

Teaching Considerations ▪ Although the name "Underground Railroad" is familiar, many students lack much information about its specifics and its place in the long history of the struggle to be free. In particular, they are often unaware of the extensive role free blacks played in helping fugitives to safety. This book was designated a Notable Children's Trade Book in the Field of Social Studies for 1994. It contains photographs, maps, illustrations, and a timeline of significant dates from 1518 through 1865.

After Reading: Suggested Student Activities

1. Discuss with your class the role of the Underground Railroad in helping fugitive slaves and its effects on both the North and the South.

2. Develop an idea map to illustrate the various components and activities of the Underground Railroad. (Teacher Note: See the guidelines in chapter 1 for this literature involvement strategy.)

3. Select one or two individuals described in this book whom you admire and use a creative medium to illustrate their actions.

4. Choose an event described in this book. Then write two newspaper accounts of it, one from the perspective of antislavery forces and the other from a proslavery perspective.

**Hooks, William H. Paintings by James Ransome. *Freedom's Fruit.*
Alfred A. Knopf, 1996. 40 pages, unnumbered.**

> The master left Mama Marina's cabin. She closed the
> door and hid the small gold piece in a money belt she
> wore under her clothes. Through the years as a conjure
> woman, she managed to collect gold pieces here and
> there. But she was a long way from a hundred pieces.
> She settled the money belt back in place and went about
> her business among the grapevines. (p. 3, unnumbered)

At a Glance ▪ This beautifully illustrated picture book combines
the story of a conjure woman with the desire of a mother to see her
daughter freed from slavery. This book could be read and enjoyed
by students at all levels.

Summary ▪ Capitalizing on the oral tradition of Carolina "Low
Country," William Hooks uses a conjure woman who outsmarts
her owner to buy freedom for her daughter and the man she loves.
Conjure women (or men) have special powers that are used to cast
spells or to protect people from spells. Mama Marina is asked by
her master to "conjure the grapes," so that his slaves will not eat
his valuable crop before he can have it harvested and made into
wine. She agrees and is paid by him. She is saving money to buy her
daughter Sheba's freedom, but freedom means nothing to Sheba
without the man she loves, Joe Nathan. The master plans to rent
him out to other plantations because he is an accomplished leather
worker. Knowing that this plan would keep them apart, they go to
Mama Marina for help. She has them eat conjured grapes from the
vine before they have ripened. Mama Marina promises the lovers
that they will become ill, but they will not die and in the spring they
will recover and then they will be free.

Teaching Considerations ▪ Younger students will need background about both conjuring and about the whole oral tradition
from which this story comes. This book is a great springboard for
writing experiences. Older students can be helped to see the connection with Greek mythology, especially the story of Persephone. The
wonderful paintings that illustrate this book deserve special attention.

After Reading: Suggested Student Activities

1. Interview an older member of your family or a close family friend. Have them share examples of myths from their family's history. Write a story based upon what you have learned.

2. In small groups discuss the role of superstition in our society. What kinds of beliefs do people have? How does the concept of mind over matter apply to this situation? Be prepared to share your findings with the whole class.

3. In preparation for whole class discussion, prepare answers to the following questions. What do the paintings contribute to this book? Are they effective? Why or why not?

4. Research the practices and tradition of conjurers. Share your findings with the class.

Hopkinson, Deborah. Paintings by James Ransome.
Sweet Clara and the Freedom Quilt.
Alfred A. Knopf, 1993. 38 pages, unnumbered.

Sunday I went to my favorite place on the little hill and looked out at the people's cabins and the fields. I took a stick and started making a picture in the dirt of all I could see.

But how could I make a picture of things far away that I *couldn't* see? And how could I make a map that wouldn't be washed away by the rain—a map that would show the way to freedom?

Then one day I was sewin' a patch on a pretty blue blanket. The patch looked just the same shape as the cow pond near the cabins. The little stitches looked like a path going all round it. Here it was—a picture that wouldn't wash away. A map! (p. 16)

At a Glance ▪ This picture book presents quilting as a type of storytelling, as Clara designs a quilt that maps the escape route for slaves to get to the Underground Railroad. As with other outstanding picture books, this one can be used with students at all levels.

Summary ▪ Clara is sold away from her mother and her home on North Farm to be a field hand on the Home Plantation before she is twelve years old. But Clara is determined to find a way to escape and go back to her mother. An older woman, Aunt Rachel, looks after Clara and realizes that she isn't strong enough to be a field hand. Aunt Rachel has an idea. She teaches Clara to sew. Clara practices hard to learn to make tiny stitches so she can work in the Big House as a seamstress. While working there, she overhears other slaves talking about the troubles some people have in trying to escape. They say that they need a map. Clara thinks about a map and wonders how she could make a map to help people escape. She decides to put the route on a quilt so she can work on it and no one from the Big House will have any idea about what she is doing. Once her map is done, Clara doesn't need it; she knows it by heart. She and young Jack leave to seek their freedom. But Clara cannot leave without going back for her mother.

Teaching Considerations ▪ The paintings by James Ransome give a vitality to this book. It was selected to be a Reading Rainbow Book. Additionally, it received the International Reading Association Children's Book Award; it was a Notable Children's Trade Book in the Field of Social Studies, and was chosen as a Children's Book-of-the-Month Club selection.

After Reading: Suggested Student Activities

1. Design a quilt that tells the story of some event from the Civil War period.

2. Research the patterns on quilts and their meanings. Specifically gather information about military quilts. Share your findings with your class.

3. Discuss the relative benefits of being a house slave. Would it be better or worse than working in the fields or working with animals? Be prepared to present your choices to the class.

4. To be a slave was to be considered less than human. In this type of dehumanizing environment, it took a special kind of courage

to escape. In a journal entry, imagine that you have been a slave. What would you have to do in order to flee?

Johnson, Dolores, author and illustrator.
Now Let Me Fly: The Story of a Slave Family.
Macmillan, 1993. 32 pages, unnumbered.

I will never forget how it felt to be forced to walk, bound and beaten, for endless miles, each step taking me farther away from my mother and father. As I was marched, hundreds of other shackled and stumbling black men, women, and children, taken as prisoners of war or kidnapped like me, joined us. We were herded by slave catchers like Dongo across Western Africa up to the edge of the western shore. (pp. 10–11, unnumbered)

At a Glance ▪ *Now Let Me Fly: The Story of a Slave Family* traces the experiences of slaves from their capture in Africa to their captivity on a Southern plantation. This picture book has wonderful color illustrations that complement the text. As with most picture books, it can be used with students at all grade levels. It would also be an appropriate teacher read-aloud.

Summary ▪ This is the story of two African children stolen from their families to be taken to the United States in chains. Minna and Amadi take care of one another on the ship that carries them into slavery. They are sold together to be field hands on a plantation, where they slave in the cotton fields. When they are older, Minna and Amadi are allowed to "jump the broom," the marriage ceremony for slaves. They have four children before Amadi is sold away. Minna wants to keep the rest of her family together, but within a year her eldest child is sold. Eventually, Minna and her younger daughter are the only members of the family left on the plantation.

Teaching Considerations ▪ Johnson provides author's notes that frame the content of this book. This story provides many of the details about slavery and the circumstances that people went through. Teachers should be aware that because the book is an overview, the significance and horror of slavery are somewhat minimized.

After Reading: Suggested Student Activities

1. In whole class discussion respond to the following: What does the title of the book mean? How is the image of flying used throughout the book?

2. In the book, Minna and Amadi "jump the broom" as their wedding ceremony. Read about other African American traditions or rituals and trace their origins. Prepare a written entry on each ritual. All the entries will be compiled in a class book.

3. Mason found freedom, not in the North, but with the Seminoles. Write a research report on the role that the Seminoles played in helping fugitive slaves.

Lasky, Kathryn. *True North: A Novel of the Underground Railroad.* Scholastic, 1996. 267 pages.

> Her grandfather was a doctor and a scholar. Was he a warrior, too?
> She knew he hated slavery, hated the fugitive slave law, but was he in fact a warrior against it? Would he break the law of the land himself and help slaves or help others to help fugitive slaves? There were fines, there was prison, you could be arrested!
> Her ancestors had written the laws of the Commonwealth—would they dare break them?
> Suddenly her whole world was turning upside down. There was so much to think about. (p. 125)

At a Glance ▪ Set in 1858, this historical novel intertwines the stories of a privileged fourteen-year-old girl in Boston, influenced by her abolitionist grandfather, and a fugitive slave girl from Virginia attempting to escape to freedom. Filled with intrigue and tough ethical issues, this book is appropriate for junior high/middle school students and able upper elementary school readers.

Summary ▪ The prologue and epilogue to *True North* are set in 1917, with flashbacks to the events in the lives of Lucy and Afrika during the year of 1858. Afrika is a pregnant slave girl fleeing with Harriet Tubman and other runaways from an abusive master in Virginia. When her baby is born prematurely and dies en route, Afrika stays behind in the swamp to bury the infant. She must then, by herself, find her way to the Underground Railroad stations on her way to freedom. Lucy Bradford, rebellious fourteen-year-old daughter of a prominent Boston family, bored with the narrow, confining lives of her four older sisters, looks to her grandfather for intellectual stimulation and moral guidance. Confused when she discovers that he is breaking the law to help fugitive slaves, she then becomes involved in activities that eventually result in meeting Afrika. Together they engage in dangerous and life-threatening actions as they try to get Afrika to safety in Canada.

Teaching Considerations ▪ A well-written book filled with suspense and danger, *True North* presents a number of moral and ethical issues and dilemmas that can be examined both in the context of the pre-Civil War era and of contemporary times. The physical and sexual abuse of slaves by their masters is presented in a sensitive yet historically accurate manner. Students may benefit from additional background information about the social attitudes and mores of the times as well as more details about the Fugitive Slave Law. While this book is not written at a difficult reading level, Lasky uses several literary devices, such as symbolism and time shifts, that add even more to the richness of the story. The author's section at the end of the book about why she wrote it provides fascinating insights.

After Reading: Suggested Student Activities

1. Lucy and Afrika come from very different backgrounds, yet they have some important things in common. Write a paper comparing and contrasting them and their lives. Create a visual representation of them to accompany your paper.

2. Symbols are used by authors to create meaning on several different levels. Lasky uses several symbols, such as *ship, true north,*

owl/owling, and *North Star*. Select one of these symbols or another one you found in the book and explain its meaning and significance in the story.

3. Debate with your class the pros and cons of the following issue: Laws are the legal foundation of a democratic society. Is it justifiable, therefore, to break a law you think is wrong? (Teacher's Note: This activity also could be used with a whole class by implementing it as a discussion continuum. See the guidelines in chapter 1 for this strategy.)

4. Many of the characters in this book behave in a deceptive manner. Choose two of them—one whose actions you agree with and one whose actions you disagree with. Describe and analyze their actions, using specific examples from the book. Then try to persuade your classmates to view the characters the way you do.

Lester, Julius. *To Be a Slave*. Scholastic, 1968. 160 pages.

To be a slave. To be owned by another person, as a car, house, or table is owned. To live as a piece of property that could be sold—a child sold from its mother, a wife from her husband. To be considered not human, but a "thing" that plowed the fields, cut the wood, cooked the food, nursed another's child; a "thing" whose sole function was determined by the one who owned you.

To be a slave. To know, despite the suffering and deprivation, that you were human, more human than he who said you were not human. To know joy, laughter, sorrow, and tears and yet be considered only the equal of a table.

To be a slave was to be a human being under conditions in which that humanity was denied. They were not slaves. They were people. Their condition was slavery. (p. 28)

At a Glance ▪ This award-winning and powerful book of what it was like to be a slave is told in the words of the men and women who endured slavery. Appropriate for secondary students and able junior high/middle school students, excerpts could also be used for teacher read-alouds.

Summary ▪ Lester drew upon two sources to compile this document of voices from slavery. The first source, recorded by Northern abolitionists during the first half of the nineteenth century, was the stories of blacks who escaped from the South. These narratives were used to build public opinion against slavery. The second source was work undertaken by the Federal Writers' Project during the 1930s. Lester intersperses the narratives with historical perspectives and commentary.

Teaching Considerations ▪ This highly acclaimed book has received the following awards: Newbery Honor Book, ALA Notable Children's Book, *School Library Journal* Best Book of the Year, Lewis Carroll Shelf award, *Horn Book* Fanfare Honor List, and *New York Times* Outstanding Book of the Year. Because it personalizes slavery, it could be used effectively as an accompaniment to a history text.

After Reading: Suggested Student Activities

1. This book uses a combination of a chronological and a thematic approach to tell the story of slavery. Select one or two narratives from each chapter that you consider to be representative and analyze their message and their implications. What common themes do you find throughout the book? Compare your responses with your learning partner's.

2. Select a chapter and prepare the narratives in it for use with Readers Theatre.

3. Compare this book of personal narratives with another book or excerpt from another book that you also have read about slavery. Analyze their effectiveness and describe your reactions to each one in your response journal.

4. Choose two or three narratives that particularly had an impact on you. Use a creative form to demonstrate their message and its effect.

Lyons, Mary E. *Letters from a Slave Girl: The Story of Harriet Jacobs*. Aladdin Paperbacks, 1992. 175 pages.

$300 REWARD! Ran away from the subscriber, an intelligent, bright mulatto girl, named Harriet, 21 years of age. Five feet four inches high. Dark eyes, and black hair inclined to curl; but it can be made straight. Has a decayed spot on a front tooth. She can read and write, and in all probability will try to get to the Free States. All persons are forbidden, under penalty of law, to harbor or employ said Slave. $150 will be given to whoever takes her in the state, and $300 if taken out of the state and delivered to me, or lodged in jail. Dr. Norcom (p. 70)

At a Glance ▪ A powerful, award-winning book based on the life of Harriet Jacobs, a North Carolina slave woman who hid in an attic for seven years before she was able to escape to freedom. Although the reading level is not difficult, the content is more appropriate for junior high/middle school age students and could provide valuable insights into slavery for high school students.

Summary ▪ Told in the form of letters written by Harriet Jacobs from 1825 to 1842 while she was a slave, followed by a summary of her life after her escape in 1842 until her death in 1897, this book helps the reader to experience the degrading powerlessness of a young woman in slavery and her incredible indomitable spirit to survive and to protect her children. Harriet is eleven years old when the mistress dies. She had cared for Harriet since her mother's death, taught her to read, and promised her and her family freedom. Harriet eagerly awaits a new life. But when the will is read, Harriet grimly discovers that she has been given to her mistress's niece, the three-year-old daughter of Doctor Norcom and his wife. Life in the Norcom household is difficult for Harriet and her brother, but it becomes almost intolerable when she reaches puberty. Refusing Harriet permission to marry the freedman she loves, Norcom relentlessly and cruelly pursues her, until she bears a child with another, more kindly, white man. After a second child is born, Harriet and her children are sent to the plantation of Norcom's son. There she devises a plan to save her children and to escape to freedom, but it takes seven long years in hiding, and many more twists of fate, before she realizes her dream.

Teaching Considerations ▪ Mary Lyons's book about Harriet Jacobs has won numerous awards, including the Golden Kite Award, and has been named an ALA Notable Children's Book, a Best Book for Young Adults, and a *Horn Book* Fanfare Book. Lyons's book is based on Harriet's own book, *Linda: Incidents in the Life of a Slave Girl, Written by Herself*, written under the pseudonym of Linda Brent and published three months before the Civil War began in 1861, and Harriet's other correspondence. Lyons also used additional sources, including letters written by Harriet's brother and the Norcom family papers. Part III of the book, the summary of Harriet's life from 1842 to 1897, while not written in letter form, is a compelling glimpse into the life of this courageous woman. It is followed by photographs, drawings, and an author's note. Some students may want to read a reprint of the original version of Harriet's book:

> Jacobs, Harriet Ann. *Incidents in the Life of a Slave Girl: Written by Herself*. Reprint, with introduction and notes by Jean Fagan Yellin. Cambridge: Harvard University Press, 1987.

> Brent, Linda. *Incidents in the Life of a Slave Girl: An Authentic Historical Narrative Describing the Horrors of Slavery as Experienced by Black Women*. Edited by L. Maria Child with new introduction and notes by Walter Teller. Harcourt Brace & Co., 1973

After Reading: Suggested Student Activities

1. Write a tribute to Harriet Jacobs using poetry or prose.

2. Discuss with your class examples of how Harriet and other

members of her family displayed courage in the face of cruelty and inhuman treatment.

3. Develop an annotated timeline illustrating the significant events in Harriet's life.

4. Select two of the people from Harriet's life, one that you admire and one that you dislike. Develop a character sketch of each, providing specific examples from the book of their actions and characteristics. (Teacher's Note: See the guidelines in chapter 1 for this strategy.)

McKissack, Patricia C., and Fredrick L. McKissack. *Christmas in the Big House, Christmas in the Quarters.* Scholastic, 1994.

The men gather in the study to smoke and talk politics. One young Marine under Colonel Robert E. Lee's command was at Harpers Ferry when the abolitionist John Brown and his men led a raid. He holds everyone's attention as he describes John Brown' s hanging earlier in the month. "His eyes blazed like those of a madman!" A toast is proposed: "God bless Colonel Robert E. Lee for saving Harpers Ferry." (p. 48, from the Big House)

But first the news. A driver who was with his master when John Brown was hanged describes it. "I was there that Friday morning. His eyes were filled with strength and determination. He stopped on his way to the gallows to kiss a black baby. My massa say John Brown was crazy. I say John Brown was Truth marching on. Slavery's coming to an end . . . and soon! Amen! Amen!" (p. 50, from the Quarters)

At a Glance ▪ This is a powerful book of contrasts, giving readers a sense of plantation life during Christmas in 1859. The book provides the final look at a way of life that would soon be altered irrevocably. The book, with its wonderful illustrations, is appropriate for a wide range of students.

Summary ▪ This book shows the festivities of the Christmas holidays, juxtaposing the opulent celebration in the master's home with the guarded celebration in the slave quarters. While those in the Big House speculate about the future and the importance of states' rights and the possibility of secession, they are secure in their lifestyle. In the Quarters, the days off from labor, the return visits of old friends and relatives, the celebrating are all welcome, but there is the pervasive desire to be free. While those in the Big House are satisfied with their lives, those in the Quarters are sure that freedom will come soon.

Teaching Considerations ▪ The book includes song lyrics, poems, and recipes from the antebellum period. Among the awards it has received are the Coretta Scott King Award and Orbis Pictus.

After Reading: Suggested Student Activities

1. Identify two customs practiced by those in the Big House and two practiced by those in the Quarters. Trace their origins. Report your findings to the class.

2. In whole class discussion, examine how irony is used in this book, giving examples. What does it contribute to the book?

3. Imagine that you are living in 1859. Write two journal entries, one as if you were living in the Big House and one as if you were living in the Quarters, for Christmas Day and for New Year's Day. How are our celebrations of these holidays today different from then?

4. In this book, the authors present two distinct points of view. Imagine that you are a visitor from New England. Report your reaction to these differing perspectives as if you are a reporter for your hometown paper.

5. Using the dual-perspective point of view demonstrated by the McKissacks in this book, select an issue or event that you have been reading about and create a scenario that represents the view of those who lived in the Big House and those who lived in the Quarters.

McPherson, James A. *Marching Toward Freedom: Blacks in the Civil War, 1861–1865.* Facts on File, 1991. 142 pages. Originally published in a different form by Alfred A. Knopf in 1967.

> Thousands of slaves in areas near the Northern army camps left their plantations and went over to the Yankees the first chance they had. This action by slaves, "voting with their feet" for freedom, forced the Union army to define these escaped slaves as "contrabands." Thus, the slaves themselves took the first step to achieve their freedom. (p. 23)

At a Glance ▪ Noted historian James A. McPherson uses a wealth of primary sources such as eyewitness accounts, diaries and journals, newspaper articles, songs, and photographs to provide a fascinating description of the little-known role of African Americans in the Civil War. This book is part of the Library of American History series and is appropriate for secondary students and able junior high/middle school students.

Summary ▪ Until recently, most Americans were unaware of the active and vital part that African Americans played in winning their freedom. This involvement included keeping the issue of freedom for slaves before the public, providing services and labor to support the war effort, serving in the navy and army, and working behind the lines as scouts and spies. Among the free African Americans in the North was the prominent orator and writer Frederick Douglass, who opposed the prevailing sentiment that "this is a white man's war" and urged that blacks be allowed to enlist in the army. An ardent and persuasive abolitionist, he argued that without slave labor, the South could not win the war. Beginning early in the war and continuing throughout it, escaped slaves who made their way to the Union lines were labeled as "contraband of war" and given shelter and work. It was not until after the Emancipation Proclamation was issued in 1863, however, that blacks were allowed to serve in the army, although they were already serving in the navy. Even though they served with bravery and distinction, they frequently experienced prejudice and discrimination. African Americans' efforts were also crucial in providing education to those for whom learning to read and write had been forbidden, securing suffrage through the Fifteenth Amendment, and organizing freedmen's aid associations.

Teaching Considerations ▪ McPherson's book is a highly readable and credible source of information on a frequently neglected topic. Students who have seen the film, *Glory*, may have some knowledge that African Americans fought in the Civil War. This book, however, will broaden and extend readers' understanding of the multiple roles of African Americans during this period. Prior to reading the book, review with students the status of blacks in both the North and South at the onset of the Civil War.

After Reading: Suggested Student Activities

1. Analyze the significance of the following terms: white man's war; voting with their feet; abolitionists; contraband of war; Emancipation Proclamation.

2. Construct an idea map, poster, or collage illustrating the major concepts you learned from reading this book. Write an accompanying essay describing and interpreting it. (Teacher's Note: See the guidelines in chapter 1 for this strategy.)

3. Find an excerpt from this book that challenged you or made you look at an event, issue, or person from a different perspective. Explain your choice and its significance.

4. Research Frederick Douglass's political and social positions; write a persuasive paper either in support of or in opposition to his ideas. As you write your paper, imagine that you are preparing it to deliver as a speech.

Meriwether, Louise. *Fragments of the Ark.* Simon & Schuster, 1994. 342 pages.

"Slaves stealing a gunboat?"

"Yes, suh."

Peter gave the *Onward's* captain a full account, reporting that they also had on board four cannons earmarked for Middle Ground Battery but they had successfully delayed their delivery in order to hand them over to Uncle Sam.

By noon Peter was back on the *Swanee*, now flying the Stars and Stripes, with officers and seamen from the Union gunboat aboard. (p. 77)

At a Glance ▪ Inspired by the bravery of Robert Smalls, the Sea Island slave who secretly piloted a Confederate gunboat out of the Charleston harbor to the Union navy, Meriwether has created a powerful and complex novel. Appropriate for secondary students with a strong background in the history of the Civil War, this novel creates vivid characters who struggle to free themselves from the internal and external demons created by slavery.

Summary ▪ Peter Mango—ship pilot, husband, friend, and slave—longs for freedom for himself and for his family. Seizing an opportunity during the siege of Charleston, Peter, his family, and a group of other runaway slaves steal the Confederate gunboat *Swanee* under cover of darkness, and sail it out of the harbor. Delivering it to the Union navy, Peter is rewarded by being accepted into the navy where he rises to the rank of captain. But his success carries a price for himself and his family. Peter must learn to navigate not only the treacherous seas but the treacherous life of a former slave in the South during and immediately after the Civil War.

Teaching Considerations ▪ *Fragments of the Ark* gives readers an opportunity to explore the conflicts, issues, events, and personalities of the Civil War from yet another perspective. Providing students with some background information about Robert Smalls, although not essential, could add to their understanding of the historical context. Some obscenities are used as well as the word, "nigger," but these uses are within the context of the times and do not detract from this high-quality piece of literature.

After Reading: Suggested Student Activities

1. Peter Mango is a complex character who grows and changes significantly throughout this novel, yet in some ways remains the same. Write a paper comparing and contrasting how Peter

is portrayed in the opening chapters with how he is depicted at the end of the book.

2. Identify a major theme of this novel and chart how it is developed throughout the book.

3. Discuss with your class the meaning of the title of this book, *Fragments of the Ark*, its symbolism, and implications.

4. Choose a character or an episode from *Fragments of the Ark* that had an impact on you. Use a creative medium of expression to demonstrate its significance.

5. Research the life of Robert Smalls. How closely does this book reflect fact? Meriwether, as do all novelists, uses poetic license in telling her story. Do you think the novel is more effective than the real story? Why or why not? Write a persuasive paper stating your position.

Paulsen, Gary. *Nightjohn*. Delacorte Press, 1993. 92 pages.

> Waller he brought Nightjohn into the main yard near the quarters out in the open, yelling and swearing at him. Yanking on the rope. Nightjohn he didn't have any clothes on, stood naked in the sun. I was by the quarters, carrying water to wash the eating trough before it was time for the evening feeding and I saw them. . . . His back was all over scars from old whippings. The skin across his shoulders and down was raised in ripples, thick as my hand, up and down his back and onto his rear end and down his legs some. (pp. 26–27)

At a Glance ▪ Set in 1850, this short historical novel deals with the cruelty of life in the slave quarters and the slaves' intense desire to learn to read, even though it is forbidden and dangerous. The book is appropriate for upper elementary and junior high/middle school students.

Summary ▪ Life on the Waller plantation is difficult for the slaves. Told through the eyes of a twelve-year-old slave girl, Sarny, this book focuses on the bitter cruelty of slavery. Nightjohn is brought to the plantation naked and in chains. His back is a mass of scars from beatings from previous owners. A slave like that means trouble because he refuses to be submissive. But Nightjohn's pride and undaunted manner tells Sarny that he is special. She learns that one of the things that makes him special is that he can read and write. Sarny convinces him to teach her. Both Sarny and Nightjohn risk everything as he teaches her to read. They both know that all hope for the future lies in slaves being able to read so that they will be able to function when they are free.

Teaching Considerations ▪ Paulsen is a prolific author, but this is his first work of historical fiction. *Nightjohn* is a deceptively simple book that children much younger than twelve would be able to read; however, the realistic accounting of the brutality that some slaves encountered would be inappropriate for younger readers because it is extremely disturbing. On the other hand, the book also presents a very strong message about reading, its value, and its importance. The character development of Sarny, Nightjohn, and Mammy is well done; however, Waller and his family are presented as one dimensional. They are portrayed as stereotypically cruel and hateful, without a glimmer of kindness, sensitivity, or decency. Teachers should be cautious about any book that presents only negative stereotypes of a group. Among the awards *Nightjohn* received are ALA Best Book for Young Adults, ALA Notable Children's Book, and IRA-CBC Children's Choice. The sequel to this book, *Sarny: A Life Remembered*, describes life after the end of the Civil War (see entry in chapter 7).

After Reading: Suggested Student Activities

1. Critically examine the uses of stereotyping in this book. How is it used to present both the owners and the slaves? How does that impact the effectiveness of this book?

2. Research the laws and conditions of literacy for slaves. Analyze the impact of these laws, based on historical information. Present your findings in a chart.

3. Imagine that it is summer of 1865 and pretend that you are either Nightjohn or Sarny. Write a journal entry of what your life is now like.

4. Create a character portrait of Sarny. (Teacher's Note: See the guidelines in chapter 1 for this strategy.)

Ringgold, Faith. *Aunt Harriet's Underground Railroad in the Sky.* Crown Publishers, 1992. 30 pages, unnumbered.

"Come on, Cassie," Be Be said, jumping up on the train. "Let's take a ride."

"Get off that train, Be Be! I'll tell Mommy and Daddy, and you will be in a world of trouble," I yelled.

But the train quickly moved off through the sky and disappeared. All I could see now were flashing lights, sending a threatening message through a sea of clouds: GO FREE NORTH OR DIE! GO FREE NORTH OR DIE! GO FREE NORTH OR DIE! (pp. 3–4)

At a Glance ▪ This is a wonderfully imaginative picture book. When she was close to death, Harriet Tubman dreamt that she was flying to freedom. Ringgold uses her dream as the basis for this book. This book could be enjoyed by students at any level. It could also be an effective teacher read-aloud.

Summary ▪ Using the dream motif, Ringgold tells the story of slavery, escape, Harriet Tubman, and the Underground Railroad. Cassie and her little brother Be Be are flying when they see an old train in the sky. Its conductor, a woman, calls: "All aboard!" Be Be gets on the train and is gone, and Cassie is left calling for him. The conductor, Harriet Tubman, talks with Cassie and sends her on her way to follow the route of the Underground Railroad. Harriet says that every 100 years the old train follows the route that she used to lead others to freedom so that people will not forget. In order to get her brother back, Cassie has to experience what her ancestors went through to be free, by following the North Star along the same path that so many slaves took years before. As directed by Harriet, Cassie makes all the stops along the route of the Underground Railroad in search of both her brother and her heritage.

Teaching Considerations ▪ Faith Ringgold includes a photograph of Harriet Tubman, background information about her life, and a map showing the routes of the Underground Railroad. This information will provide readers with a helpful context for understanding the times. This book can be used with students of all ages. It provides a good introduction to time travel books because students see Cassie transported into the time of slavery. (See chapter 4 for more detailed books about the life of Harriet Tubman).

After Reading: Suggested Student Activities

1. Imagine that you are able to time-travel to the Civil War era. Select a specific time and place. Relying on historical fact, report what you might see and experiences you might have in your journal.

2. In small groups, select an event from the Civil War and create a picture book to tell its story.

3. Read a biography of Harriet Tubman and share the information about her with the class.

4. Do a VIP map, highlighting the life and accomplishments of Harriet Tubman. (Teacher's Note: See the guidelines in chapter 1 for this strategy.)

Winter, Jeanette. *Follow the Drinking Gourd.* Alfred A. Knopf, 1988. 46 pages, unnumbered.

> Joe had a plan.
> At night when work was done,
> he'd teach the slaves a song
> that secretly told the way
> to freedom.
> Just follow the drinking gourd, it said.
> (p. 8, unnumbered)

At a Glance ▪ In this wonderfully illustrated picture book, Winter tells the story of one of the conductors on the Underground Railroad, a sailor with one leg, called "Peg Leg Joe." An effective teacher read-aloud, this book could be enjoyed by students at any level.

Summary ▪ Peg Leg Joe went from plantation to plantation, working as a handyman. At each of his stops, he befriended slaves and taught them a "simple" song, "Follow the Drinking Gourd." It was not just a simple song. The lyrics provided directions for escaping to the North by using the Big Dipper as a guide. Once Joe taught his song, it was time to move on. In this picture book, his song became the road map to freedom for Molly and James, their son Isaiah, old Hattie, and her grandson George. They followed the drinking gourd along the Underground Railroad.

Teaching Considerations ▪ Winter prefaces the story with "A Note about the Story," which provides readers with helpful background information and an historical context for the story.

After Reading: Suggested Student Activities

1. Using the song lyrics and the introductory notes, trace the route on a map that the slaves probably used.

2. Research the role that the stars have played as a basic navigational tool. Report your findings to the class.

3. Find out more about the Underground Railroad. Imagine that you have one of the "safe houses" that is a stop along the way. What do you do and how do you make sure that you won't be discovered?

4. Since slaves were forbidden to learn to read and write, oral tradition and music were important ways of transmitting their culture, beliefs, and traditions. Research the role of either oral tradition or music in this period.

More Books

Bial, Raymond. *The Underground Railroad*. Houghton Mifflin, 1995. 48 pages.

The Underground Railroad was the escape route for slaves to find their way to freedom. For these escapees, a number of routes wound through the northern states and into Canada. The Underground Railroad was surrounded by secrecy because it was illegal to help slaves escape. A slave was considered to be the property of his or her owner; thus, to help a slave escape was considered to be thievery. The number of slaves that were helped to freedom along the Underground Railroad is unknown, but we do know that the railroad existed for sixty years prior to the Civil War. It is estimated that 3,200 people assisted the escaping slaves. Many of these helpers were escaped slaves themselves who felt the need to give others the chance that they had. A number of others were freedmen, while others were white people from all levels of society. These people shared a commitment to the concept of "freedom for all," regardless of race. This book combines contemporary photographs with reproductions of documents from the times and historical prints to complement the text, which tells of the people who helped the slaves and the places along the many routes of the Underground Railroad. This nonfiction account provides a good factual understanding of the Underground Railroad for students in upper elementary or junior high/middle school.

Brill, Marlene Targ. Illustrated by Janice Lee Porter. *Allen Jay and the Underground Railroad*. Carolrhoda Books, 1994. 48 pages.

Brill and Porter have created an illustrated easy-to-read book based upon the actual lives of Allen Jay and his family in Ohio in the 1840s. The Jay family belonged to the Society of Friends, or Quakers, and was part of the Underground Railroad. In this story, eleven-year-old Jay demonstrates his courage when he helps an escaped slave to freedom. The illustrations are colorful and enhance the text. This book could be used as a teacher read-aloud or is appropriate for upper elementary school students who have difficulty reading.

Clark, Margaret Goff. *Freedom Crossing*. Scholastic, 1980. 148 pages.

Laura was eleven when she went to Virginia to live with her aunt and uncle for four years after her mother died. Her aunt and uncle, who treated their slaves well, hated the Underground Railroad, and thought it was wicked to help slaves escape. Now that Laura's father has remarried, he has brought her back to New York to live.

Learning About the Civil War

Everything seems different and strange to Laura, especially when she discovers that their home is a station on the Underground Railroad and that her younger brother Bert is keeping it a secret from her because he doesn't trust her. Laura is angry, frightened, and confused. When the sheriff and his men arrive unexpectedly at their house looking for a runaway slave boy, Bert hides him in Laura's room, and she must decide what to do. This novel is appropriate for upper elementary school students and junior high/middle school students.

Edwards, Pamela Duncan. Illustrated by Henry Cole. *Barefoot: Escape on the Underground Railroad*. HarperCollins Publishers, 1997. 29 pages, unnumbered.

This lovely picture book is an unusual artistic representation of the experience of runaway slaves using the signs of nature to help them escape on the Underground Railroad The dark, muted illustrations show people through the eyes of animals and suggest a mysterious relationship between nature and humans. The author paints word pictures of this same relationship that are beautifully interwoven with the illustrator's images.

> The heron's keen eyes had spotted the Barefoot moving furtively toward the pathway. The heron's warning cry had been a signal to the other animals.
> They had seen many Barefeet along their pathway. And they had seen some of them being led away in ropes by the Heavy Books. (p. 4, unnumbered)

Barefoot: Escape on the Underground Railroad can be experienced on many different levels and is highly recommended for readers of all ages.

Gorrell, Gena K. Foreword by Rosemary Brown. *North Star to Freedom: The Story of the Underground Railroad*. Originally published in Canada by Stoddard, 1996. First American edition by Delacorte Press, 1997. 168 pages.

The title of this fine book is slightly misleading as it does not indicate the full scope of its valuable contents. Beginning with a brief history of slavery in ancient times and its expansion into the New World, it also describes the horrible sea voyages from Africa aboard slave ships and the establishment of slavery in North America as an integral part of its economic development. The majority of the book describes protests and actions against slavery with an emphasis on the role of the Underground Railroad in helping escaped slaves to freedom. Stories of specific acts of bravery and daring as well as the actions of leading figures in the antislavery movement are accompanied by photographs and illustrations. Written by a Canadian author, an interesting feature of the book is the inclusion of the history of slavery in Canada, its role in the Underground Railroad, and the Canadian-U.S. relationship. Appropriate for upper elementary and junior high/middle school students, this book would also be a useful resource for secondary students.

Herschler, Mildred Badger. *The Walk into Morning.* A Tor Book, 1993. 318 pages.

Herschler's first novel intertwines the complex and confusing human, social, and military relationships and events in Louisiana during 1862–63 with the compelling story of Chad, Anna, and a host of other fascinating black and white characters. Chad, a young slave who flees the plantation at Sweet Haven to join the Union forces, promises to return when the South is split in two. Herschler uses lyrical prose, vivid characterization, and frequent time shifts to convey a sense of the times. This book would be appropriate for college-preparatory secondary students who enjoy quality literature and have a strong historical knowledge of the Civil War.

Lester, Julius *Long Journey Home.* Scholastic, 1972. 149 pages.

Julius Lester frames stories rooted in substantiated fact with additional characters and details consistent with the period to tell six stories of courage of African Americans who wanted to be free. Four of the six stories are from the Civil War period. One story tells of the delicate balance on a plantation when the owner dies and an overseer is brought in. Conditions suddenly become unbearable, and Ben, who knows more about running the plantation than anyone else, escapes. In each of these stories, the characters face the hardships of slavery with a sense of dignity and determination. Lester includes notes as an afterword to identify the sources of his stories. This book was nominated for the American Book Award in

1972. Lester's award-winning book, *To Be a Slave*, is a focus book in this chapter. The book should be used with students in secondary schools. Able junior high/middle school student could also read it.

Lester, Julius. *This Strange New Feeling*. Scholastic, 1981. 164 pages.

Using the same type of format that he did in *Long Journey Home*, Lester presents three true stories of African Americans, but he adds additional details to the substantiated facts. These are three love stories as well as stories of the quest for freedom. The first is the story of freedom achieved, the second of freedom lost, and the third of freedom fulfilled. This last story about Ellen and William Craft is also related in Freedman's *Two Tickets to Freedom*, a focus book in this chapter. Lester's award-winning book, *To Be a Slave* also is a focus entry in this chapter. The book should be used with students in secondary schools. Able junior high/middle school student could also read it.

Levine, Ellen. Illustrated by Larry Johnson. . . . *If You Traveled on the Underground Railroad*. Scholastic Books, 1988. 64 pages

This is a nonfiction book designed to provide elementary students with basic background information about what the Underground Railroad was and what it did for people. It uses the format of frequently asked questions about the Underground Railroad, the concept of slavery, and the escape from it. This informative book begins by giving readers explanations about what the Underground Railroad was and why it was necessary. As the book progresses, Levine essentially takes the reader on a guided tour of using the Underground Railroad. She identifies key people such as Harriet Tubman, Harriet Beecher Stowe, and William Lloyd Garrison. This slim volume includes a wealth of fundamental information about the conditions that African Americans faced during slavery and in their efforts to be free. This book is appropriate for elementary students.

Marston, Hope Irvin. *Isaac Johnson: From Slave to Stonecutter*. Cobblehill Books, 1995. 80 pages

Isaac Yeager was born on a farm in Kentucky owned by his white father. His father and a slave named Jane lived as man and wife.

They had four sons together, the second of whom was Isaac. While the father was a successful farmer, his neighbors ignored him and disapproved of his relationship with Jane. When Isaac was seven, his father decided to sell his farm. He left on a trip to sell his horses, and while he was gone, the local sheriff took Jane, Isaac, and his three brothers to the slave auction. From that point, Isaac's life became very difficult because he was sold to cruel masters. He struggled until he was able to run away to join the Union forces as a member of the 1st Michigan Colored Infantry. After the war, Isaac looked for his family. He never found any trace of them; however, he did find out that his father had authorized his sale and that of his mother and brothers. From that point on, Isaac refused to use his father's name, Yeager. Instead he took his mother's surname. He moved to Canada, where he married, raised a family, and spent the remainder of his life working in border towns in Canada and New York State. Isaac Johnson became a highly respected stonecutter who worked on many buildings, homes, bridges, municipal buildings, and churches in these communities. Many of his buildings remain today as tributes to his workmanship. He wrote an account of his experiences, entitled *Slavery Days in Old Kentucky*, which was privately printed in 1904. This book is appropriate for junior high/middle school students.

McKissack, Patricia C. *A Picture of Freedom: The Diary of Clotee, A Slave Girl*. Scholastic, 1997. 195 pages.

One of the books in the Dear America series, this novel is written in the form of diary entries by Clotee, a slave girl on the Belmont Plantation in Virginia, in 1859 and 1860. Although it is against the law to teach slaves how to read and write, Clotee has secretly learned how while fanning her young master, William, during his lessons. When Clotee discovers that Mr. Harms, William's tutor, is secretly an abolitionist and involved with the Underground Railroad, she must decide what action to take. At the end of the book, a short informational section and photographs about life in America in 1859 are provided. This book is appropriate for upper elementary and junior high/middle school students and provides readers with a view of plantation life, its social relations and living conditions, immediately prior to the Civil War.

Rappaport, Doreen. *Escape from Slavery: Five Journeys to Freedom.* **HarperCollins, 1991. 117 pages.**

This collection of biographical sketches dramatizes the courage and resourcefulness that slaves used to escape from bondage to find freedom. It could be used effectively with upper elementary and junior high/middle school students. Each of the accounts in this book can be read independently of the others. Each presents stories of courage, daring, and an unstoppable desire to be free that will appeal to many readers. Because the selections are relatively short, teachers could also use them as effective read-alouds with younger students. Students who enjoy this book should be directed to *Two Tickets to Freedom* by Freedman. This more detailed account of the escape of Ellen and William Craft is a focus book in this chapter.

Riggio, Anita. *Secret Signs Along the Underground Railroad.* **Boyd Mills Press, 1997. 29 pages.**

This picture book is the story of the courage of a deaf boy. Luke's mother needs to give information about a new safe house on the Underground Railroad. She is to meet her contact when she and Luke are selling the sugar eggs he decorates at a local store. While they are making the eggs, a slave catcher comes to their house and accuses them of hiding slaves. While his mother denies it, the man doesn't believe her. He won't let her leave the house, but he takes Luke to sell his eggs at the store. Communicating in sign language, Luke tells his mother that he will deliver the message. She tells him to be brave. At the store Luke takes the parchment paper and paints a miniature of a white house with a red barn. When the young girl comes looking for his mother, Luke gives her the egg and helps her to look inside it. She sees the white house, which has a row of bricks painted white on its chimney, a sign of safety on the Underground Railroad. The book has an afterword that gives readers information about the education of the deaf in this country as well as about the Underground Railroad. This book could be read and enjoyed by all readers.

Robinet, Harriette Gillem. *If You Please, President Lincoln.* **Atheneum Books for Young Readers, 1995. 149 pages.**

Based on the little-known historical plan to take former slaves and free-born people of African descent from this country and colonize them elsewhere, this novel tells the story of fourteen-year-old Moses, a runaway slave who becomes part of the group to go to Cow Island off the coast of Haiti in 1864. Ill-conceived and poorly planned, this colonization effort involves crowding over 400 people onto a ship with inadequate supplies and then leaving them to face starvation and disaster on Cow Island. Moses demonstrates courage and leadership as he helps the group survive and with the help of a friend, makes rescue possible. This book is appropriate for upper elementary and junior high/middle school students.

4

Those Who Made a Difference

Traditionally, in times of war there are military and political figures who emerge as heroes. While their fame may be from a single act or a series of acts, their role as hero is far more significant. Heroes provide a symbolic function in the society that they serve. Military and political leaders are the "expected" heroes, those who by education and job experience have been groomed to assume leadership under any circumstances. The Civil War period certainly was populated with numerous men who accepted leadership mantles with grace and acumen. The North was led by Abraham Lincoln, who was arguably the greatest president that this nation ever had. Jefferson Davis was a figurehead who certainly did not compare with Lincoln, but he did select General Robert E. Lee to lead the Confederate forces. Lincoln and Lee, probably more than any other leaders of their time, were the symbols of the opposing sides of the Civil War. Lincoln, the self-made man, overcame humble beginnings to become a successful attorney, legislator, and powerful orator. On the other hand, Lee, the son of a revolutionary war hero, epitomized the courtly Southern tradition. Lee was as different from Lincoln as he was from his Union military counterpart, Ulysses S. Grant; yet both these men were the most successful military strategists of their time.

These men were, by their career choices, thrust into positions of leadership in which they made a difference to those around them and ultimately to the nation, but there were numerous others during the period who by their acts also became heroes. These "unexpected" heroes were not trained in the military or politics. They were people who made choices in their lives that ultimately had an impact on many others. This impact might have been from a single act, like that of Barbara Frietchie's alleged protection of the flag in the face of Confederate soldiers. The immortalization of this action in a poem by John Greenleaf Whittier was a popular testimony to patriotism. Others made a difference by their selfless devotion to helping the ill and wounded, like Clara Barton and Walt Whitman. The medical conditions during the war were deplorable, but volunteers like Barton and Whitman provided help and comfort to soldiers from both sides.

Perhaps there is no rallying cry for action like a horrible injustice. Reaction against slavery became such a cause for many people in the North. Perhaps the best-known abolitionist was the controversial John Brown, whose judgment and actions may be questioned; however, he did focus attention on the atrocity of slavery.

In addition to the actions of abolitionists, Northern opinion was galvanized against slavery by the activities of former slaves, like Harriet Tubman, who had either escaped or were freed and then worked to help free others. Certainly those who worked with the Underground Railroad were among those who significantly affected the lives of others. Two former slaves who led the efforts for emancipation were Frederick Douglass and Sojourner Truth. Both of them were powerful and persuasive speakers, and they carried the antislavery message to halls and churches throughout the North. Both Douglass and Truth spent their early years as slaves, and neither had the opportunity to get an education. Douglass, who was largely self-taught, became a powerful writer as well as an effective orator. Each had a genius for touching others with their message and a true understanding of the power of human dignity.

Perhaps the ability to make that connection with others is the fundamental bond that all of these people who made a difference share. Whether we look to the expected heroes like Lincoln or Lee or to the unexpected heroes like Barton and Douglass and the others, each of them serves to touch the minds and hearts of others and give them hope and purpose.

Prior to Reading: Think About . . .

Young people need to do some preliminary thinking and talking to prepare them to understand what they read or what is read to them about the Civil War. They need opportunities to ask questions and to raise issues and concerns. The following questions and activities can be used to prompt this discussion:

- Make a list of names of people whom you associate with the Civil War period.

- What do you already know about military leaders of the Union and Confederacy?

- What do you already know about those who opposed slavery?

- Who are you interested in learning more about from the Civil War period?

- How do biographers learn about their subjects?

- What do you think makes a person a hero? Make a list of the characteristics that you consider to be heroic and discuss it in class.

- Choose a quotation taken from one of the books described in this chapter. What do you think it means? What does it make you curious about in the book?

Focus Books

Archer, Jules. *A House Divided: The Lives of Ulysses S. Grant and Robert E. Lee.* Scholastic, 1995. 184 pages.

"I met you once before, General Lee," Grant said, "while we were serving in Mexico . . . I have always remembered your appearance, and I think I should have recognized you anywhere."

"Yes," Lee replied, "I know I met you on that occasion and I have . . . tried to recollect how you looked,

but I have never been able to recall a single feature."
(pp. 144–145)

At a Glance ▪ Archer portrays the public and private lives of two of our most famous military leaders, Grant and Lee. Their biographies are interwoven with the significant events of the Civil War and accompanied by vintage photographs. Junior high/middle school students and secondary school students will find this book about Grant and Lee an interesting study in contrasts.

Summary ▪ Archer's fascinating biography of Grant and Lee offers the reader insights into both of these men against the backdrop of our country's history during the 1800s. Chapters alternate between Lee and Grant, beginning with Lee, who was fifteen years older than Grant. Archer starts with a description of their early years and factors that influenced each of their development and concludes with their lives after the Civil War and then their deaths. Differences in upbringing, temperament, and style are skillfully interwoven with a description of other significant figures, historic events, and major battles. Archer's description of their appearances at the surrender at Appomattox symbolizes the contrast between the generals:

> . . . Lee dressed in a new, immaculate gray uniform, a red silk sash, and ornamented boots. He buckled on a dress sword with a carved hilt in a gold-embroidered scabbard. Mounting Traveller, he left for the McLean farmhouse accompanied by two generals. There they entered the parlor and conversed quietly while waiting for Grant to arrive.
>
> Grant had left his camp that morning in "rough garb." He wore a dusty, unbuttoned, army-blue ordinary soldier's blouse for a coat, with only shoulder straps to indicate his rank. His pants and boots were mud-spattered. And, as usual, he wore no sword when on horseback. (p. 143)

Teaching Considerations ▪ Jules Archer is a renowned and prolific writer with a strong interest in the Civil War. Students will benefit more from this study of Grant and Lee if they first have some background in the history of the Civil War. This book then can be used to answer more specific questions that students generate about the two military leaders and how they came to symbolize the North and South. Other biographies about Grant and Lee with entries in this chapter are:

Brown, Warren. Introductory Essay on Leadership by Arthur M. Schlesinger, Jr. *Robert E. Lee.* Chelsea House Publishers, 1992.

Greene, Carol. *Robert E. Lee: Leader in War and Peace.* Children's Press, 1989.

Marrin, Albert. *Unconditional Surrender: U.S. Grant and the Civil War.* Atheneum, 1994.

Sell, Bill. *Leaders of the North and South.* Metro Books, 1996.

After Reading: Suggested Student Activities

1. Analyze how Grant symbolized the North and Lee the South. Provide specific examples to illustrate your points. Present your findings to the class.

2. Use a Venn diagram to compare and contrast Grant and Lee. Then use that information to write a description of the two men and their roles in our country's history. (Teacher's Note: See the guidelines in chapter 1 for this strategy.)

3. With your learning partner, select an issue, an event, or an incident from the Civil War. Based on your knowledge of these men and the history of the times, create a dialogue between Lee and Grant.

4. Military leaders are often called "heroes." Does this term apply to either or both Grant and Lee? In a persuasive essay, present and document your position.

Brown, Warren. Introductory Essay on Leadership by Arthur M. Schlesinger, Jr. *Robert E. Lee.* Chelsea House Publishers, 1992. 111 pages.

Lee shared with the rest of the U.S. Army a difficulty in adjusting to the placid life of peacetime. His restlessness deepened so that in 1849 he even considered serving with a group of Cuban revolutionaries planning to overthrow the Spanish colonial government. Despite his frustration, however, Lee felt unable to leave the army, which had given him a sense of purpose and of belonging he had not found in civilian life. (p. 42)

At a Glance ▪ This biography presents an overview of the life of one of this country's most beloved and revered military leaders. It focuses on his accomplishments as a military leader. This book is appropriate for able upper elementary and junior high/middle school students.

Summary ▪ Perhaps Robert E. Lee's entire life was a preparation for the day at Appomattox Courthouse, Virginia, when he would surrender to the Union forces under the leadership of General U. S. Grant. Lee was the son of Light-Horse Harry Lee, a hero of the revolutionary war, but a man who was never committed to responsible membership in civilian society. He was imprisoned in debtor's prison, disgracing his family and especially his wife's family. Young Robert was a direct contrast to his father; he was responsible, serious, and courtly. A graduate of West Point, Lee made a career in the military. He distinguished himself in battle in Mexico and later served as superintendent of West Point. When he was not promoted as rapidly as he wished in the engineers, he welcomed a transfer to the cavalry. He led the government troops to Harper's Ferry, Virginia (now West Virginia), to quell the uprising by John Brown and his men. Lee remained in charge of the troops there until after Brown was executed. When the Civil War broke out, Lee had the choice of assuming a leadership position with either the Union or Confederate forces. He was opposed to both slavery and secession, yet he chose to command the Confederate forces out of loyalty to his home state of Virginia.

Teaching Considerations. ▪ As biographies go, this one presents the factual information about Lee in a straightforward manner; the emphasis is on his military life, rather than his personal life.

After Reading: Suggested Student Activities

1. Discuss in a small group or with your class why you think Robert E. Lee was so revered in the South.

2. Compare and contrast the images of Lee and Grant from their encounter at Appomattox Courthouse, Virginia, on the day of the surrender. (Teacher's Note: See the guidelines in chapter 1 for this strategy.)

3. From your knowledge of history, did Lee make the right choice when he decided to lead the Confederate forces? Do you think he would have been as revered if he had fought for the Union? Write a short paper discussing your position on this topic.

4. Do further research about Lee's life and career. Be prepared to discuss with your class whether or not you think his reputation is deserved.

Douglass, Frederick. *Escape from Slavery: The Boyhood of Frederick Douglass in His Own Words.* Edited by Michael McCurdy. Knopf, 1994. 63 pages.

Very soon after I went to live with Mr. and Mrs. Auld, she very kindly commenced to teach me the A, B, C. After I had learned this, she assisted me in learning to spell words of three or four letters. Just at this point of my progress, Mr. Auld found out what was going on, and at once forbade Mrs. Auld to instruct me further, telling her, among other things, that it was unlawful, as well as unsafe, to teach a slave to read. To use his own words, he said, ". . . A nigger should know nothing but to obey his master—to do as he is told to do. Learning would *spoil* the best nigger in the world. Now," said he, "if you teach that nigger [speaking of myself] how to read, there would be no keeping him. It would forever unfit him to be a slave. He would at once become unmanageable, and of no value to his master."

These words sank deep into my heart, stirred up sentiments within that lay slumbering, and called into existence an entirely new train of thought. I now understood what had been to me a most perplexing difficulty—to wit, the white man's power to enslave the black man. From that moment, I understood the pathway from slavery to freedom. It was just what I wanted, and I got it at a time when I the least expected it. (pp. 12–13)

At a Glance ▪ While there are a number of good biographies of Frederick Douglass for young readers, this edited version of the first part of his autobiography has the advantage of helping the reader to hear Douglass's own voice as he relates his experiences. While this book can be read easily by many middle school students, older students may also find it an interesting account.

Summary ▪ Frederick Bailey was born on a Maryland plantation and separated from his mother as an infant. He spent his early years in difficult circumstances, but when he was eight years old, his life was changed considerably. He was sent to work for a relative of his master's in Baltimore. The living conditions were better, but most important, his new master's wife began teaching young Frederick to read. His master found out and ordered the lessons to stop, but the door had been opened, and Frederick's life changed. From then on he was self-taught. His life in slavery became even more difficult; he was sent from one member of the master's family to another, each one treating him worse than the one before. At sixteen he was sent to work as a field hand for the first time in his life. Although he was big and strong, Frederick was not prepared for that type of physical labor. His master was a cruel man who beat Frederick regularly for the first six months he was with him, but one day Frederick fought back. The fight lasted for over two hours, and when it was over, Frederick was never beaten again. But he was still a slave. For the next few years he worked on other farms, where he began teaching other slaves to read. He also planned to escape with four other slaves, but they were betrayed. Frederick was jailed, but he was later allowed to return to Baltimore to live in the home where he first learned to read. He was sent to work for a ship-builder, where he learned to be a caulker, one who seals the wooden planks on ships so that they will not leak. While he earned a wage for his owner, Frederick dreamed and planned to be free. Frederick did not tell how he escaped from slavery in his narrative in order to protect others who had helped him. His escape to freedom gave the abolitionist movement one of its most articulate voices.

Teaching Considerations ▪ Any definition of a hero can aptly be attributed to Frederick Douglass. Not only did he overcome the horrible circumstances of slavery, but he then devoted his life to trying to improve conditions for women as well as other blacks. This brief account could be accompanied by the unedited version or the other two parts of his autobiography. Among the other books written about Frederick Douglass for young people are the following:

Adler, David A. Illustrated by Samuel Byrd. *A Picture Book of Frederick Douglass.* Holiday House, 1993. (Appropriate for elementary students)

Davis, Ossie. *Escape to Freedom, Play about Young Frederick Douglass.* Puffin Books, 1976, Intro. 1989. (See entry in this chapter.)

Girard, Linda Walvoord. Paintings by Colin Bootman. *Young Frederick Douglass: The Slave Who Learned to Read.* Albert Whitman, 1994. (Picture book appropriate for all readers)

McKissack, Patricia, and Fredrick McKissack. *Frederick Douglass, the Black Lion.* Children's Press, 1987. (Appropriate for upper elementary and junior high/middle school students)

Miller, William. Illustrated by Cedric Lucas. *Frederick Douglass: The Last Day of Slavery.* Lee and Low Books, 1995. (See entry in this chapter.)

Woods, Andrew. *Young Frederick Douglass: Freedom Fighter.* Troll, 1996. (See entry in this chapter.)

After Reading: Suggested Student Activities

1. Do a VIP map of Frederick Douglass's life. (Teacher's Note: See the guidelines in chapter 1 for this strategy.)

2. Frederick Douglass's achievements are tributes to the strength and power of the human spirit. Use a "Profile of . . ." chart to list the characteristics that you think helped him to achieve all that he did. (Teacher's Note: See the guidelines in chapter 1 for this strategy.)

3. Do further research about Frederick Douglass's career as a human rights advocate. Write an account of some aspect of his work that you find particularly interesting. Share your findings with members of your class.

4. Write a poem or compose a song in honor of Frederick Douglass.

Ferris, Jeri. Illustrated by Peter E. Hanson.
Walking the Road to Freedom: A Story About Sojourner Truth.
Carolrhoda Books, 1988. 64 pages.

> Sojourner went alone to Ohio, Illinois, Indiana, and Michigan, to sing and speak against slavery and in support of women's rights. Her friends worried that she would be hurt or killed by mobs, but Sojourner said, "The Lord will preserve me . . . for the truth is powerful and will prevail." (p. 48)

At a Glance ▪ An illiterate former slave, Sojourner Truth was a woman of tremendous conviction and determination who greatly influenced people's thinking about the evils of slavery. Her biography is set against the backdrop of the turbulent antebellum period and the Civil War era. It is appropriate for elementary students or could be used as an effective teacher read-aloud.

Summary ▪ Born into slavery at the end of the 1700s in the northern part of the state of New York, Sojourner Truth was named Isabella by her mother. Slavery was still legal in New York at that time, and slaves were given the surname of their master. Belle, as she was called, was sold away from her mother when she was nine years old and then sold several more times as she was growing up. Each time she was given a different surname, until later in her life, when she had secured her freedom, she decided to choose her own name: Sojourner Truth. *Walking the Road to Freedom* describes her battle to secure her own freedom and that of her children. Because it was forbidden to educate slaves, Sojourner Truth never learned to read and write. But she spoke both Dutch and English and was an eloquent and persuasive speaker. She told the story of her life to a friend, and in 1850, *The Narrative of Sojourner Truth: A Northern Slave* was published. Six feet tall, deeply religious, and a powerful singer, she traveled extensively and spoke and sang at religious, abolitionist, and women's rights meetings. During the Civil War Sojourner Truth met with President Lincoln and worked with former slaves teaching them skills they needed in their new lives. She continued her work after the war, and when conditions for blacks grew worse, she lobbied President Grant and Congress for help. She died in 1883.

Teaching Considerations ▪ Students can learn much from the life of Sojourner Truth. Spanning over eighty years of some of our nation's most significant history, her life provides a personal context for understanding this time. On another level, her bravery and strength make her an authentic hero from whom we can all learn important lessons about overcoming the adversities of life. This book received the Carter G. Woodson award. Other books about Sojourner Truth with entries in this chapter are:

Macht, Norman L. *Sojourner Truth: Crusader for Civil Rights.* Chelsea House Publisher, 1992.

McKissack, Patricia C., and Fredrick McKissack. *Sojourner Truth: Ain't I a Woman?* Scholastic, 1992.

After Reading: Suggested Student Activities

1. Develop a timeline that shows both major events in our country's history and in Sojourner Truth's life over the same period of time.

2. Construct a graphic representation that shows the changes that occurred for black people during the span of Sojourner Truth's life.

3. Find a creative way to demonstrate what you have learned about Sojourner Truth. For example, dramatize an incident from her life or write a poem about her or write a song similar to one she might have sung.

4. Complete a "Did You Know . . . ?" chart while reading this book. (Teacher's Note: See the guidelines in chapter 1 for this strategy.)

Freedman, Russell. *Lincoln: A Photobiography.*
Clarion Books, 1987. 150 pages.

"As I would not be a slave, so I would not be a master," Lincoln declared. "This expresses my idea of democracy. Whatever differs from this, to the extent of the difference, is not democracy." (p. 52)

"This government was instituted to secure the blessings of freedom," said Lincoln. "Slavery is an unqualified evil to the Negro, to the white man, to the soil, and to the State." (p. 59)

At a Glance ▪ Freedman's superb biography of Lincoln is enhanced with ample vintage photographs and illustrations. Well-written and thoroughly researched, Freedman's portrayal of Lincoln makes him come alive for the reader. Appropriate for upper elementary and junior high/middle school students, it could also be used as an effective teacher read-aloud.

Summary ▪ Freedman's first chapter about Lincoln is aptly titled, "The Mysterious Mr. Lincoln," and sets the stage for the engrossing biography. For as Freedman states, "In his own time, Lincoln was never fully understood even by his closest friends. Since then, his life story has been told and retold so many times, he has become as much a legend as a flesh-and-blood human being. While the legend is based on truth, it is only partly true. And it hides the man behind it like a disguise" (p. 2). Freedman then precedes to show us the man behind the disguise. Lincoln was a man of contrasts. While he is thought of as a common man, by the time he ran for president he was wealthy from his law practice and investments.

Lincoln was a complex man and not easy to live with, but he genuinely liked people and was devoted to his family and friends. Freedman provides us with a thorough account of Lincoln's attitudes toward slavery and the changes in his political stance through the years. Throughout this biography, major public events are interspersed with personal episodes and insights into Lincoln's character.

Teaching Considerations ▪ While there are numerous biographies written about Lincoln, Freedman's is one of the best for teachers to use in the classroom or to recommend to students for independent reading. Well-organized, it is an excellent addition to the curriculum. Included in the book are additional resources: "A Lincoln Sampler," with quotes from Lincoln's speeches and writings; "In Lincoln's Footsteps," with information about historic sites; and "Books About Lincoln." Among the awards *Lincoln: A Photobiography* received are the Newbery Medal award, Jefferson Cup award, and International Board of Books for Young People. Other books about Lincoln with entries in this chapter are:

d'Aulaire, Ingri, and Edgar Parin d'Aulaire. *Abraham Lincoln.* Bantam Doubleday Dell, 1939, 1957.

Greene, Carol. *Abraham Lincoln: President of a Divided Country.* Children's Press, 1989.

Hargrove, Jim. *Abraham Lincoln: Sixteenth President of the United States.* Children's Press, 1988.

Jakoubek, Robert E. *The Assassination of Abraham Lincoln.* The Millbrook Press, 1993.

Kent, Zachary. *The Story of Ford's Theater and the Death of Abraham Lincoln.* Children's Press, 1987.

Lincoln, Abraham. Illustrated by Michael McCurdy. Foreword by Garry Wills. *The Gettysburg Address.* Houghton Mifflin, 1995.

Sandburg, Carl. Illustrated by James Daugherty. *Abe Lincoln Grows Up.* Harcourt Brace & World, 1926, 1956.

Sell, Bill. *Leaders of the North and South.* Metro Books, 1996.

Shorto, Russell. *Abraham Lincoln and the End of Slavery.* The Millbrook Press, 1991. 30 pages.

Winnick, Karen B. *Mr. Lincoln's Whiskers.* Boyds Mills Press, 1996. 30 pages, unnumbered.

After Reading: Suggested Student Activities

1. Lincoln was a man of contrasts. In a journal entry describe three examples of these contrasts and analyze how they affected his political career.

2. Summarize Lincoln's attitudes toward slavery. Then use a timeline to trace the changes in his political stance toward it and what he believed was the proper role of the federal government.

3. Use a creative medium to pay tribute to Lincoln.

4. Freedman presents Lincoln, the real person, in this book. In a chart list three common myths about him and in a parallel column, list the true information. In a short essay, discuss whether or not the facts enhance or diminish his image.

5. The popularization of photography during this period created a new way for the American people to "see" history as it was made. Lincoln was the most frequently photographed person of the time. Study the photographs of him in this book, and in a class discussion describe the changes you see.

Fritz, Jean. *Harriet Beecher Stowe and the Beecher Preachers.* G.P. Putnam's Sons, 1994. 144 pages.

Without realizing it, Harriet Beecher Stowe had written America's first protest novel, the first book written against a law. She meant it to be realistic. . . . Most important, Harriet had done what she wanted to do: she had used a novel to criticize and denounce a society.

Uncle Tom's Cabin was published on March 20, 1852. The publisher must have known that Harriet's characters were believable, her plot fast-paced, and her subject timely, yet never in his wildest dreams did he foresee that *Uncle Tom's Cabin* would be an immediate smash hit. By mid-June 10,000 copies of the book were being sold every week. In order to keep up with the demand, the publisher had three power presses running twenty-four hours a day, one hundred and twenty-five to two hundred bookbinders at work, and three mills going full tilt to supply the paper. (pp. 70–71)

At a Glance ▪ Award-winning author Jean Fritz has written a fascinating biography of Harriet Beecher Stowe, author of *Uncle Tom's Cabin,* within the framework of her influential family of famous preachers and reformers. Appropriate for upper elementary and junior high/middle school students, it may also be interesting to less able secondary readers.

Summary ▪ Harriet was born into the large, influential Beecher family in 1811. Her father, Lyman, an influential and well-known preacher, wanted more sons to follow in his footsteps. At that time, opportunities for women were limited; they might teach, but for the most part, they were expected to care for the home and children. Harriet enjoyed writing, but had few outlets for it. When she was in her early twenties, her father, a fiery orator and a reformer, moved his family to Cincinnati, where he was to be president of Lane Theological Seminary. Harriet was always rather shy. Her older sister involved her in teaching and they co-authored a geography book. Joining a small social group that encouraged its members to write, Harriet began to write more and even had some of her pieces published. While living in Cincinnati she met fugitive slaves as well as many people for and against slavery. Marriage and babies kept her busy, however; but as the debate over slavery grew, she became frustrated at her limited opportunities to express her fierce opposition to it. She and her family moved to Maine the year the Fugitive Slave Act was passed. When her sister-in-law suggested she use her writing to express the outrage the abolitionists were feeling, she began mulling ideas over in her mind. One Sunday in church she was struck with a vision of what was to become *Uncle Tom's Cabin*. Life was never the same after its publication, for "the little housewife with a houseful of children" became one of the most famous people of her time.

Teaching Considerations ▪ In today's media-drenched world, students may need help to realize the tremendous impact that a single book, *Uncle Tom's Cabin,* had on public attitudes towards slavery prior to the Civil War. Find a copy of it and read excerpts to the students to familiarize them with it. Fritz's biography of Harriet Beecher Stowe includes photographs and an afterword which summaries the life of each member of the Beecher family. Other biographies written about her include:

Bland, Celia. *Harriet Beecher Stowe: Antislavery Author.* Chelsea Juniors, 1993. (Appropriate for elementary students)

Johnston, Norma. *Harriet: The Life and World of Harriet Beecher Stowe.* Simon & Schuster, 1994. (Appropriate for secondary students)

After Reading: Suggested Student Activities

1. Prepare a VIP map of Harriet Beecher Stowe. (Teacher's Note: See the guidelines in chapter 1 for this strategy.)

2. Discuss with the class why you think Harriet Beecher Stowe and *Uncle Tom's Cabin* had such a powerful impact on public attitudes about slavery.

3. Prepare an annotated timeline of significant events in Harriet Beecher Stowe's life.

4. In a journal entry, describe the differences between opportunities for women in Harriet's lifetime and now.

Hamilton, Virginia. *Anthony Burns: The Defeat and Triumph of a Fugitive Slave.* Alfred A Knopf, 1988. 193 pages.

At noon on June 2, 1854, not a cloud marred the blue sky. The sun was bright and warm. Eighteen hundred men of the volunteer militia stood in the sunshine, carrying loaded guns. They were stationed in the streets and lanes all the way from the Court House to Long Wharf. More troops took up positions on either side of State Street, armed against Anthony Burns. Fifty thousand citizens lined the streets also, hissing and booing every time there was a troop movement. (p. 163)

Church bells in the vicinity began a sad tolling, and soon bells chimed all over Boston. The mournful toll rang out from town to town, from Plymouth to Salem, to Haverhill and on. Throughout the coast of New England, it was as if the hills chimed: *Anthony Burns is taken back to slavery. We toll for him and thee. And for shame, and shame again.* (p. 165)

At a Glance ▪ Virginia Hamilton has recreated the life of Anthony Burns in this powerful narrative of the escaped slave, captured in Boston, tried under the Fugitive Slave Act of 1850, and returned to slavery. This miscarriage of justice so enraged the public that laws were passed to prevent it from ever happening again in Massachusetts. This book is appropriate for secondary students and able junior high/middle school readers.

Summary ▪ Born as a slave in Virginia, Anthony Burns escaped to Boston on a ship in 1854 when he was almost twenty. Unfortunately, his master found him and had him arrested and thrown in jail. Tried under the Fugitive Slave Act of 1850, Burns was defended by leading abolitionist lawyers. The case so inflamed public opinion that some supporters even tried to storm the courthouse to free him. Even though he lost the case and was returned to his owner, the case resulted in the passage of the Massachusetts Personal Liberty Law—no other fugitive slave was ever again returned to bondage from this state. After friends of Burns located him in the South and bought his freedom, he returned to Boston and lectured about his life and mistreatment as a slave. Later he moved to Canada and became a minister, but died from illness at age twenty-eight.

Teaching Considerations ▪ While records exist about the trial of Anthony Burns and its aftermath, little is known about his earlier years. Hamilton uses a combination of historical records and historical narrative to recreate his life and the impact it had on the struggle to abolish slavery. The final section of this book contains selections from the Fugitive Slave Act of 1850 that might be helpful to discuss with students before reading about Burns's life. Among the awards this important book has received are: Boston Globe-Horn Book Award for Nonfiction, Jane Addams Children's Book Award, *School Library Journal* Best Book of the Year, and ALA Best Book for Young Adults.

After Reading: Suggested Student Activities

1. Anthony Burns lived for only twenty-eight years and died almost 150 years ago. In a small group or class discussion, describe the significance of his life and why we should care now about the events he was involved in then.

2. Imagine that you are defending Anthony Burns. Write a persuasive essay arguing that he should not be returned to bondage.

3. Prepare to debate the pros and cons of the following issue: Laws are the legal foundation of a democratic society. Is it justifiable, therefore, to break a law you think is wrong? (Teacher's Note: This activity also could be used with a whole class by implementing it as a discussion continuum. See the guidelines in chapter 1 for this strategy.)

4. Develop a tribute to Anthony Burns using a creative medium of expression.

Hargrove, Jim. *Abraham Lincoln: Sixteenth President of the United States.* Children's Press, 1988. 97 pages.

I believe this government cannot endure, permanently half slave and half free. I do not expect the Union to be dissolved—I do not expect the house to fall—but I do expect it will cease to be divided. It will become all one thing, or all the other. (p. 58)

At a Glance ▪ Hargrove provides a readable account of Lincoln's life accompanied by numerous vintage photographs and drawings.

Abraham Lincoln: Sixteenth President of the United States is part of the Encyclopedia of Presidents series. Appropriate for upper elementary and junior high/middle school students, it could be used as a teacher read-aloud.

Summary ▪ Hargrove's book is a concise overview of Abraham Lincoln's life with enough details and personal information to keep the reader interested. The first chapter describes Lincoln's decision to issue the Emancipation Proclamation and provides preliminary information about the Civil War and slavery. The remainder of the book presents Lincoln's life in chronological order, with the major emphasis on his life before his election as president. Numerous other historical figures and the issues and events of this tumultuous period in history are introduced and provide the context for understanding Lincoln's significance as president. A chronology of American history, with the events in Lincoln's life shaded in gray, provides a useful reference guide at the end of the book.

Teaching Considerations ▪ It will be helpful to provide students with an overview of the various views toward slavery from our country's beginning through the Civil War. Lincoln's own views as presented in this book will need more explanation and discussion.

After Reading: Suggested Student Activities

1. Construct a timeline of the significant events in Abraham Lincoln's life.

2. In a journal entry, explain what the Emancipation Proclamation did and why Abraham Lincoln issued it.

3. George Washington and Abraham Lincoln are frequently called the two greatest presidents in the history of the United States. In a persuasive essay, evaluate this statement and make a case for or against it.

4. In a small group or class discussion, describe how various groups in the Union and Confederacy responded to the Emancipation Proclamation and analyze the short-term and long-term implications of this key decision.

Lincoln, Abraham. Illustrated by Michael McCurdy.
Foreword by Garry Wills. *The Gettysburg Address.*
Houghton Mifflin, 1995. 25 pages, unnumbered.

The world will little note, nor long remember what we
say here, but it can never forget what they did here. (p.
18, unnumbered)

At a Glance ▪ The combination of Lincoln's immortal Gettysburg
Address and Michael McCurdy's striking illustrations make this
picture book a powerful experience for all ages.

Summary ▪ The Battle of Gettysburg, July 1–3, 1863, was the
turning point of the Civil War. In November of that year a national
cemetery was dedicated to the soldiers who perished in the terrible
battle. Although Lincoln was not the principal speaker at the dedication, his brief "remarks" of 272 words gave the loss of fifty thousand Union and Confederate soldiers a higher meaning and
connected it to the preservation of the Union. This picture book
includes a foreword and afterword that provide additional historical context.

Teaching Considerations ▪ Lincoln's immortal three-minute
speech encapsulates the essence of the Civil War conflict. An effective way to present Lincoln's Gettysburg Address is to provide a
dramatic reading of it accompanied by Michael McCurdy's illustrations. Make students aware that Lincoln wrote out six copies of the
Gettysburg Address with slight differences; five copies are known
to still exist.

After Reading: Suggested Student Activities

1. Select a phrase or sentence from Lincoln's Gettysburg Address
   that you think is especially significant and explain its significance in terms of the conflict between the North and South.
   Present your explanation to the class.

2. Evaluate and discuss the use of illustrations to accompany Lincoln's words. Explain whether you think they enhance or detract from the text and why.

3. It has been said that Lincoln's Gettysburg Address is one of the greatest speeches in our nation's history. In an essay explain its importance.

4. Identify an ideal or value that Lincoln presents in this speech. Prepare a Values map. (Teacher's Note: See the guidelines in chapter 1 for this strategy.)

Marrin, Albert. *Unconditional Surrender: U.S. Grant and the Civil War.* **Atheneum, 1994. 200 pages.**

He [Grant] habitually wears an expression as if he had determined to drive his head through a brick wall, and was about to do it. (p. 4)

At a Glance ▪ Marrin's fascinating story of Grant's life is effectively placed within the larger context of the history of the pre-Civil War and Civil War years in our nation. More than a biography of Grant, it is a splendid account of the times and the people who figured so prominently in it, accompanied by vintage photographs and excerpts from letters, diaries, and newspapers. This book is appropriate for secondary school students and able junior high/ middle school students.

Summary ▪ Marrin's biography of Grant spans his life from his birth on April 27, 1822 in Ohio to his death at age sixty-three on July 23, 1885 in New York. Grant was a complex man, full of contradictions. He was a failure at everything he did, except for being a soldier. His appearance and dress were unimposing, and frequently he looked quite seedy. He didn't seem to have strong antislavery views and didn't see himself as a liberator. He hated war, yet he was the only general Lincoln could count on to fight. His public popularity rose and fell with his success or failure on the battlefield. Newspaper headlines either praised him, saying U.S. Grant was actually "Unconditional Surrender" Grant, or condemned him, calling him a mad butcher. While Grant's life during the Civil War years constitutes the major portion of this book, the issues, events, and other prominent individuals of the time also receive ample attention. Additional topics range from a cogent overview of slavery in the United States to a harrowing description of medical and sanitary conditions on the battlefields. Particularly fascinating, also, are the sections of the book devoted to other principals, such as William Tecumseh Sherman and Philip Sheridan.

Teaching Considerations ▪ *Unconditional Surrender: U.S. Grant and the Civil War* is so much more than a biography; it is a rich source of well-written information about the Civil War era. Students who declare that they do not like history may learn it in spite of themselves with this engrossing book. Marrin occasionally quotes speakers who use mild profanity and the word "nigger" in a derogatory manner. Descriptions of some battle scenes and a few photographs are grim, but realistic. This use of language is not gratuitous and is placed within the context of the times and events. *Unconditional Surrender: U.S. Grant and the Civil War* received the International Reading Association Young Adults' Choices Award.

After Reading: Suggested Student Activities

1. Keep a journal of your impressions of Grant, analyzing how they change or remain constant as you read about his life from childhood to death.

2. Compare and contrast how Grant and Lee felt about slavery and secession. Analyze their perspectives in light of the major roles they each played in the Civil War. Prepare a chart highlighting the achievements of each of these men.

3. In a speech prepared for your class, evaluate Grant's role in the Union winning the Civil War. Use specific historical data to support your position.

4. While this book is a biography of Grant, it also describes other significant individuals, events, or issues of the times. Select one of these that is particularly interesting to you. Do further research about it and present your findings to the class.

McKissack, Patricia C., and Fredrick L. McKissack. *Rebels Against Slavery: American Slave Revolts.* Scholastic, 1996. 181 pages.

From generation to generation slave children were taught that they were inferior beings meant to be servants, and white children were taught that they were superior to all others. In time, large numbers within each group came to believe what they'd been taught. On any plantation there were more than a few slaves who were loyal and faithful to their masters or afraid to disobey them. But there were always a few—and current research shows the number was much larger than ever expected—who stubbornly refused to relinquish their right to be free, and no amount of coercion or kindness could change them. (p. 18)

At a Glance ▪ Based on meticulous research, the McKissacks refute the popular misconception that African slaves in America placidly accepted their condition. Their book describes the day-to-day resistance and early revolts as well as events and figures that had a major impact on the struggles of African slaves in the United States to be free. It is appropriate for able junior high/middle school students and secondary students.

Summary ▪ While slavery is as old as recorded history, slaves from Africa were first brought to the Americas with the sixteenth-century European colonization. The first recorded large-scale revolt of African slaves occurred in 1522 on the island of Hispaniola, on the plantation of Christopher Columbus's son. Other significant revolts occurred in the Caribbean, Mexico, and Central and South America during the 1500s. In 1619 African slaves were first brought into what later became the United States. They came to Virginia initially as indentured servants, but by 1641, the legal enslavement of Africans began. When slaves and indentured servants conspired to overthrow their masters, slave laws were adopted that restricted the rights of both free blacks and slaves. Runaways increased, and *maroons,* hidden communities of runaways in remote locations, were secretly organized. Gabriel Prosser, David Walker, Nat Turner, Cinque, and others provided important leadership in the struggle to be free during the early 1800s. In addition to the text, *Rebels Against Slavery: American Slave Revolts* has numerous illustrations and a listing of important dates.

Teaching Considerations ▪ Many students have a narrow perspective of slavery in the Americas. This book can help to broaden their

knowledge and understanding although they do need to be aware
that while this information is not comprehensive, it does provide
an excellent representation of the various ways in which slaves
struggled for their freedom as well as insightful profiles of several
significant leaders.

After Reading: Suggested Student Activities

1. Select one of the acts of rebellion described in this book that you
   found particularly significant. Find a creative way to portray it
   for someone who has not yet read this book. (Teacher's Note:
   See the guidelines in chapter 1 for this strategy.)

2. In your class discuss why so little is generally known about rebellious acts by slaves and why it is important to learn about
   this aspect of history.

3. Find an excerpt from this book that challenged you or made you
   look at an event, issue, or person from a different perspective.
   Write an accompanying essay explaining your choice and how
   it has affected you.

4. Do more research on a person or event described in this book.
   Write a report and prepare an accompanying visual to present
   to the class.

McKissack, Patricia C., and Fredrick McKissack. *Sojourner Truth: Ain't I a Woman?* Scholastic, 1992. 186 pages.

Soon word spread that Sojourner Truth was a stirring
and inspirational speaker. When she came into a camp
meeting, people rushed to greet her; and after hearing
her speak, people were so filled with emotion that they
often cheered and cried.

At first, Sojourner was taken with the notion that
whites would sit still and listen to anything she had to
say. Later, her goal became clearer. All her life Sojourner
had been a victim of oppression, despised because of her
race, and disregarded because of her sex. It was out of
the fog of this life that she emerged at age forty-six, ded-

icated to the elimination of human suffering. She would speak out against slavery! (p. 84)

At a Glance ▪ This award-winning biography traces the life of Sojourner Truth, born in slavery as Isabella Van Wagener. Sojourner Truth became one of the most effective spokespersons for the abolition of slavery. This book could be read by junior high/middle school students and would also be enjoyed by secondary students.

Summary ▪ Isabella Van Wagener took control of her life after spending her first twenty-eight years as a slave. A devoutly religious woman, Belle was sustained by her faith in God during the difficult years. After gaining her freedom, Belle was dismayed to learn that her only son, Peter, had been sold. A child of six, he eventually was sold to a family from Alabama. New York was in the process of abolishing slavery, and so it was unthinkable to have a child sold and taken to a state where slavery was for life. With the help of some Quakers, Belle went to court and ultimately won her son back, but he had been severely beaten and never really recovered. She was one of the first black women to win a court case in this country. After witnessing the abolition of slavery in her home state of New York, Belle sought a new life where she could have her family together, but things didn't work as she had hoped. Belle changed her name to Sojourner Truth to reflect who she was. She became a preacher who quoted scriptures, although she never learned to read. She also became a powerful voice in speaking against slavery and campaigned for equal rights for both women and blacks. Sojourner Truth was a powerful presence and a dynamic speaker who made a difference to those she encountered.

Teaching Considerations ▪ While the reading level of this biography is not difficult, the story of Sojourner Truth's life and trials will hold the interest of a wide range of readers. The book is a Coretta Scott King Honor Book. There are a number of photographs and illustrations that complement the text effectively. The brief biographical sketches of people that Sojourner Truth knew will be both interesting and informative for readers.

After Reading: Suggested Student Activities

1. Do a VIP map of Belle/Sojourner's life. (Teacher's Note: See the guidelines in chapter 1 for this strategy.)

2. From your knowledge of history and your reading, write a persuasive paper either supporting or rejecting the notion that Sojourner Truth has not received the recognition that she deserves for her contributions to the struggle for human rights.

3. Select one of the people who is included in the biographical sketches at the end of the book, do further research, and share your findings with the class.

4. There are a number of accounts of Sojourner Truth's life. Read another one and compare and contrast the portrayal of her in both.

Miller, William. Illustrated by Cedric Lucus.
Frederick Douglass: The Last Day of Slavery.
Lee and Low Books, 1995. 28 pages, unnumbered.

Frederick saw the anger in Covey's eyes and knew no magic would save him now. He knew that any man— slave or free—had to defend himself. (p. 21)

At a Glance ▪ This picture book is written for elementary students, but it could be used with students of any age and make an effective teacher read-aloud. It tells the story of the early years of Frederick Douglass's life and has wonderful illustrations.

Summary ▪ This book tells of Frederick Douglass's early years in slavery. As a young man he dreamed of freedom, but he felt trapped. A turning point in his life was when a slave breaker whipped him, and Frederick fought back. From that point on, he knew that he would be free.

Teaching Considerations ▪ This picture book could be used effectively to introduce Frederick Douglass to students unfamiliar with this remarkable man.

After Reading: Suggested Student Activities

1. Prepare a Did You Know . . . ? chart based on your reading of this book. (Teacher's Note: See the guidelines in chapter 1 for this strategy.)

2. Discuss what changed Douglass's life. How did he take action?

3. In your response journal discuss whether or not the illustrations add to the impact of this book? How or how not?

4. Read either Douglass's autobiography or a biography about him. Compare it with this book.

Petry, Ann. *Harriet Tubman: Conductor on the Underground Railroad.* HarperCollins, 1995. 247 pages.

She had announced her arrival in the quarter by singing the forbidden spiritual—"Go down, Moses, 'way down to Egypt Land"—singing it softly outside the door of a slave cabin, late at night. The husky voice was beautiful even when it was barely more than a murmur borne on the wind.

Once she had made her presence known, word of her coming spread from cabin to cabin. The slaves whispered to each other, ear to mouth, mouth to ear, "Moses is here." "Moses has come." "Get ready. Moses is back again." (p. 133)

At a Glance ▪ This biography tells the story of the courageous life of Harriet Tubman, the "Moses" of the Underground Railroad who also served as a spy and nurse during the Civil War. Appropriate for upper elementary and junior high/middle school students, this book will also be enjoyed by less able readers at the secondary level.

Summary ▪ Born into slavery in Maryland around 1821, Harriet's birth name was Araminta which was shortened to "Minta" or "Minty" when she was a child; later she was called Harriet and when she led other slaves to freedom, she became known as "Moses." She was born at a time when there were increased stirrings and whisperings about freedom among the slaves and increased fear on the part of the owners. Her mother, Old Rit, worked in the Big House and wanted that way of life for Minty, rather than the rough life of a field hand. Her father, Ben, respected for his honesty and knowledge of nature, taught her what he knew. Beginning when she was six years old, Minty was hired out by her master for a series of different house jobs, but she succeeded at none of them. Mistreated, beaten, and frequently ill, she finally ended up working in the fields. Harriet became as strong as a man; she also heard stories about an "underground road" that led slaves to freedom. One fall while helping another slave run away, she was struck in the head by the overseer with a two-pound weight, which nearly killed her and left her subject to strange dreams and unexpected sleeping spells the rest of her life. Later she married a freedman, John Tubman, but when she could no longer endure the life of slavery and made plans to run away, he threatened to tell the master. After several abortive attempts to flee with others, she finally escaped by herself into the free state of Pennsylvania. There she worked while she arranged for the escape of some of her family members; later she returned to the plantation to guide others out to safety. When the Fugitive Slave Act was passed and life was no longer safe for her in Pennsylvania, she established a home in Canada but kept returning to the Eastern Shore to lead others out of slavery. She became a legend, and although there were large rewards for her capture, she, and the people she guided, were never caught.

Teaching Considerations ▪ While telling the story of Harriet Tubman, the author skillfully interweaves into the narrative information about other people Harriet will encounter later in her life or events that will affect her. An ALA Notable Children's Book, this biography of Harriet Tubman effectively recreates her life and is a valuable addition to a classroom library. Another easier biography appropriate for elementary school students is:

McMullan, Kate. Illustrated by Steven James Petruccio. *The Story of Harriet Tubman, Conductor of the Underground Railroad.* A Yearling Book, 1991.

The following picture books based on Harriet Tubman's life can be used with students of all ages and are described in the chapters noted:

Lawrence, Jacob. *Harriet and the Promised Land*. Simon and Schuster, 1993. (See entry in this chapter.)

Ringgold, Faith. *Aunt Harriet's Underground Railroad in the Sky*. Crown Publishers, 1992. (See entry in chapter 3.)

Schroeder, Alan. Illustrations by Jerry Pinkney. *Minty: A Story of Young Harriet Tubman*. Dial Books, 1996. (See entry in this chapter.)

After Reading: Suggested Student Activities

1. Prepare a VIP map of Harriet Tubman and the significant events in her life. (Teacher's Note: See the guidelines in chapter 1 for this strategy.)

2. Prepare a tribute to Harriet Tubman using a creative means of expression.

3. Select an event from her life to dramatize. Prepare a script and perform it with some of your classmates.

4. Harriet Tubman could have lived in safety once she reached Canada. Discuss with your class why you think she continued to risk her life by returning to the South to lead others out of slavery.

Quackenbush, Robert. *Clara Barton and Her Victory Over Fear*. Aladdin, 1995. 36 pages.

The sensitive nature will always remain. She will never assert herself for herself—she will suffer wrong first—. But for others she will be perfectly fearless. (p. 16)

At a Glance ▪ This short biography written for elementary school students presents an overview of Clara Barton's early life, but then focuses on her successful careers as a teacher, as the first female government worker, as a nurse in the Civil War, and as the founder of the American Red Cross.

Summary ▪ Clarissa (Clara) Barton was ten years younger than the next youngest of her siblings. She was treated like a special gift by her brothers and sisters. Each one looked after her and taught her various things, and she was an eager pupil. When she began school at age four, she was far more advanced than the other children her age. She enjoyed learning, but she was very shy and did not make friends easily. She used her love of learning to become a teacher when she was almost seventeen. As a teacher, she was able to overcome her shyness. After a successful teaching career, she moved to Washington, D.C., where she worked for the Patent Office, the first woman to work for the government. When the Civil War began, she volunteered to be a nurse. She helped both Union and Confederate soldiers. After the war, she worked with the European Red Cross. She was impressed by the organization, and after returning to the United States, she worked to establish the first chapter of the Red Cross in this country. After considerable effort, she was allowed to begin a chapter. It was soon followed by others, and in the years that followed, Clara Barton and the Red Cross responded to every national disaster. Today the work she began continues, and the American Red Cross has over one million volunteers.

Teaching Considerations ▪ This book presents an effective account of Clara Barton's accomplishments as a nurse during the Civil War and as the founder of the American Red Cross after the war. The brevity of the book may be a bit misleading because Quackenbush provides lots of information about Clara Barton.

After Reading: Suggested Student Activities

1. Imagine that you are Clara and that you regularly write in a journal. Write entries expressing what you suspect her life was like during the following periods: when she moved to the farm with her parents; when she was teaching; during the Civil War; and when she was retired and reflecting on her contributions.

2. Select an event from Clara's life. In your collaborative learning group, write a scene dramatizing the event.

3. Create a mural with key events from Clara's life.

4. Contact your local chapter of the Red Cross and interview its director about the organization's activities in your community.

Schroeder, Alan. Illustrations by Jerry Pinkney. *Minty.* Dial Books, 1996. 40 pages, unnumbered.

As Minty reached for the bowl, she accidentally knocked over a pitcher of cider. Mrs. Bodas jumped to her feet. "Now look what you've done!" Angrily, she turned to her husband. "Do you see, Edward? It's spite, pure and simple! Well, I won't stand for it. I don't want her in the house anymore. From now on, she's a field slave. That'll fix her." (p. 6)

At a Glance ▪ "Minty" is a nickname for young Harriet Tubman. Schroeder presents the story of her early days in slavery. As is true of many of today's picture books, this book will appeal to readers of all ages. This book is also an effective teacher read-aloud.

Summary ▪ The story that is often told of Harriet Tubman is of her work with the Underground Railroad in rescuing slaves. This book relates some of the stories that are known of her childhood on a plantation on the Eastern Shore of Maryland. One of the on-going fears that all slaves lived with was the possibility of being "sold south," sent to another plantation further south, away from family and friends as a punishment. Minty was a willful child who was banished from being a house slave to do field work. As a child she was determined to escape, and she learned how to follow the stars, the Big Dipper, which was known as the "drinking gourd"; how to read trees to know direction; and what to eat and what not to eat in the wild. She also learned to swim. All of this was in preparation for her own escape from the plantation many years later.

Teaching Considerations ▪ This book is one of many that relate the remarkable life and accomplishments of Harriet Tubman. It could be used to introduce her to students and get them interested in what she did with her life.

After Reading: Suggested Student Activities

1. Read other accounts of Harriet Tubman's life (including other picture books or biographies) and compare the information.

2. Dramatize an event from her life as it is presented in this book.

3. Select an illustration that you particularly like and discuss in your response journal why you like it and how it makes you feel. What does it contribute to the text?

4. Develop a "Did You Know . . . ?" chart while reading this book. (Teacher's Note: See the guidelines in chapter 1 for this strategy.)

Stepto, Michele, editor. *Our Song, Our Toil: The Story of American Slavery as Told by Slaves*. Millbrook Press, 1994. 95 pages.

> The story of slavery is American history, and it is one of the most important stories that can ever be told in the United States. Whatever color we may be, wherever our families may have come from, as Americans we can all learn from it. Knowing our past, knowing how we have come to be who we are, we can enter the future with greater strength and understanding. (p. 16)

At a Glance ▪ This nonfiction account uses excerpts from actual narratives of former slaves. Too often with any group, we see only a few people, the heroes who publicly make a difference. For every well-known hero there are numerous others whose contributions have also made an impact. This book is the story of many who made a difference by valuing freedom. This book is appropriate for junior high/middle school students, but it might also provide secondary readers with good introductory material.

Summary ▪ In this well-researched volume, Stepto presents a chronological view of slavery in this country from 1640, when an African American indentured servant in Virginia unsuccessfully escaped and was sentenced to a lifetime of servitude, to the early days of freedom. By using excerpts from narratives by former slaves, she is able to make the times dramatically come alive. The book deals with the capturing and transporting of slaves, being born to a life of slavery with its implications for families, the economic implications of slavery, acts of resistance and escape, and freedom. Another chapter addresses the significance of literacy and its role in keeping a people enslaved.

Teaching Considerations ▪ The book combines stories of well-known former slaves, such as Frederick Douglass and Harriet Jacobs, with those who are little known, such as Annie L. Burton and Henry Bibb. Each of the time periods is illustrated by the words of former slaves who experienced it. Stepto provides margin notes to help young readers with unfamiliar vocabulary.

After Reading: Suggested Student Activities

1. Select one of the people featured in this book, find out more about the person, and prepare a report for the class.

2. Do a timeline of the major events in the history of slavery in this country. Make sure that you include the dates when each state allowed and then outlawed slavery.

3. Research the antiliteracy laws and their implications. Imagine that you were living during the time they are enforced. Write an editorial, newspaper column, or a letter to the editor reacting against these laws.

4. In a class discussion, be prepared to examine the following question: "What does it mean to be courageous?" Identify three acts of courage that impressed you in this book. Why were you impressed by them?

Whittier, John Greenleaf. Illustrated by Nancy Winslow Parker.
Barbara Frietchie. **Greenwillow Books, 1992. 32 pages.**

> "Shoot, if you must, this old gray head,
> But spare your country's flag," she said.
> A shade of sadness, a blush of shame,
> Over the face of the leader came;
> The nobler nature within him stirred
> To life at that woman's deed and word;

"Who touches a hair of yon gray head
Dies likes a dog! March on!" he said.

(pp. 21–23)

At a Glance ▪ John Greenleaf Whittier's famous poem with the oft-quoted lines shown here is colorfully illustrated and accompanied by maps, flags, and biographical, military, and historical notes. This edition could be used effectively with readers of all ages.

Summary ▪ First published in the *Atlantic Monthly* in 1863, Whittier's poem is set in Frederick, Maryland, in September 1862 when General Stonewall Jackson and his Confederate troops marched through the city on their way to the Battle of Antietam at Sharpsburg. Maryland was a border state, and the citizens of Frederick were divided between loyalty to the Union and sympathy for the South. According to legend, Barbara Frietchie, ninety-five years old, risked her life to demonstrate her loyalty to the Union.

Teaching Considerations ▪ Although there is disagreement as to the historical accuracy of the poem, Barbara Frietchie has become a legendary figure symbolizing the ordinary citizen who takes a dangerous stand and makes a difference. One of America's most honored poets, Whittier was a Quaker and an ardent abolitionist who wrote "Barbara Frietchie" based on newspaper reports and other popular accounts of the day. A few years before his death he wrote a defense of the poem, asserting that he did not make up the events. Readers of all ages can enjoy this stirring poem for its own sake and as an example of poetry written during the Civil War. Older readers can also be helped to understand its role in creating a legend.

After Reading: Suggested Student Activities

1. Discuss why the actions of Barbara Frietchie as portrayed in this poem had such a strong impact on supporters of the Union during the Civil War. Why does it continue to inspire and move many readers?

2. An event can be reported as a series of facts and observations, or it can be translated into a creative form that captures the

hearts and imaginations of people. Legendary figures who become an important part of a country's national identity usually have some basis in fact; often, however, the facts are changed, distorted, or embellished in the process. Decide your position on the following statement: U.S. History should be taught using only documented facts. Be prepared to debate the topic in class. (Teacher's Note: This activity also could be used with a whole class by implementing it as a discussion continuum. See the guidelines in chapter 1 for this strategy.)

3. Evaluate Parker's illustrations. Do you think her style enhances or detracts from Whittier's poem? Write a paper stating your position and your rationale.

4. Research more about the life and works of John Greenleaf Whittier, especially his role as an abolitionist. Compare "Barbara Frietchie" with some of his other poetry. Try to find other illustrated editions of "Barbara Frietchie" to compare with this one.

More Books

Bains, Rae. Illustrated by Jean Meyer. *Clara Barton: Angel of the Battlefield*. Troll Associates, 1982. 48 pages.

This book is an easy-to-read biography of the famous Civil War nurse, Clarissa Barton, and is appropriate for elementary students. The fifth and youngest child in her family, Clara was shy but loved to learn. She became a teacher while a teenager, which helped her to overcome her shyness. Later she worked for the Patent Office in Washington, D.C., and was the first woman to work for the federal government. She volunteered to be a nurse during the Civil War and helped both Union and Confederate soldiers. After the war, she established the first chapter of the Red Cross in this country.

Bentley, Judith. *"Dear Friend" Thomas Garrett and William Still*. Cobblehill Books, 1997. 119 pages.

This nonfiction account relates the parallel relationship between two men with very different backgrounds who were united by a single cause, helping fugitive slaves to find freedom and safety. The subtitle of the book is *Collaborators on the Underground Railroad.* Still was a free black man living in Philadelphia. He worked for the Anti-Slavery Society, the most effective of the abolitionist organizations in Pennsylvania. In this role he was a bridge between the predominately white community that worked in the abolitionist movement and the black community, which was involved more in activities directly involving escaped slaves. Thomas Garrett was a white Quaker, living in the slave state of Delaware and acting as one of the primary conductors on the Underground Railroad. Garrett helped slaves escape from bondage and then turned them over to Still and the Philadelphia Vigilance Committee, who helped them continue their passage into Canada. This book is appropriate for able junior high/middle school students and secondary students.

Collins, James L. *John Brown and the Fight Against Slavery.* Millbrook Press, 1991. 32 pages

This informational book, replete with photographs and illustrations, presents a brief overview of John Brown's life, including a timeline of major events. The emphasis of the book is on his anti-slavery activities, first in Kansas where he and his followers (including four of his sons) sought revenge for the violence against abolitionists in Lawrence. The swift, violent killings that Brown committed made him a hero to some but a murderer to others. Brown then decided to make a stand at Harper's Ferry, Virginia (now West Virginia). He and his followers took command of the armory and arsenal, claiming that they were there to free all the blacks in the state. A battle ensued and Brown was captured, tried, convicted, and sentenced to death. This is an easy biography appropriate for elementary school students. (See also chapter 4.)

d'Aulaire, Ingri, and Edgar Parin d'Aulaire. *Abraham Lincoln.* Bantam Doubleday Dell, 1939, 1957. 54 pages, unnumbered.

The 1940 Caldecott Award winner, this picture book tells the life of Abraham Lincoln by interweaving popular stories and legends about him with historical facts. Using beautiful illustrations and detailed text, the book focuses on his early life, with the section on his presidency ending before his assassination. Written less than seventy-five years after his death, it will interest anyone who wants to see how Abraham Lincoln has been portrayed for children through the years.

Davis, Ossie. *Escape to Freedom, A Play About Young Frederick Douglass.* **Puffin Books, 1976; Introduction, 1989. 89 pages.**

This play, winner of the Coretta Scott King Award, tells the inspiring and harrowing story of the childhood of Frederick Douglass. Using narrative, dialogue, and songs, the telling of the events of his early years captivates us as we view his determination to learn to read and write, the determination of his master to break him, and his courageous escape to freedom. Appropriate for school audiences, it is an excellent vehicle for making history come alive.

Greene, Carol. *Abraham Lincoln: President of a Divided Country.* **Children's Press, 1989. 46 pages.**

Part of the Rookie Biography series, *Abraham Lincoln: President of a Divided Country* is appropriate for young readers or upper elementary students who have difficulty reading. Written in a simple style, the text is enhanced with vintage photographs and drawings. Greene tells Lincoln's life from his early years, through his important role as president during the Civil War, to his untimely death.

Greene, Carol. *Robert E. Lee: Leader in War and Peace.* **Children's Press, 1989. 48 pages.**

Robert E. Lee: Leader in War and Peace is part of the Rookie Biography series and is appropriate for young readers or upper elementary students who have difficulty reading. Written in a simple style, the text is enhanced with vintage photographs, drawings, and quotations. Greene tells Lee's life story, beginning with his father, who fought in the revolutionary war and was governor of Virginia, through Lee's role as the great Civil War general, to his death in 1870.

Jakoubek, Robert E. *The Assassination of Abraham Lincoln.* **Millbrook Press, 1993. 64 pages.**

The Assassination of Abraham Lincoln is one of the books in the Spotlight on American History series and is appropriate for upper elementary and junior high/middle school students. Jakoubek provides enough details about Lincoln and additional information about other historical figures to keep the reader's attention. Almost every page is enlivened with vintage photographs and other illustrations. A brief chronology from 1860 to 1865 is provided at the end of the book.

Kent, Zachary. *Jefferson Davis*. Children's Press, 1993. 31 pages.

This short biography of Jefferson Davis is part of the Cornerstones of Freedom series for elementary school students. It provides an overview of Davis's life and his presidency during the Civil War and uses photographs, paintings, and drawings to enhance the text. Born in Kentucky and educated at West Point, Davis later became a Mississippi plantation owner. He served as a colonel in the U.S. Army during the 1846–47 war with Mexico, then became a senator from Mississippi, and was chosen by President Franklin Pierce to be U.S. Secretary of War in 1853. Davis was unanimously elected president of the Confederate States of America in 1861. As author Zachary Kent states, "Perhaps more than anyone, Davis symbolized the hopes and stubborn spirit of the Confederacy" (p. 5).

Kent, Zachary. *The Story of Ford's Theater and the Death of Abraham Lincoln*. Children's Press, 1987. 32 pages.

As part of the Cornerstones of Freedom series for elementary school students, this volume presents one of the closing chapters of the Civil War, the assassination of Lincoln. The book presents the details of one of the most infamous acts in our history. It includes the president's premonition about his assassination. It also mentions his reluctance to go to the theater that night. In the end, his sense of obligation to not disappoint those who expected to see him overshadowed his uneasiness. The book also tells of the activities of John Wilkes Booth and his followers, who had failed in their earlier plans to kidnap President Lincoln. There were nine alleged conspirators: Booth and four others were hanged, and the others were sent to prison.

Lawrence, Jacob. *Harriet and the Promised Land*. Simon and Schuster, 1993. 30 pages, unnumbered.

This picture book is a verse biography of Harriet Tubman. It tells of her early years as a slave, her desire to be free, and about her hearing the Bible story of Moses leading the slaves out of Egypt. After her escape, she became a "Moses" for her people. The book, wonderfully rhythmic with powerful illustrations, would be enjoyed by students of all ages.

Macht, Norman L. *Sojourner Truth: Crusader for Civil Rights*. Chelsea House Publishers, 1992. 79 pages.

Sojourner Truth: Crusader for Civil Rights is a Junior Black Americans of Achievement book, part of the Junior World Biographies series. Appropriate for elementary students or junior high/middle school students who need an easier text, this biography tells the moving and inspiring story of the former slave who became a champion for civil rights causes. Photographs and other illustrations—as well as suggestions for further reading, a glossary, and a chronology of Sojourner Truth's life, enhance the clearly written text.

Reef, Catherine. *Walt Whitman*. Clarion Books, 1995. 148 pages

While this biography covers Whitman's whole life, it was the Civil War years he spent in Washington that had a great impact on him as a poet. When his brother was wounded in battle, Whitman left New York to help nurse him. While his brother's injury was slight, Whitman was moved by the suffering he saw in the hospitals. He served as a volunteer for the U.S. Christian Commission, going to hospitals and helping to nurse the wounded. He wrote letters for the patients, entertained them, and gave comfort to them. He frequently saw President Lincoln, a man whom he admired, on the streets of Washington. The experiences during the war and his admiration of the president served as inspiration for some of his most successful poetry. The book might be used with junior high/middle school students or even as an introduction to Whitman's poetry for secondary students.

Sandburg, Carl. Illustrated by James Daugherty. *Abe Lincoln Grows Up*. Harcourt Brace & World, 1926, 1956. 222 pages.

Through the years Carl Sandburg's classic *Abe Lincoln Grows Up* has been read and enjoyed by readers of all ages. It will still be enjoyed today by those seeking to understand how Lincoln was viewed a little more than sixty years after his death. This book for children was taken from Sandburg's two-volume *Abraham Lincoln: The Prairie Years,* first published in 1926 to celebrate Lincoln's birthday. It tells the story of Lincoln's early years until he leaves home at age nineteen.

Sell, Bill. *Leaders of the North and South.* **Metro Books, 1996. 128 pages**

This nonfiction collection of biographical sketches includes fourteen leaders from the Civil War period, seven from the Union and seven from the Confederacy. On the Union side, Sell profiles Lincoln, Grant, Sherman, McClellan, Chamberlain, Sickles, and Farragut; from the Confederacy, he profiles Davis, Lee, Jackson, Longstreet, Stuart, Semmes, and Forrest. The profiles provide an overview of each man's career within the context of a more indepth view of his role during the Civil War. All profiles are complemented by numerous illustrations and photographs. Able junior high/middle school students and secondary students will find this a valuable resource.

Shorto, Russell. *Abraham Lincoln and the End of Slavery.* **Millbrook Press, 1991. 30 pages.**

Part of the Gateway Civil Rights series, this concise biography of Lincoln is appropriate for elementary school students or junior high/middle school students who have difficulty reading. It could be used as a teacher read-aloud. The clearly written text is enhanced with vintage photographs, illustrations, maps, inserts with related information, a chronology of important dates, and a list of additional resources. Shorto focuses on Lincoln's adult years, beginning with his trip to New Orleans at age eighteen where he sees black men, women, and children treated like animals as they are auctioned off to the highest bidder.

Sullivan, George. *Mathew Brady: His Life and Photographs.* **Cobblehill Books, 1994. 136 pages.**

In this biography, Sullivan captures a sense of a man whose true genius was his ability to recognize the huge potential of photography as a new art form. In this realistic account, Brady's gifts for recognizing opportunities are counterbalanced by his extremely poor business sense and his almost obsessive need to be in control. The majority of the thousands of photographs taken during the Civil War that bear Brady's name were, in fact, taken by the legions of photographers that he hired to cover both sides of the war. The credit that he deserves is for recognizing the importance of capturing the images of this brutal war. Virtually every major political and military leader of the time flocked to his studio to sit for Brady, which is a tribute to his influence. Upper elementary students and junior high/middle school students will enjoy this book. It gives a perspective about the early days in the field of photography as well as looking at Brady's career.

Winnick, Karen B. _Mr. Lincoln's Whiskers_. Boyds Mills Press, 1996. 30 pages, unnumbered.

A charming picture book illustrated with rich oil paintings, _Mr. Lincoln's Whiskers_ tells the true story of eleven-year-old Grace Bedell, who may have been responsible for Lincoln's decision to grow a beard. Grace wrote Lincoln a letter when he was campaigning for the presidency suggesting that he would look much better and get more votes if he grew whiskers. Much to everyone's surprise, he wrote back to her. After the election, while traveling from Springfield, Illinois, to Washington, D.C., to be sworn into office, he asked to see Grace when his train made a brief stop for wood in her town. Lincoln was the first president to wear a beard. Appropriate for all ages, this picture book concludes with reproductions of the letters Lincoln and Grace exchanged.

Woods, Andrew. _Young Frederick Douglass: Freedom Fighter_. Troll Communications, 1996. 32 pages.

This short biography, written for beginning readers, relates the story of one of the greatest champions of freedom for African Americans, Frederick Douglass. Born into slavery as Frederick Bailey, he spent his early years on a plantation, but when he was eight he was sent to work for a family in Baltimore and stayed there for eight years. He was treated well and even learned to read, which was against the law for slaves. After he was returned to the plantation, Fred's life became more difficult. He was treated badly by his owners. This treatment increased his desire to be free. At twenty-one, he escaped to New Bedford, Massachusetts, where he changed

his name to Frederick Douglass to avoid being captured and returned to slavery. In the North, Douglass became a leading abolitionist. He traveled extensively and spoke eloquently for freedom
for slaves. Teachers will need to add background information because the information in this book is so brief.

5

War Experiences

The devastation of the Civil War can be described in various ways—loss of homes, farms, crops, livestock—but nothing is as chilling as the casualty statistics. In the four years of war from 1861 until 1865, more than 620,000 lives were lost at a time when the population of the country was around 29 million people. Twenty percent of the American population at the time was killed during the Civil War, which means that one in every twelve men and boys from ages fifteen to fifty died. For every death on the battlefield, two soldiers died from disease. Of the soldiers who survived, many were crippled from wounds that resulted in amputated limbs. After returning home, many of the wounded from the North suffered from the "soldier's disease," an addiction to morphine induced by the medical treatment they had received. The South was spared this problem because its supplies of medicines were very limited.

In the wake of the war, virtually every American community was affected. The Civil War was fought primarily by volunteers on both sides. Military companies were organized regionally. For example, the much-lauded 20th Maine under the command of Joshua Chamberlain was composed of men from a narrow strip along the Maine coast from Portland to Friendship. The men from communities like those, both North and South, enlisted together, fought together, and too often died together. If a company was involved in a particularly fierce campaign, then every member from a community might be killed. The scars were deep on both sides, and the healing was gradual.

Beyond these grim statistics, the Civil War has left a two-fold legacy: the words and images of life at war. The soldiers of the Civil War were, up to that time, the most literate soldiers ever, with 90 percent of the white Union forces and 80 percent of the Confederate able to read and write. Additionally, nineteenth-century American society avidly read newspapers, so the forces of both sides were highly informed and interested in the events of the day. This interest is reflected in the letters, diaries, and journals from the period. Additionally, the war was covered by reporters and artists who sketched battle scenes or anything else they observed. The telegraph also conveyed battle results quickly, thus creating a sense of immediacy for people on the homefront. Beyond the steady flow of information, the second part of the legacy was based on the role of photography in capturing the images of people and events of the war. The teams of photographers that Mathew Brady sent to cover the war were on the battlelines, in the camps, and with the soldiers. As a result, we have the most comprehensive photographic coverage of any war to that time. The words and images from the Civil War remain a part of our heritage.

The names of battles are deeply ingrained in our collective memory: Bull Run (first and second), Antietam, Shiloh, Vicksburg, and others. Many Americans recognize that these places are connected with the Civil War, but they frequently have forgotten the details or even the outcomes of these battles. The exception in most people's minds would be the battle of Gettysburg, one of the most significant events in our history and the most decisive battle of the Civil War.

The Civil War was in many respects the first modern war because of the improvement in weapons. Unfortunately, the leaders of both sides had been trained in classical warfare techniques that involved precision maneuvers, bayonet charges, and encounters in the open. In earlier conflicts, infantry used muskets, which were accurate only for short distances. The improvements of arms by 1860 allowed the infantry to hit targets 500 yards away and fire three shots a minute. This "improvement" shifted the emphasis of the war. The open warfare tactics of the past combined with improved weaponry had a disastrous impact, causing significant casualties.

In this chapter we examine books that reflect many aspects of the war experience—the battlefields, the camps, and the soldiers. The photographs of the warriors and their letters reveal that this was a national tragedy that affected every region, every state, and virtually every community, North and South. The tragedy pitted West Point classmates against each other on the battlefield; it lured boys too young to fight to seek glory as drummer boys; it encouraged blacks to fight for the Union with the promise that their freedom would mean equality when the war ended; and it divided families and communities as individuals stood up for their beliefs. Young and old, white and black, North and South, it was a war that reflected who we were and who we would become.

Prior to Reading: Think About . . .

Young people need to do some preliminary thinking and talking to prepare them to understand what they read or what is read to them about the Civil War. They need opportunities to ask questions and to raise issues and concerns. The following questions and activities can be used to prompt this discussion:

- What do you already know about the major battles of the Civil War? Have you ever visited a Civil War battlefield or seen a monument to the soldiers of the Civil War?

- There are many books written about the Civil War. Why do you think these war experiences still command so much attention and interest?

- What do you already know about the role of blacks as soldiers during the Civil War? What else would you like to learn?

- What do you already know about the role young boys and teenage boys played in the Civil War? What else would you like to learn?

- What do you already know about the health and medical conditions of soldiers during the Civil War? What else would you like to learn?

- What do you already know about what the ordinary soldier's life was like during the Civil War? What else would you like to learn?

- What are the differences between an informational book and an historical novel written about the Civil War? Which would you rather read? Why?

Focus Books

Beatty, Patricia. *Charley Skedaddle.* Troll Company, 1987. 186 pages.

Now the truth flooded Charley's consciousness. Gone were thoughts of heroism and revenge. He had shot a man! He was only twelve years old, and he'd shot and killed a human being. What should he do now? He didn't know. He cried out wordlessly, threw down Jem's musket, and with the useless drum banging at his hip, sprinted for the wooded clearing to the left. Musket balls speeding toward him hummed beelike and tore away fragments of cloth from his sleeve and trousers. (pp. 79–80)

At a Glance ▪ Beatty presents the conflict between courage and cowardice in this story of a young boy who seeks the glory of war only to find its horrors instead. This novel raises many issues that will help junior high/middle school students and able upper elementary school students to examine war and its consequences.

Summary ▪ Twelve-year-old Charley Quinn is a member of the Bowery Boys, the roughest of New York City's street gangs, so fighting for the Union Army seems like just what he should do. After Johnny, his older brother, is killed at Gettysburg, Charley wants to fight even more to avenge the death. He runs away, hoping to join the 140th New York, Johnny's old company, but he is too young. He enlists as a drummer boy, and spends months learning to play the drum and doing drills and practice. Charley, however, always dreams of being in battle, where he could avenge Johnny's death. His chance comes in his first battle, in The Wilderness.

Caught in an ambush, the Union troops are pinned down. After a bullet punctures Charley's drum, he watches the battle, waiting for a chance to fight. When his friend is shot, Charley grabs his rifle and shoots a Confederate soldier. Suddenly, the reality of the war hits him, and he knows that it is more than he can deal with. Charley runs; he "skedaddles." He runs from the Confederates, but he also runs from his comrades. He keeps running until he is taken in by an odd old mountain woman who gives him a home. While in the mountains, Charley learns to come to terms with running away and to decide whether or not he is a coward.

Teaching Considerations ▪ Patricia Beatty has written a number of novels about the Civil War era that are appropriate for use with upper elementary or middle school students. Each of her books concludes with a commentary that provides an historical context for the book. In these commentaries, she identifies fact and fiction for the reader. *Charley Skedaddle* won the Scott O'Dell Award for Historical Fiction.

After Reading: Suggested Student Activities

1. After reading this book, read *The Boy's War* by Jim Murphy. Discuss whether or not boys have an appropriate place in war. Be prepared to support your position.

2. Write a position paper addressing whether or not you believe Charley is a coward. (Teacher's Note: This activity also could be used with a whole class by implementing it as a discussion continuum. See the guidelines in chapter 1 for this strategy.)

3. Discuss whether or not war is an appropriate measure of one's courage.

4. In small groups, trace the changes that Charley goes through in the book. Do the literature involvement strategy, character portraits. Are these changes believable? Why or why not? (Teacher's Note: See the guidelines in chapter 1 for this strategy.)

Beatty, Patricia. *Jayhawker.*
William Morrow, Beech Tree, 1995. 214 pages.

For the rest of his life, Lije Tulley would remember that September day at Wilson's Creek, Missouri, remember it as he would remember John Brown's blessing and his pa's death. He could not recall any details, but memories of the brutal heat and swarms of flies, his thirst, the shouts of men and screams of wounded horses, and his wordless terror would haunt him always. (p. 137)

At a Glance ▪ This novel presents the western frontier and the conflict between free and slave states joining the Union. Students will need a sense of historical context to understand the events and the people of this story. This book is appropriate for junior high/middle school students as well as able upper elementary school students. The lively adventure and Elijah's courage will make this an appealing book for male readers.

Summary ▪ In the days prior to the beginning of the Civil War, the Kansas Territory was a center of abolitionist activity. The Tully family admires and follows the activities of abolitionist John Brown. Elijah's father belongs to a group of guerilla fighters called "Jayhawkers," who raid Missouri slaveholders. Elijah is excited when he is finally big enough to accompany his father and his partner on these raids. On his second mission, the slave owners are waiting, and they shoot both Elijah's father and his partner. After his father's death, Elijah Tully continues his activity as a Jayhawker. While he is away on a raid, the Tully family farm is burned. The family then moves to Lawrence, Kansas. As the Civil War begins, Elijah continues his abolitionist activities by accepting a challenging and dangerous mission behind enemy lines, going underground as a spy in Missouri to gather information. He joins the followers of the Confederate raider, Quantrill, to collect information about the activities of the raiders. As a member of the Quantrill gang, Elijah sees action at the battle of Wilson's Creek and then is recruited for a raid on Lawrence.

Teaching Considerations ▪ Frequently, the western involvement of Kansas and Missouri in the Civil War is not discussed. Providing students with an historical context for the events of the book will help them get more from it.

After Reading: Suggested Student Activities

1. Identify the historical perspectives that are presented in the novel. Compare and contrast the positions of the people from Kansas and those from Missouri. (Teacher's Note: See the guidelines in chapter 1 for this strategy.)

2. There are a number of well-known figures mentioned in this book, including John Brown, Charley Quantrill, Frank and Jesse James, and James "Wild Bill" Hickok. Select one for further research and prepare a report for the class about one of these people.

3. What was the impact that spies had during the Civil War? What made Elijah an effective spy?

4. Identify a core value that is inherent in this book and create an Ideals/Values map. (Teacher's Note: See the guidelines in chapter 1 for this strategy.)

5. In war many actions are taken against civilians because the soldiers feel that they have aided the enemy. Using a discussion continuum, decide where your position is relative to the following statements:

Soldiers have the right to punish civilians they think are assisting their enemies.	Civilians should not be punished by military authorities.

(Teacher's Note: See chapter 1 for additional information about using the discussion continuum.)

Bolotin, Norman, and Angela Herb. *For Home and Country: A Civil War Scrapbook.* Lodestar Books, 1995. 98 pages.

Almost every camp, Confederate or Union, had an informal "homemade" band composed of every size and shape of instrument the men could manage to carry from home. Large camps assembled formal music and theatrical groups that performed for the general public as well as for military audiences. In a letter to his fiancee in Illinois, one Union soldier described such an event: "There is to be a large ball . . . on the evening of the 16th. I think some of attending. I have no doubt but that it will be a very elegant affair. Oh, how I wish you were here to go with me! . . . A great many ladies from Washington, Philadelphia, and Baltimore are expected to be there . . . Still my thoughts would wander to the dear girl . . . on whom my affections are already placed." (pp. 80–81)

At a Glance ▪ This fascinating book provides a vivid overview of the lives of the soldiers in both the Union and Confederacy during the Civil War, accompanied by a multitude of illustrations, including photographs and newspaper clippings of the times and excerpts from diaries and letters of soldiers and their loved ones at home. Appropriate to use at all levels, this valuable resource would also appeal to a wide range of ages.

Summary ▪ Part of the Young Readers' History of the Civil War series, this book begins with an annotated timeline for the years 1860 and 1865. It provides an excellent visual and verbal overview of numerous topics related to soldiering. Some of these topics— such as the soldiers' clothing, food, and entertainment—include little-known information and help to develop an overall perspective of this time.

Teaching Considerations ▪ A real strength of this book is its wealth of visual information. With its sparse but captivating text, it is a commendable scrapbook that could be used effectively to provoke curiosity and interest in learning about the Civil War. It could also be used as an accompaniment to a more substantial text.

After Reading: Suggested Student Activities

1. Develop an idea map that presents in a succinct manner the important points about the life of a soldier during the Civil War. (Teacher's Note: See the guidelines in chapter 1 for this strategy.)

2. Often when reading a book like this, we find new and unusual information and then say to someone else, "Did you know . . . ?" Find five to seven new or unusual pieces of information from this book that you would like to share with other members of your class. Then prepare a visual or creative means of presenting that information. (Teacher's Note: See the guidelines in chapter 1 for this strategy.)

3. Compare and contrast this book with another book that you have read about soldiers during the Civil War that uses fewer illustrations. Evaluate the strengths and weaknesses of each book in helping you learn about this aspect of Civil War life.

4. Choose one topic from this book that you would like to know more about and then find other books about it.

Bunting, Eve. Illustrated by Ned Bittinger. *The Blue and the Gray*. Scholastic Press, 1996. 28 pages, unnumbered.

In 1862 this was a battleground,
and here two armies fought
and soaked the grass with blood.
I guess the flowers were red instead of white that night. (p. 6)

My father knows the history of this place,
and he tells us that we must
remember and revere.
I don't understand the word
but he explained.
It means that we must honor all that happened here. (p. 8)

At a Glance ▪ Award-winning author Eve Bunting and illustrator Ned Bittinger have created a hauntingly beautiful picture book set in contemporary times that tells the experiences of two young boys, one white and one black, as they explore a former Civil War battlefield, now the building site of their new houses. Deceptively simple, this picture book could be experienced on many levels and is appropriate for all ages.

Summary ▪ A young boy, his friend J.J., and his dad explore the fields and meadows around where their new homes are being built.

The father explains that this beautiful, calm pastoral scene wasn't always the case. In 1862, this ground was the scene of a battle between the North and the South. Their discussion of the Civil War, specifically, and war, in general, is intermingled with the sights and sounds they encounter during their walk. At first, the boys think it isn't fair that there is no marker commemorating the battleground, but then they decide their lives and friendship can be a monument of sorts. Throughout the picture book, illustrations of the area as it appeared during the battle are alternated effectively with scenes from the present.

Teaching Considerations ▪ This book can be enjoyed by younger readers as an engaging story connecting Civil War times with present times. Older students can be helped to appreciate both the story and the literary and artistic techniques that convey a more sophisticated message.

After Reading: Suggested Student Activities

1. Discuss what it means when the father says, "*We'll* be a monument of sorts."

2. Do you agree or disagree with the boy's decision not to keep the bullet as a souvenir? Why? What would you have done?

3. Discuss why you think it is important to "remember and revere" what happened during the Civil War.

4. Describe how the author and illustrator have used words and images to create a mood and express a message. Provide specific examples.

Cox, Clinton. *Undying Glory.* Scholastic, 1991. 167 pages.

"Without the military help of black freed men," President Lincoln declared, "the war against the South could not have been won." (p. 150)

At a Glance ▪ This account of the role of the 54th Massachusetts Regiment is a stirring depiction of bravery and valor under extremely difficult conditions. It is appropriate for secondary school and able junior high/middle school students.

Summary ▪ While the North had abolished slavery, it was not able to eliminate racial bigotry and prejudice against the blacks. This attitude became obvious when freed blacks sought to enlist in the army to fight the Confederacy and were refused. There were Northerners who were appalled by the prejudice and thought that black soldiers should be allowed to serve in the Union Army. One of the most articulate supporters of blacks was the governor of Massachusetts, John Andrews, who had long been seeking an end to slavery. He seized the opportunity to act when Abraham Lincoln issued the Emancipation Proclamation. He petitioned and was granted the authority to raise companies of "colored" soldiers. He asked Captain Robert Gould Shaw of the 2nd Massachusetts Infantry Regiment to become the commander of this unit. With the help of Frederick Douglass and others, black recruits from throughout the North were brought together, and in thirteen weeks ten companies of the regiment were filled. Recruitment and service did not automatically improve the lot of the blacks. They did not receive the same pay as white soldiers, and their families suffered real hardships at home because the men were not there to help support them. Regardless of the conditions, the men of the 54th and other regiments of black soldiers fought valiantly for the remainder of the war.

Teaching Considerations ▪ This is a fascinating, readable account of the significant role that African Americans played in the Union victory over the Confederacy. It presents a realistic perspective of the trials as well as the triumphs for this group of military pioneers.

After Reading: Suggested Student Activities

1. What were the short-term and long-term consequences of blacks serving in the Union Army? What were the consequences for African Americans, for Southerners, and for Northerners?

2. In a graph, present the comparative data about the number of African American soldiers, the number of disabilities, and the

number of deaths, with the same figures for white Union soldiers and Confederate soldiers.

3. Develop a "Did You Know . . . ?" chart as you read this book, recording new information from this book. (Teacher's Note: See the guidelines in chapter 1 for this strategy.)

Crane, Stephen. Historically annotated edition by Charles LaRocca. *The Red Badge of Courage*. Purple Mt. Press, 1995. 212 pages.

He was being looked at by a dead man who was seated with his back against a columnlike tree. The corpse was dressed in a uniform that once had been blue, but was now faded to a melancholy shade of green. The eyes, staring at the youth, had changed to the dull hue to be seen on the side of a dead fish. The mouth was open. Its red had changed to an appalling yellow. Over the gray skin of the face ran little ants. One was trundling some sort of a bundle along the upper lip.

The youth gave a shriek as he confronted the thing. (p. 57)

At a Glance ▪ This classic war novel is the story of young Henry Fleming, who enlisted in the Union Army. The young private has long dreamt of the glories of battle, but he is soon confronted with the reality of war. This book is frequently used as required reading for secondary students.

Summary ▪ Probably most soldiers wonder how they will acquit themselves when they are under fire for the first time, and so it was for young Henry Fleming as he anticipated the long-awaited battle. Among the most difficult periods for soldiers are the long times between battles when they sit idly waiting. As his company waits to go into battle, Henry hears stories and images of war that collide with his childhood dreams of the glory of war. Henry starts second guessing himself, and he is tested. In the heat of combat, as other Union soldiers flee, Henry assumes that the battle is lost, and he flees, too. The battle is a rout for the Union, and Henry is filled with guilt. From this point, Henry must make decisions about honor and courage.

Teaching Considerations ▪ This classic novel is often taught in high school American Literature survey courses. Nevertheless, the introspective intensity that Henry experiences makes this book difficult for all but the most-sophisticated high school readers. There are also language issues that teachers should be aware of. First, the text includes slang and dialect that again may be difficult for all but the most able readers. Also, there are some mild profanities that some parents might find objectionable.

After Reading: Suggested Student Activities

1. Discuss why Henry is always referred to as "the youth."

2. Write a paper discussing how the theme of illusion versus reality is developed in this novel. (Teacher's Note: This activity also could be used with a whole class by implementing it as a discussion continuum. See the guidelines in chapter 1 for this strategy.)

3. Discuss whether or not you believe that Henry is a coward when he flees during his first battle.

4. Do a values map, identifying a value or ideal of American society that is presented in this book. Cite supporting incidents for the presence of this value from the text of the book. (Teacher's Note: See chapter 1 for guidelines for this strategy.)

5. Examine and discuss the development of Henry's character in the novel.

Fleischman, Paul. *Bull Run*. Scholastic, 1993. 102 pages.

I'm a Boston man myself, and I snatched up a martyr's gun, hot for revenge. The company was ordered to fire on the mob. I joined them. There were screams, and further shots. We quick-stepped through a hailstorm of stones, finally reached the Camden Street station, then had to wait for a locomotive. Three valiant volunteers were dead. Many others were injured. I burned to put upon paper the faces of the taunting traitors and the fallen heroes, took up a pencil, tried to draw—but couldn't. My hands were shaking, with fury. (p. 12)

At a Glance ▪ Using sixteen different characters, all speaking for themselves, Fleischman provides a readable accounting of the Battle of Bull Run. While upper elementary and junior high/middle school students will be able to read the book with ease, they may need help understanding the context of the times.

Summary ▪ This historical novel has the unusual structure of presenting the story of the first major battle of the Civil War through the perspective of sixteen characters. Representing a microcosm of society at the time—both black and white, Northern and Southern, male and female—each reveals feelings and thoughts about Bull Run.

Teaching Considerations ▪ The sixteen different voices, while a strength of this book, may be confusing for younger readers. It might be best used as a culminating experience after students are more knowledgeable about the war and its circumstances. It would serve as an excellent vehicle for Readers Theater; Fleischman includes a note on page 103, listing characters and the pages on which they appear.

After Reading: Suggested Student Activities

1. Select one of the characters, and write a character sketch of him or her.

2. Bull Run was the first battle of the war. Select one character from the book and imagine what his or her life is like at the end of the war.

3. Practice and prepare to do an oral reading of the selections of one character.

4. With your learning partner, select two of the characters and write a dialogue between them in which they try to share their perspectives about the war with each other.

5. Analyze how the use of multiple perspectives adds to your understanding of both the issues and the feelings about the war.

Kent, Zachary. *The Story of the Battle of Bull Run.* Children's Press, 1986. 32 pages.

———. *The Story of the Battle of Shiloh.* Children's Press, 1991. 32 pages.

———. *The Story of the Battle of Chancellorsville.* Children's Press 1994. 32 pages.

———. *The Story of Sherman's March to the Sea.* Children's Press, 1987. 32 pages.

———. *The Story of the Surrender at Appomattox Court House.* Children's Press, 1987. 32 pages.

General Sherman made no apology to Southerners for his ruthlessness. "If the people raise a howl against my barbarity and cruelty," he stated, "I will answer that war is war, and not popularity-seeking." To an officer he later grimly added, "The more awful you can make war, the sooner it will be over . . . war is hell, at the best." (*The Story of Sherman's March to the Sea*, p. 30)

At a Glance ▪ These books are all part of the Cornerstones of Freedom series. Each of these books provides young readers with information about specific events, from the first major battle of the war to its final chapter at Appomattox. Each book has a single focus and is designed for elementary school aged students.

Summary ▪ In each of these books, Kent seeks to put a human face on the major events that shaped the war. He accomplishes this by using a number of quotations from both leaders and everyday soldiers and citizens. Also each of the books has a number of illustrations, photographs, drawings, and maps.

Teaching Considerations ▪ Inherent in any account written for young readers, is the problem of how to simplify detailed and complex issues. In this type of simplification, it is easy to have generalizations that may not present the whole picture. Teachers should be prepared to provide students with a broader context than these books provide. Sections of each of these books might be appropriate for teacher read-alouds.

After Reading: Suggested Student Activities

1. Prepare a timeline of major events in the Civil War.

2. Select an event from one of the books and illustrate it.

3. Using one of these books as a springboard, do further research on an event described in it. Then write an entry for a class book on the times.

Mettger, Zak. *Till Victory Is Won: Black Soldiers in the Civil War.* Lodestar Books, 1994. 118 pages.

By the time the Union won the Civil War in April 1865, black soldiers had fought on 449 different battlefields and had played an important role in 39 major engagements, including the Union's final assaults on the Confederacy. In several battles, their contributions made the difference between Union victory and loss. (p. 75)

At a Glance ▪ Illustrated with vintage photographs and drawings and enlivened with first-person accounts, Mettger tells the story of how blacks gained the right to fight in the Civil War and describes their contributions during and immediately after that terrible struggle. *Till Victory Is Won* is part of the Young Readers' History of the Civil War series and is appropriate for junior high/middle school students and able elementary students. Excerpts could also be used effectively as teacher read-alouds.

Summary ▪ *Till Victory Is Won* is a highly readable account of black soldiers during and immediately after the Civil War. It begins with accounts of the attempts of African American men in the

North to enlist in the army or form their own regiments at the onset of the war and the rebuffs and discrimination they faced. Mettger tells little-known stories of units that did succeed in forming in the Sea Islands of South Carolina, in Louisiana near New Orleans, and in Kansas, even before official approval was granted for the recruitment of African American men. When Lincoln became convinced that the only way to win the war was to take away the South's source of labor by liberating the slaves, approval was granted for recruitment of blacks in both the North and South. Again Mettger tells little-known stories of the experiences of black soldiers that demonstrate both the benefits and the abuses of recruitment and life in the army. Other accounts in the book describe the courageous battlefield deeds of African Americans, including the 54th Massachusetts Regiment at Fort Wagner and the Louisiana Native Guards at Port Hudson. The concluding portion of the book describes how serving in the army transformed the lives of African American men, and how it continued to affect them after the war.

Teaching Considerations ▪ Mettger uses the word "nigger" in several instances throughout the book when quoting speakers from the era. Generally the term is used in a derogatory manner; i.e., "We want you d———d niggers to keep out of this," officials told a group of black citizens trying to organize a military company in Cincinnati, Ohio (p. viii). While this terminology should not act as a deterrent to using this fine book, care must be taken to help students understand the times and context in which the word was spoken.

After Reading: Suggested Student Activities

1. Identify the multiple perspectives of the significance of the assault on Fort Wagner in July 1863 and the Fort Pillow Massacre in April 1864 for both whites and blacks.

2. This book describes the many ways in which African Americans demonstrated their courage both on and off the battlefield during and immediately after the Civil War. Select two examples to describe to your classmates. Compare and contrast these examples using a Venn diagram. Also evaluate why you selected these

particular events. (Teacher's Note: See chapter 1 for guidelines for this strategy.)

3. Select an incident from this book to interpret and dramatize. Create a script with some of your classmates to perform for other students.

Murphy, Jim. *The Boy's War: Confederate and Union Soldiers Talk About the Civil War.* Clarion, 1990. 110 pages.

> T.G. Barker, then thirteen, was attending a small private school in South Carolina. "We were in class," Barker remembered, "all bent over our books, when Headmaster Hammond entered. He did not knock to announce himself, which was unusual, and he not speak to our teacher either. This was also unusual. He went instead to the middle of the room and said in a serious voice: 'We have had word this morning. Fort Sumter has surrendered and is now a part of the Confederate States of America.' Then he smiled. A second passed and not a sound. Then, as if shot from a cannon, the class stood as one and cheered Hooray! Hooray!" (p. 6)

At a Glance ▪ This award-winning book has over fifty vintage photographs from the Civil War. Murphy presents the stories of scores of young boys who enlisted on both sides of the war. Students in junior high/middle school and upper elementary school could certainly read and enjoy this book; however, the stories are so effectively told that even older students would enjoy it.

Summary ▪ Jim Murphy tells the stories of a number of Union and Confederate soldiers aged sixteen and under who enlisted to serve in the Civil War. This book is replete with photographs and with the actual words of these youthful soldiers from their letters, journals, diaries, company records, and newspaper accounts. While the image of war was appealing, its reality was painful; many of the boys are shocked by the reality. The words of these young boys, relating their experiences, gives the book a special vitality.

Teaching Considerations ▪ This book is excellent. Among the awards it has received are the ALA Best Book for Young Adults and the Golden Kite Award Book for Nonfiction. It could be used effectively with historical fiction based on the lives of boys who served in the Civil War. Among the other recommended books with entries in this chapter are:

Beatty, Patricia. *Charley Skedaddle*. Troll Company, 1987.

Nixon, Joan Lowry. *A Dangerous Promise*. Bantam Doubleday Dell, 1994.

Polacco, Patricia. *Pink and Say*. Scholastic, 1994.

Weinberg, Larry. *The Drummer Boy*. Avon Books, 1996.

Wisler, G. Clifton. *The Drummer Boy of Vicksburg*. Lodestar Books, 1997.

———. *Mr. Lincoln's Drummer*. Lodestar Books, 1995.

———. *Red Cap*. Lodestar Books, 1991.

———. *Thunder on the Tennessee*. Scholastic, 1983.

After Reading: Suggested Student Activities

1. Select one of the photographs from the book that made an impression on you and analyze its impact.

2. Imagine that you are a fifteen-year-old in the war. Describe what you imagine your experiences would be like. Make sure that your response reflects historical accuracy.

3. Do research on an event, battle, or leader mentioned in the book. Share your findings with the class.

4. Select an image of two young soldiers, one from the Union Army and the other from the Confederate. Imagine that they meet *prior* to the war and create a dialogue between them. Then imagine that they meet again *during* the war. Write a second dialogue between the two.

Murphy, Jim. *The Long Road to Gettysburg.* Scholastic, 1995. 116 pages.

> Everything became terrifically quiet. For the quiet that precedes a great battle has something of the terrible in it. Everyone knows that there must be fought a bloody battle and all are therefore anxious to save our strength for the contest. Hence the extraordinary quiet. (p. 37)

At a Glance ▪ Murphy provides a highly readable account of the Battle of Gettysburg, complete with firsthand accounts, photographs, maps, and other illustrations. Appropriate for upper elementary and junior high/middle school students, *The Long Road to Gettysburg* engages readers of all ages.

Summary ▪ Murphy begins and concludes this book by describing the dedication of the National Soldiers Cemetery in Gettysburg, using it to establish a framework for understanding the significance of the Battle of Gettysburg. Throughout the book he uses firsthand accounts from the diaries of eighteen-year-old John Dooley, a Confederate lieutenant, and fifteen-year-old Thomas Galway, a Union corporal, to bring a personal dimension to this historic event. Dooley and Galway contend with heat, dust, and fatigue as they march toward Gettysburg with their units. They each experience the fury and destruction of the three-day battle, writing about it at brief intervals. Dooley is seriously injured and lies unattended on the battlefield for two nights and a day. When the Confederate Army retreats, Dooley is left behind and becomes a prisoner of war. Injured when the fighting ends, Galway serves on burial detail before his company is ordered to pursue Lee's retreating army. *The Long Road to Gettysburg* provides an overview of the major events of the three-day battle without becoming bogged down in too many details. The major Union and Confederate army officers, their roles in the battle, and the decisions they made come alive through Murphy's skillful descriptions.

Teaching Considerations ▪ The Battle of Gettysburg resulted in the loss of approximately 50,000 men in one of the deadliest battles of the Civil War. Some of the photographs and battle descriptions reflect this carnage. While the historical figures and military action are intriguing to history buffs, the significance of Gettysburg lies both in its role as a turning point in the war and as a defining event in our nation's history.

After Reading: Suggested Student Activities

1. Analyze the significance of the Battle of Gettysburg for both the Union and the Confederacy. Construct a visual representation that illustrates its importance.

2. Develop a Venn diagram to demonstrate the similarities and differences between Confederate soldier, John Dooley, and Union soldier, Thomas Galway. Use the Venn diagram as the springboard for a brief comparison/contrast paper. (Teacher's Note: See guidelines in chapter 1 for this strategy.)

3. Write a poem that expresses your feelings about Gettysburg.

4. Since Gettysburg was one of the most significant battles of the Civil War, imagine that you are a civilian living in the area in July, 1863. Develop a master list of pertinent information using the strategy, "What Would It Have Been Like to Live in _____?" (Teacher's Note: See guidelines in chapter 1 for this strategy.)

Nixon, Joan Lowry. *A Dangerous Promise*. Bantam Doubleday Dell, 1994. 148 pages.

Funny, Mike thought as Corey left. He had just wished good luck to a Confederate soldier who'd soon be in combat against Mike's own army. Well, it was no crazier than Federal sympathizers owning slaves, or generals countermanding each other's orders, or fathers and sons on opposite sides. Mike shut his eyes, recalling the two men, young and old, who lay dead in each other's arms, father in blue and son in gray. (p. 83)

At a Glance ▪ Mike Kelly and his best friend, Todd, are caught up in the excitement and patriotic fever sweeping the country after the surrender of Fort Sumter. They run away from home, and lying about their ages, enlist in the 2nd Kansas Infantry, only to discover that war is not the glorious adventure they had imagined. *A Dangerous Promise* is part of the Orphan Train Adventures series and is appropriate for junior high/middle school and upper elementary school students.

Summary ▪ Mike Kelly, not quite thirteen, lives in Kansas with his foster parents, Captain and Mrs. Taylor. When Captain Taylor and the father of his best friend, Todd, are sent to Virginia to fight, Mike and Todd decide to run away from home and enlist in the Union Army. Too young to be soldiers, they lie about their ages and become part of the drum and bugle corps. They soon learn that army life is not the great adventure they had imagined, but instead is filled with boredom and drudgery, hunger and hardships, homesickness, and the unimaginable horrors of battle. Todd makes Mike promise that if he dies, Mike will take his watch and return it to his sister. Todd is killed during a fierce battle; and Mike, wounded in the leg and left behind Rebel lines when the army retreats, sees a Rebel soldier steal Todd's watch. Another Rebel soldier, Corey, recognizes Mike and secretly carries him to a safe house where he can hide until his wounds heal. Mike's determination to fulfill his promise to Todd leads him into many risky and dangerous experiences during which he learns some important lessons about himself and about the confusing complexities of the issues and feelings surrounding the Civil War.

Teaching Considerations ▪ Prior to reading this book or in conjunction with it, provide students with background information about the Missouri-Kansas conflict within the larger context of the Civil War. Also, it may be helpful for students to understand the importance of the drum and bugle corps in relaying information to soldiers in an age when current methods of communication did not exist. Joan Lowry Nixon, author of this book, is also author of the Orphan Train Adventures series, which is based on true stories of children from the slums of New York City who were sent by train to find new homes in the Midwest and West between 1854 and 1929. Other titles in this series reflect the times immediately before and after the Civil War.

After Reading: Suggested Student Activities

1. Mike makes tough choices throughout this book that frequently lead him into danger. Select two examples and analyze what other alternatives he might have used. The alternatives must be realistic and in accordance with the times. Discuss these examples and your rationale for them in a small group or class discussion.

2. Imagine that you are Mike and are keeping a journal of your experiences. Write in your journal for a five-day period of time. Make certain that your entries are historically accurate and contain historical facts about the Civil War.

3. Develop character sketches of both Mike Kelly and Jiri Logan that compare and contrast the two people.

4. Mike joins the army with high expectations about the glory of war. With your learning partner, discuss and document the changes that he undergoes as he faces the realities of war.

5. Create a visual that depicts the meaning of the book's title. Write an accompanying explanation of your artwork.

Phillips, Charles, and Alan Axelrod. *My Brother's Face: Portraits of the Civil War in Photographs, Diaries, and Letters.* Foreword by Brian C. Pohanka. Chronicle Books, 1993. 153 pages.

America's Civil War was the first conflict in which photographers consciously sought to capture war in all its horrors. (p. 3)

At a Glance ▪ *My Brother's Face* is an extraordinary collection of eighty photographs from the Civil War accompanied by historical commentaries and passages from letters, diaries, and firsthand accounts. This book is a valuable resource and appropriate for all ages, although older students may benefit more from the written text than younger ones.

Summary ▪ The earliest permanent photographic images were recorded in the 1820s, and although other conflicts had been photographed, the Civil War was the first one to be documented extensively with a pictorial record. Ordinary soldiers as well as famous generals posed for their photographs. Advances in the photographic process allowed photographers to travel to the battlefields and hospitals and record their horrors. The prevailing romantic view of war was dispelled when these photographs were displayed in galleries for the public to view. *My Brother's Face* begins with an introductory chapter that provides a lucid and fascinating overview of the Civil War. The remainder of the book chronicles the Civil War from the fall of Fort Sumter to the surrender at Appomattox. Photographs of the well known, such as Clara Barton, Grant, and Lee, are interspersed with those of the little known, farmers turned soldiers, young boys turned "powder monkeys." Each photograph is enhanced with text that places it within an historical context and explains its personal significance.

Teaching Considerations ▪ The photographs selected for this book put a human face on the Civil War; however, the number of photographs of African Americans is limited. The accompanying text helps to portray the spirit of the times and personalizes the tragic nature of the war. The photographs shown in *My Brother's Face* are not graphic or offensive in nature.

After Reading: Suggested Student Activities

1. Select five photographs that had a special impact on you. Analyze their significance and explain what they mean to you in a class discussion.

2. Do more research about photography and specific photographers, such as Mathew Brady, during the Civil War. Prepare your findings to share with your classmates.

3. Select one of the photographs and write a description of what you think the individual's life was like before and after the photograph was taken. Base your description upon available historical data about life during the Civil War.

Polacco, Patricia. *Pink and Say.*
Scholastic, 1994. 52 pages, unnumbered.

That night I couldn't sleep.

"What's wrong, child?" Moe Moe Bay said from her chair.

"I don't want to go back," I blurted out.

"I know, child," she said. "Of course you don't."

"You don't understand. I took up and run away from my unit. I was hit when I was runnin'." I sobbed so hard my ribs hurt. "I'm a coward and a deserter." (p. 27, unnumbered)

At a Glance ▪ Appropriate for all ages, *Pink and Say* is a beautifully illustrated picture book with strong emotional appeal. Two boys with the Union Army, one black and the other white, are wounded and left behind the lines in Georgia. They form a deep bond of friendship as they seek refuge. *Pink and Say* lends itself well to a teacher read-aloud.

Summary ▪ Using an oft-retold incident from her own family history, Polacco tells the story of Pinkus Aylee (Pink) and Sheldon Curtis (Say), two boys caught up in the Civil War. Say is wounded during a battle in Georgia and left for dead when Pink, also injured, discovers him and carries him to the safety of his mother's cabin. Pink's mother, Moe Moe Bay, cares for the boys, who share their experiences in the Union Army. Say carried the staff for the Ohio 24th, but after so many men were killed, even the boys were given guns. Pink served with the Forty-eighth Colored and tells about having to fight, first with sticks and hammers and sledges because the black soldiers weren't trusted with guns, and then with old muskets that frequently failed to fire properly. Sharing other important experiences and secrets, Pink and Say become close friends. When marauders come to the cabin, Moe Moe Bay hides the boys, but she is shot and killed. The boys leave to try to rejoin their units, but are captured and sent to the notorious Confederate prisoner-of-war camp at Andersonville. They are separated and Say survives, but Pink is hanged. Say returns home after the war and lives to be old man who keeps the memory of Pink alive.

Teaching Considerations ▪ *Pink and Say* is a powerful picture book that touches the reader deeply while telling an interesting story with an important message.

After Reading: Suggested Student Activities

1. Compare and contrast the two boys, Pink and Say. Create a Venn diagram of their similarities and differences. (Teacher's Note: See guidelines in chapter 1 for this strategy.)

2. Dramatize *Pink and Say* with a small group of classmates or prepare a scene from it for use as Readers Theatre.

3. Select a topic from this picture book for further research, such as boys in the Civil War, black soldiers, marauders, or Andersonville.

Ray, Delia. *Behind the Blue and Gray: The Soldier's Life in the Civil War.* Scholastic, 1991. 101 pages.

Whenever soldiers from the North and South did manage to hold serious conversations, they were strangely moved by how much they had in common. They often shared the same backgrounds, the same likes and dislikes, the same fear. Their respect for one another often outweighed their resentments. One Confederate soldier, after a long talk with a Union man, wrote home sadly, "We could have settled the war in 30 minutes had it been left to us." (pp. 29–30)

At a Glance ▪ This informational book, replete with vintage photographs, gives readers an opportunity to look at the Civil War from the perspective of the daily lives of soldiers from both sides. It has numerous quotes from diaries and the correspondence of soldiers. Appropriate for upper elementary, junior high/ middle school students, it could also be used with some secondary school students.

Summary ▪ There is a tendency to attempt to glorify war, but there is nothing glorious about it. In this nonfiction account, the realities of day-by-day existence are presented. In a primarily chronological approach, the Civil War unfolds from its early days, when recruits entered with enthusiasm and high expectations, to the aftermath as the war ends. Particularly effective are two chapters, one examining life in the camps and the other dealing with hospitals and prisons.

Teaching Considerations ▪ Ray's fine book can be used to help history come alive for students and to put a human face on the overwhelming facts and figures associated with the battles and losses in the Civil War.

After Reading: Suggested Student Activities

1. Select one aspect of a soldier's life and do further research about it, making sure that your report reflects history accurately.

2. Select one of the photographs from the book. Imagine that you are there. Describe what the experience is like in a journal entry.

3. Identify five issues, concepts, or ideas that you learned from this book. Discuss in class how they help you to understand the Civil War better.

4. Create a dialogue with your learning partner in which you imagine life in both the Union and Confederate camps. Convey what is it like waiting, drilling, marching, and not knowing where and when the next battle will be.

Shaara, Michael. *The Killer Angels*. Ballantine Books, 1974. 355 pages.

Lee knelt and began to pray. His engineer's mind went on thinking while he prayed. He could find no flaw: we will go up the center and split them in two, on the defense no longer, attacking at last, Pickett and Hood and McLaws. By the end of the prayer he was certain: he felt a releasing thrill. This was the way, as God would have it. Face to face with the enemy, on grounds of his own choosing. End with honor. (pp. 269–70)

At a Glance ▪ *The Killer Angels* is a popular and widely read historical novel of the Civil War. Appropriate for secondary school students, it tells the compelling story of the Battle of Gettysburg through the perspective of the major Union and Confederate military figures.

Summary ▪ Shaara's sweeping novel of the Battle of Gettysburg covers four days as experienced by the major players on both sides. It begins with a foreword that introduces the men and concludes with an afterword that summarizes what happened to those who survived the battle. Shaara dramatically recreates the bloody action with its incredible bravery and horrible mistakes. Major figures, like Lee and Longstreet of the Confederacy and Chamberlain and Buford of the Union, become real people with all their human frailties. *The Killer Angels* makes history come alive and provides intriguing insights into the most significant battle of the Civil War, if not of our country's entire history.

Teaching Considerations ▪ Students will need to be reminded that while *The Killer Angels* is based on primary source documents, it *is* fiction; the author has written his own interpretation, thoughts, and words for the characters. Readers who have seen the film, *Gettysburg,* may also find that passages from this novel evoke scenes from the film.

After Reading: Suggested Student Activities

1. This novel gives you an excellent opportunity to consider a major event from multiple perspectives. Select one incident and show how the key figures' differing perspectives of the conditions affected the outcome.

2. Compare and contrast Shaara's portrayal of General Robert E. Lee with those in other books you have read about Lee.

3. Find five examples illustrating the difference between historical facts and historical interpretations.

4. Dramatize a scene from the book that you see as a turning point in the battle.

5. Write a dialogue between two Union soldiers looking over the battlefield at the conclusion of the battle. What do they see? How do they feel? Then write a second dialogue from the position of Confederate soldiers. What do they see? How do they feel?

Wisler, G. Clifton. *Red Cap*. Lodestar Books, 1991. 160 pages.

Our high hopes of good treatment at Andersonville faded into disappointment. Our clothes were mere rags, and there was scant hope of any replacement. . . . Rations continued to dwindle, and they'd be cut off entirely on the poorest excuse.

I was hungry. No, more than that. I was starving. My fist could plunge into my hollow belly and close to come out the other side. There never had been all that much of me, but what was left threatened to melt away. (p. 83)

At a Glance ▪ Based on the life of Ransom J. Powell, this historical novel tells the story of a thirteen-year-old boy who runs away from home to join the Union forces, becomes a drummer, and then is captured and sent to the infamous Confederate prison camp at Andersonville. This book will appeal to upper elementary and junior high/ middle school students, especially boys.

Summary ▪ When the Civil War is declared, its effects are immediately felt in Allegheny County in western Maryland where thirteen-year-old Ransom J. Powell and his family live. The community is divided in its loyalties, and some of R.J.'s friends and neighbors join the Confederates, while others join the Union. R.J.'s parents tell him he is too young to enlist, but he runs away and becomes a drummer with the Union forces. Small for his age, but feisty and determined, R.J. suffers hardships and the disillusionment of discovering what army life and battle are really like. He perseveres and even makes friends with some of the older men, but when his best friend Danny, another drummer, is killed in battle, he feels that things can't get much worse. Unfortunately, it is only the beginning of horrible suffering. Captured by Rebel forces, R.J. and a small group from his regiment are sent first to Libby Prison in Richmond and then to the infamous prison camp near Andersonville, Georgia. Nicknamed "Red Cap," R.J. remains loyal to his friends and to the Union even when given an opportunity to secure his own release. Red Cap suffers horribly, but survives through the friendship of a Confederate guard and his own wits. He helps his fellow soldiers as much as possible, but one by one, they die. Finally, barely alive, Red Cap gains his freedom through a prisoner exchange agreement.

Teaching Considerations ▪ While *Red Cap* captures the grim realities of being a prisoner of war, it also vividly portrays a feisty, courageous teenager who demonstrates admirable values and maintains his honor under the worse conditions. Although descriptions of the prisoners' conditions are difficult to read, this book presents an aspect of the Civil War experience that is not well known. The epilogue and author's note at the end of the book provide interesting information about what happened to Ransom Powell during the rest of his life, including a letter he wrote about his prison experience. It also gives more information about the prison camp at Andersonville. Among the awards *Red Cap* has received are ALA Best Book for Young Adults and Child Study Association Book of the Year.

Also recommended is Wisler's *Thunder on the Tennessee* (Scholastic, 1983) which received the Golden Spur Award. This book tells the story of fifteen-year-old Willie Delamer who joins the 2nd Texas Regiment with his father to fight the Yankees. Imagining that war will be a glorious experience, he discovers its horrors and suffers a terrible personal tragedy but continues to fight.

After Reading: Suggested Student Activities

1. Prepare a VIP map of "Red Cap," R.J. Powell. (Teacher Note: See chapter 1 for guidelines for doing this literature involvement strategy.)

2. Throughout this book, R.J. makes a number of important decisions that have serious consequences for himself and for others. Identify at least three of these decisions: the first, from the early part of the story before he becomes a drummer; the second, from the middle portion of the book; and the third decision

from the last part of the story. Describe and analyze each of these decisions and their consequences, then compare and contrast them.

3. Prepare a tribute to what Red Cap and his friends endured in the prison camp.

4. While Red Cap was in the prison camp, he encountered several instances of kindness and compassion from soldiers on both the Union and Confederate sides. Choose an example from both sides and create a visual representation of them.

5. While the Confederate prison camp at Andersonville was notorious for its terrible conditions and mistreatment of prisoners, other camps in both the North and South were not much better. Research what life was like for captured soldiers and present this information to your class.

More Books

Beller, Susan Provost. *Cadets at War*. Shoe Tree Press, 1991. 95 pages.

Using primary sources, Beller describes the experiences of the celebrated Corps of Cadets from the Virginia Military Institute who fought at the Battle of New Market, May 15, 1864. The 264 boys, ages 15 to 19, were called upon by General Breckinridge to help defend the Shenandoah Valley against the much larger invading Union forces. Suffering heavy casualities, they charged up the hill to capture a Union cannon and engaged in hand-to-hand combat. The battle, although a small one, was won. The boys are still honored today for their valor and bravery. This book contains many personal vignettes of the cadets as well as photographs and maps. It will appeal to readers interested in the role boys played in the battles of the Civil War and is appropriate for junior high/middle school students and interested secondary students.

Beller, Susan Provost. *To Hold This Ground: A Desperate Battle at Gettysburg*. Margaret K. McElderry Books, 1995. 95 pages.

Beller provides an engrossing account of the battle of Little Round Top, where the 20th Maine and the 15th Alabama valiantly fought each other, placing it within the larger historical context of the Battle of Gettysburg and the Civil War. She describes the creation and experiences of each regiment and draws upon the fascinating parallels between their commanders, Colonel Joshua Lawrence Chamberlain from Maine and Colonel William Calvin Oates from Alabama. Illustrated with photographs and maps, this book is appropriate for junior high/middle school students and secondary students and also will appeal to adult readers.

Coffey, Vincent J. *The Battle of Gettysburg*. Silver Burdett Co., 1985. 64 pages.

The Battle of Gettysburg is one of the books in the Turning Points series and is appropriate for elementary and junior high/middle school students. The introduction and chapter 1 provide the reader with an overview of the historical factors and events leading to the Battle of Gettysburg. The next three chapters each cover a day of the battle from July 1 through July 3, 1863. The afterword briefly summarizes the remainder of the war and its aftermath. The text is enhanced with many vintage photographs, illustrations, and maps.

Foote, Shelby, editor. *Chickamauga and Other Civil War Stories*. A Delta Book, 1993. 241 pages.

Noted writer Shelby Foote begins this collection with Jefferson Davis's Provisional Inaugural and ends it with Abraham Lincoln's Second Inaugural. Flanked by these addresses, the ten short stories that comprise this collection stir the reader's emotions and provide a multifaceted perspective on the human dimensions of this terrible conflict. The following authors are included in this collection: Stephen Crane, F. Scott Fitzgerald, Thomas Wolfe, Ambrose Bierce, William Faulkner, Stephen Vincent Benet, Eudora Welty, Shelby Foote, John O'Hara, and Mark Twain. This collection is appropriate for secondary students.

Hansen, Joyce. *Between Two Fires: Black Soldiers in the Civil War*. Franklin Watts, 1993. 160 pages.

Part of the African-American Experience series, this fine book details the little known experiences of black soldiers in the Civil War within the larger context of the struggle for freedom. Award-winning author Joyce Hansen vividly recreates their recruitment, training, and service based on a wide range of primary and historical sources. Accompanied by photographs and other illustrations, this engrossing book describes the struggles, both on and off the battlefield, of the approximately 180,000 men of African descent who served in the Civil War. This book is appropriate for junior high/ middle school students and secondary students and would also be enjoyed by able upper elementary school readers.

Hill, Lois, editor. *Poems and Songs of the Civil War.* Barnes and Noble Books, 1996.

The drama of war, with its triumphs and tragedies, its heroes and villains, its intense action and periods of boredom, contributes to its fertile inspiration for the poet. There is something about the intensity of war that invites poetic retelling. This volume of poems reflects the impact and pain of the war for both the Union and the Confederacy. The poems in this volume are arranged thematically with the soldiers, deeds, and battles of both sides commemorated. The introduction to each of the thematic sections provides an historical framework for the poems, i.e., the first three sections are "Separation," "Soldiers," and "Deeds of Valor." A wide range of poets are represented; some of the better known include Oliver Wendell Holmes, Herman Melville, and of course, Walt Whitman. The book ends with the lyrics of songs that were popular during the Civil War. The poems in this collection could be used with junior high/middle school students or with secondary students.

Kantor, MacKinlay. *Andersonville.* Signet Classic, 1955. 733 pages.

This powerful novel portrays life in the most infamous prisoner-of-war camp of the Civil War. Andersonville was where over 50,000 Union soldiers were held and over 12,000 perished either in the squalid conditions or at the hands of the vicious camp commander, Henry Wirz. The strength of this novel is that it presents neither side as being wholly righteous; both sides had people of honor as well as those who were reprehensible. The human drama of the camp and its inmates is played out in part in the juxtaposition of Wirz and Ira Claffey, a local plantation owner whose compassion for the imprisoned soldiers directly contrasts with the camp commander's cruelty. The length and complexity of this novel make it appropriate for secondary students and adult readers.

Keith, Harold. *Rifles for Watie*. HarperCollins, 1957. 332 pages.

Based on primary source documents and personal interviews with Civil War veterans living in Oklahoma and Arkansas, this intriguing historical novel tells the little-known story of the war in the far West and of General Stand Watie, leader of the Cherokee Indian Nation Rebels. Jeff Bussey, sixteen, joins the Union Army to fight against Watie. But before the war is over, he falls in love with a Rebel Cherokee Indian girl and serves in the Confederate Army while spying for the Union. Winner of the Newbery Medal, *Rifles for Watie* provides the reader with multiple perspectives on the Civil War and will appeal to secondary school students who enjoy history.

Menge, W. Springer, and J. August Shimrak, editors. *The Civil War Notebook of Daniel Chisholm: A Chronicle of Daily Life in the Union Army 1864–65*. Orion Books, 1989. 202 pages.

In February 1864 a veteran Union officer went to western Pennsylvania to recruit infantry companies for the Army of the Potomac. Among those who volunteered were nineteen-year-old Daniel Chisholm, his brother Alex, and fellow townsman Samuel Clear. Their company fought in the final campaigns of the Civil War, including The Wilderness, Spotsylvania, Cold Harbor, Petersburg, Five Forks, and Appomattox. Chisholm was wounded and spent more than six months in various hospitals. After the war, he collected the letters he had written home and borrowed the diary of Sergeant Clear, which he then transcribed into a notebook, along with excerpts from some of his brother's letters. At the end of the notebook, he transcribed other information, including part of a diary of a prisoner of war. *The Civil War Notebook of Daniel Chisholm* provides a view of the ordinary soldier's life, thoughts, and feelings and is appropriate for secondary students and able junior high/middle school students.

Mitchell, Kirk. *Shadow on the Valley*. St. Martin's Press, 1994. 342 pages.

An exciting, well-written book, *Shadow on the Valley* is a psychological thriller set in 1864 during General Phil Sheridan's "scorch earth" campaign in the Shenandoah Valley. Surgeon Colonel Simon

Wolfe is a young Jewish doctor, born in Charleston, South Carolina, and educated at Harvard. Although his father is Solomon Wolfe, the Confederate Secretary of War, Simon serves with the Union Army. He lost an arm in a courageous act of bravery at the Battle of Antietam in 1862 and now is the chief battlefield hospital administrator for General Sheridan. Wolfe discovers that someone is murdering innocent women who are members of the Dunker Church, a German sect opposed to violence. He befriends Frau Rebekka Zelter, a Dunker widow with a young son, and sets about to learn the murderer's identity, even if it is a high-ranking officer. This book is an intriguing mystery interweaving authentic details of Civil War medical practices, the eccentric personalities of Sheridan and Custer, and the cruel Shenandoah Valley campaign with moral and ethical questions that still trouble people today. It will appeal to secondary students who are Civil War buffs and enjoy reading yet another perspective on the period.

Reef, Catherine. *Gettysburg*. Macmillan, 1992. 72 pages.

This easy reading account, part of the Places in American History series, provides young readers and upper elementary students who have reading problems with a simple historical perspective on the Civil War in general; then the focus shifts to the Battle of Gettysburg. The statistics of the bloody three days are related to convey a sense of the magnitude of the battle. The final two chapters of the book focus on the dedication of the military cemetery at Gettysburg and a visit to the national historical park at the battlefield. This book combines a few historical photographs and illustrations with a number of contemporary photographs of the monuments that have been erected there.

Smith, Carter, editor. *The First Battles: A Sourcebook on the Civil War*. Millbrook Press, 1993. 96 pages.

————. *1863: The Crucial Year: A Sourcebook on the Civil War*. Millbrook Press, 1993. 96 pages.

————. *The Road to Appomattox: A Sourcebook on the Civil War*. Millbrook Press, 1993. 96 pages.

These books are part of the American Albums from the Collections of the Library of Congress. The subtitle, "A Sourcebook on the

Civil War," accurately identifies their value to teachers and students alike. Replete with photographs, drawings, and paintings, each book begins with introductory material and a map that shows the United States during this time period. A timeline of major events follows, divided into two parallel strands—one entitled "At Home and Abroad," and the other, "Military Events." The remainder, and primary portion of each book, consists of brief sections providing more detailed information on topics related to the major theme. These books could be read by many elementary students as well as junior high/middle school students. Secondary school students looking for a succinct overview would find these books useful. Teachers also might use sections of each book to introduce a specific topic related to the war experiences.

Steele, William O. *The Perilous Road*. Harcourt Brace & Company, 1958 and 1990. 156 pages.

In this novel the Union troops forage for food in the mountains of Tennessee, taking newly harvested crops from the families living there, including the Brabsons. The Yankees also take the family's only horse. Young Chris is angry and wants to fight against the Union, but his older brother, Jethro, decides to enlist in the Union Army. Chris's anger is fueled by Silas, a neighbor, whose motives are suspect. Silas encourages Chris to work against the Union forces. When Chris reports a Union supply train in the valley, the Confederates attack it. Then Chris realizes that his brother may have been on the train. This book would be an effective selection for junior high/middle school students.

Weinberg, Larry. *The Drummer Boy*. Avon, 1996. 188 pages.

Jonathan Peasley, an officer with the 20th Maine, has been missing for months after a major battle. The family, desperate for information, sends his fourteen-year-old brother Caleb to the railroad station to talk with returning soldiers. There, Caleb is horrified to learn that some believe his brother deserted under fire. Deciding he must find his brother and learn the truth, he runs away and eventually joins the army as a drummer under an assumed name. Caleb faces many dangers until he finally locates his brother, half-dead, in a terrible Rebel prison and tries to rescue him. Appropriate for junior high/middle school students and secondary students, this novel portrays the horrors of war and the complex moral decisions that people faced during the Civil War.

Wisler, G. Clifton. *The Drummer Boy of Vicksburg.* **Lodestar Books, 1997. 133 pages.**

————. *Mr. Lincoln's Drummer.* **Lodestar Books, 1995. 131 pages.**

Wisler begins *Mr. Lincoln's Drummer* with this passage:

> A drum is the heartbeat of an army. Its tempo lets you know whether to hurry along, steady yourself, or take to your heels. It tells you when to get up, eat, and go to bed. And the fellow who taps out the calls is the very heart of every company in every regiment in every army.
>
> They call us drummer boys. (p. 1)

Based on the lives of actual boys who served as drummer boys during the Civil War, Wisler's historical novels combine powerful, moving stories with an accurate, vivid portrayal of the times. In both of these books, the boys learn that war is not the glorious adventure they imagined. They encounter destruction, death, and disillusionment but also distinguish themselves. The books are written in the first person which adds to their intensity and immediacy.

The Drummer Boy of Vicksburg tells the story of thirteen-year-old Orin Howe from Illinois who made a difference in the terrible battle of Vicksburg, Mississippi. The book opens with a photograph of Howe and Colonel Malmborg. In *Mr. Lincoln's Drummer,* eleven-year-old Willie Johnston, a skinny kid from Vermont, joins the Union Army with his father but then is assigned to a different company. Willie demonstrates unusual bravery in battle and is awarded the Congressional Medal of Honor by President Lincoln, becoming the youngest person ever to qualify for the nation's highest military decoration. Both books conclude with an epilogue and author's note summarizing what happened during the rest of the boys' lives and describing the research that had to be conducted in order to write their stories. Used in conjunction with Jim Murphy's nonfiction book, *The Boy's War: Confederate and Union Soldiers Talk About the Civil War* (see entry in this chapter), these books will hold the interest of upper elementary and junior high/middle school students, especially boys, and also help them learn important concepts about the Civil War.

6

On the Homefront

Usually when we learn about any war era, we focus on the battles, the leaders, the soldiers, and others who are directly involved with the conflict. Yet the homefront is also a crucial support area during any conflict. We may recognize the impact on residents of an occupied country; yet, when a nation is at war, all of its citizens are affected, whether they are on the immediate sidelines, trying to protect themselves and their property, or hundreds or even thousands of miles from the action. This is never truer than in the case of a civil conflict. Probably no conflicts are as destructive as those *within* countries because of the incredible impact on the whole nation. A civil conflict alters the way of life in a nation forever. In the American Civil War, as is usually the case with internal conflicts, the lines were not rigidly drawn. There were Northerners who sympathized with the South, just as there were Southerners who sympathized with the North. There were families divided on the issue with brothers fighting on both sides, with fathers and sons opposing one another, with friends turning to enemies. A vast majority of Southerners experienced the death of at least one family member in the war.

The South experienced more directly the hardships of the war because so many of the battles took place on Southern soil. Union forces, encamped in enemy territory, marched through Southern towns and countryside foraging for supplies on farms and plantations as they went. In the Shenandoah Valley, for instance, the Union forces looted and then destroyed everything they did not use, which created a significant hardship for the civilians. Northern civilians, on the other hand, had few direct contacts with the war; however, they followed the course of the battles through newspaper articles and personal accounts. Confederate forays into enemy territory were limited primarily to the border states, where many citizens were sympathetic to the South. The federal capital in Washington was so close to enemy territory that there was a constant sense of watchfulness. To capture the Union capitol would have been a major coup for the Confederates, potentially giving them a psychological edge in the war. The North did have the advantage that it did not experience the ongoing, continuous, immediate threat that the occupied South did.

The homefront during the Civil War was busy and involved on both sides. Traditional roles that men had held, such as teaching, opened up to women as schoolmasters left to serve in the military. For the first time in the history of our country, there were more women teachers than men. Women also worked in factories, making uniforms for the Union soldiers. One of the most dangerous jobs that many woman undertook was working with explosives in ordnance factories. As the war dragged on, more women had to go to work in factories and in the fields to support their families because the army pay was low or late in coming, or their husbands had been killed.

The volunteer forces provided important support to the war effort. Women from both sides took a more active role during the war than they had previously. In some cases soldiers took the homefront to war with them by having their families in camp. Women struggled to maintain a sense of normal family life in the camps. A number of other women disguised themselves as men and went into battle. The actual number of women who fought is unknown; some had their true identities discovered by doctors who treated them for injuries suffered in battle. Other women served in other ways, volunteering to accompany military units to cook, do laundry, and generally assist the soldiers.

Initially, men served as Civil War nurses, but as the casualties mounted, the need for nurses increased. The women who served as nurses constituted the largest number of women who were directly involved in the war effort. They sometimes served on or near the battlefield, but more often they worked in hospitals that were located away from the battlefront. This involvement was a radical change for women, who "genteel" society believed needed to be sheltered from the harsh realities of life. The nurses faced brutal and painful reality as they witnessed the blood, gore, and suffering of the wounded and dying.

Women also served the military as couriers and as spies. They sometimes used disguises to infiltrate enemy camps, but other times they simply ingratiated themselves to soldiers from the other side and collected as much information as they could.

The homefront provided a receptive audience for the activities of the press. Never before had so many journalists covered a war, many actually reporting from the battlefield and camps. Some traveled with the troops. Political cartoonists provided regular commentaries on leaders and battles.

Perhaps one of the most revealing events on the homefront occurred in July of 1863, when there were riots in protest of the draft in a number of Northern cities. When the draft was initiated for the Union Army, it had a provision that anyone who was drafted could "hire," for $300, a substitute to serve in his place. This clearly articulated the serious problem that the differences in social class were creating in this country. The rich could avoid serving, while the poor could not. In a number of cases it was poor immigrants who ended up fighting. This legality enraged so many people that they rioted in the streets of New York, and other cities. Their anger was also directed at the blacks. The infamous Draft Riots of 1863 became the even bloodier Race Riots.

Experiences on the homefront were as varied as life itself was at that time. The books in this chapter include stories of young women who defied tradition and assumed active involvement for the Union; it tells of those who nursed the wounded; and it provides insights about families who waited, keeping the homes together for the soldiers' return.

Prior to Reading: Think About . . .

Young people need to do some preliminary thinking and talking to prepare them to understand what they read or what is read to them about the Civil War. They need opportunities to ask questions and to raise issues and concerns. The following questions and activities can be used to prompt this discussion:

- What do you think life was like on the homefront during the Civil War? How do you think it was different in the South and North?

- What things are you interested in learning about life on the homefront during the Civil War? What questions do you have about it?

- What do you know about the roles that women played in the Civil War?

- How do you see these roles as different from roles they played in earlier wars in this country?

- How do you think that the economic conditions of the North and South influenced life on the homefront?

- What do you think life was like for someone your age during the Civil War? In what ways do you think it was the same? How do you think it was different?

- Do you have any family stories of ancestors who lived during the Civil War? What do you know about what their lives were like?

- Read the quotes listed with the book you have chosen (or that will be read to you). What do you think they mean? What do you think they reveal about the people and the times?

Focus Books

**Armstrong, Jennifer. *The Dreams of Mairhe Mehan.*
Alfred A. Knopf, 1996. 119 pages.**

March came in my dreams like the soft wind that swiftly turns bitter, and I stared many a night at my candle in the small room I had at the top of the Shinny. Or I'd sit working over my lace, building and building the delicate net rope, and as my fingers worked their well-known stitches I'd close my eyes and see Mike, how he stepped so light along the camp's corduroy streets, how he ducked into a tent to join a game of cards and drink a round of oh-be-joyful moonshine, how he drilled with his fellows in the muddy meadow where the trees were felled all around for miles and miles, a forest of stumps the witnesses to Mike's training in war.

I'd see him shoulder a gun, and drop to his knee, and sight along the bayonet at the advancing lines. And I'd try to see the Confederate lines, how they would advance, but that was where my dreams could not go. (p. 58)

At a Glance ▪ This novel presents the tale of young men who immigrated to this country and were caught up in the Civil War. One of the largest contingents of immigrant soldiers were the Irish. For Mairhe Mehan, living with her father and her older brother, Mike, the war is a serious threat. While many junior high/middle school students could read this, there is a subtlety in the dream motif that is appropriate for older students.

Summary ▪ Life is difficult in the poor Irish section of Washington, D. C., during the Civil War. The ever-present Union troops and the continuing threat of Confederate attack contribute to the difficulties that Mairhe Mehan and her family experience. She works in a tavern evenings to help support the family. Her father has lost his job; her brother, Mike, is working on the construction of the Capitol dome. She struggles to keep her family whole and dreams of better days for them all, but her father dreams of home, Ireland's County Sligo, and her brother Mike dreams of being a soldier. Her father is getting old, and he drinks too much. So the responsibility for holding the family together is Mairhe's. She is befriended by a man from Massachusetts who has come to help nurse his wounded brother and then stays to help others. The man is the poet, Walt Whitman, who becomes a good friend and gentle advisor to Mairhe. She faces a major decision after her brother volunteers to serve in the Union Army.

Teaching Considerations ▪ While this book, in its brevity, is deceptively simple, it can be read and enjoyed by more advanced readers who will understand the recurring dream motif and the juxtaposition of reality with dreams. The use of Walt Whitman as a character also provides a wonderful link to studying his poetry. Armstrong also presents the complexity of race relations and the attitudes of the times in an effective, if ironic, way.

After Reading: Suggested Student Activities

1. Some of the most powerful and moving poetry is written during wars or about the impact that war has. Walt Whitman is one of our foremost poets. Select three of his poems from different periods of his career. Compare and contrast them for style and content.

2. Discuss the role and impact of dreams in this book. What do they contribute to the meaning of the book?

3. Investigate the role of immigrants in the Civil War. How many fought? Where were they from? Why did they enlist? Which side did they fight for, primarily?

4. Mairhe essentially becomes the head of her family. What decisions did she make in that role? Do you believe that they were appropriate? Why or why not?

5. Imagine that you are living in Washington, D. C. during the Civil War. Do the strategy "What Would It Have Been Like to Live in _____?" (Teacher's Note: See guidelines in chapter 1 for this strategy.)

Beatty, Patricia. *Turn Homeward, Hannalee.* Troll Company, 1984. 193 pages.

Near noon a red-bearded Yankee officer came up to us. He climbed onto a table and read to us in a loud voice from a sheet of paper: "By order of General Sherman, commanding office of the United States Army in the seceded state of Georgia, you are all under arrest for making cloth and rope for the Confederate States of America. You are all traitors to the Union. To make sure that you will not be able to continue your traitorous work, you are all to be taken away from here to Indiana and set at liberty there. This means each and every one of you mill workers—men, women, and children."

Oh, what a groan came up from our throats. I clapped my hands over my eyes, threw my head back, and howled loud as ever I could in spite of Rosellen's tugging at me. (pp. 42–43)

At a Glance ▪ For many Southerners, the battlefield and the home-front merged at times. In this novel, a family is separated when the Union Army destroys the mill in a small Georgia town. The soldiers arrest all the mill workers and take them by train to the North to work in mills there. This book is appropriate for upper elementary and junior high/middle school students.

Summary ▪ Hannalee, her younger brother Jem, and her older brother Davy's fiancée, Rosellen, are taken from their families when the Union soldiers destroy the mill where they work. They are sent to work in the North where they are separated from each other. In their tearful farewell her mother makes Hannalee promise to "Turn your heart to me. Turn homeward, Hannalee!" (p. 34). Her mother's words are the guiding force in her life as she, Rosellen, and Jem are sent to live and work in different places in Kentucky and Indiana. Hannalee escapes from the first family she lives with. Masquerading as a boy, she sets out to find Jem. She encounters many hardships during her travels, including a meeting with Quantrill and his Raiders. When her attempt to reach her brother fails, Hannalee seeks help from Rosellen. Living under a false identity as a young boy, Hannalee, aka "Hannibal," lives with Rosellen in the Indiana home of Miz Burton, whose husband and sons are in the Union Army. "Hannibal" uses the time well, continuing with "his" schooling with Mrs. Burton and earning money in the mill. After earning some money, Hannalee decides it is time to find Jem and head back to Georgia.

Teaching Considerations ▪ Hannalee is an interesting character who breaks many stereotypical views of twelve-year-old girls of the time. Her determination, resourcefulness, and courage make her a character that male readers can appreciate. Teachers should establish an historical context for the story because it deals with little-known historical facts.

After Reading: Suggested Student Activities

1. The rules change in any war. Research the policy of the Union Army on taking civilian prisoners to the North to work in their mills and factories. Write a persuasive paper either in support of or opposition to this practice.

2. Using detailed maps of the eastern and midwestern United States, trace Hannalee's train trip north and her trip home to Georgia. Imagine that you are taking one of these trips. Keep a journal with at least five entries of your experiences.

3. Research the amount and type of manufacturing that was done in a Northern and a Confederate state during this time. How do you think the differences contributed to the outcome of the war?

4. If you were Hannalee, would you have stayed and worked in the mill in Indiana or would you have tried to get home? (Teacher's Note: This activity also could be used with a whole class by implementing it as a discussion continuum. See the guidelines in chapter 1 for this strategy.)

Chang, Ina. *A Separate Battle: Women and the Civil War.* Lodestar Books, 1991. 103 pages.

All of the women who volunteered for hospital work saw their worlds expand. Many had never ventured beyond their hometowns, and now they suddenly found themselves in strange, but fascinating surroundings. Although they would carry the images of suffering with them for the rest of their lives, they gained a taste of freedom and a sense of pride in serving their country. (p. 44)

At a Glance ▪ With clear text and vintage photographs, Chang describes the various ways that women in both the Union and the Confederacy served their cause during the Civil War. The book is part of the Young Readers' History of the Civil War series and is appropriate for upper elementary and junior high/middle school students.

Summary ▪ Women were an important part of the Civil War, but their efforts have received little attention in historical texts. Prior to the Civil War, most women led lives primarily confined to the home where they had narrowly defined roles and limited opportunities for higher education and careers. Using primary sources such as diaries and letters, Chang tells the stories of both famous and little-known women who made significant contributions to the war effort and in the process had their lives changed. Taboos still existed against women entering the medical profession, and hospitals were a man's world. The few women who were physicians and nurses encountered severe difficulties practicing their professions. During the Civil War, however, women poured enormous energy into producing clothing and medical supplies, organizing sanitation and medical efforts, serving as nurses and volunteers in the hospitals, and caring for the wounded in their homes. Other women made significant contributions as writers and orators for the abolitionist movement. A few led daring lives as spies or disguised themselves as males to become soldiers. Still others were teachers who helped freed slaves learn to read and write. As the war dragged on, some women had to work in the factories and fields to support their children. In retrospect, the Civil War was an important step in the long journey to equality for women.

Teaching Considerations ▪ While *A Separate Battle* is organized by topics, it lends itself best to reading the chapters in sequence because the author intertwines information and anecdotes about various women throughout the book. Today's students may need more information about the proscribed and limited roles and opportunities for women of that era in order to better understand the significance and courage of these women's actions. This book can serve as a simple introduction to several important female historical figures such as Harriet Tubman, Harriet Beecher Stowe, Clara Barton, Dorothea Dix, and Sojourner Truth.

After Reading: Suggested Student Activities

1. Analyze how women's lives in the 1800s were different from women's lives today.

2. Create a visual representation that interprets the major contributions of women during the Civil War.

3. Select one of the historical female figures from this book who particularly interests you. Find a biography to read about her. Then compare the perspective in the biography with the information in this book.

4. In a persuasive article, write about women as the forgotten heroes of the Civil War.

5. An event can be viewed from a number of perspectives. Discuss the role of women in the Civil War from a number of different points of view, such as social, economic, ethical, racial, geographical, and military.

Collier, James Lincoln, and Christopher Collier.
With Every Drop of Blood.
Delacorte Press, 1994. 235 pages.

"Why, you wouldn't want us to just roll over and die in front of the Yankees, would you, Johnny? The U.S. Constitution says each state is equal, and if Virginians let the Federals take away our slaves or say we can't take them into the new territories out west, there's no telling where they'll stop. Next thing you know the Federal government will try to tell us what to grow or who we can sell our cotton and tobacco to. No, Johnny. this here war isn't about slaves at all—it's about a state's right to govern itself." (p. 29)

At a Glance ▪ This historical novel is the story of one Virginia family who gets caught up in the war. It dramatizes the hardship that the Civil War created for many civilians. It is appropriate reading for upper elementary or junior high/ middle school students.

Summary ▪ The death of his father puts extra responsibility on Johnny. While his father was gone serving with the Confederate Army and even after he returned home, ailing and unable to work their small farm, Johnny did not feel the major responsibility for providing for his mother and his younger brother and sister. Granted, Johnny always worked hard on the farm, but he could rely on his father for advice and direction. As his father lies dying, he makes Johnny promise not to "get any fool notions about running off to fight." His father tells Johnny that he has done the family's duty to Virginia and now Johnny must do his duty to his mother and younger brother and sister. Johnny is fourteen and while he wants to honor his promise to his father, he also wants excitement and revenge. He agrees to be a teamster for the Confederacy using his wagon and team of mules to take supplies to Richmond as part of a wagon train. The wagons are supposed to be heavily guarded, but they cannot withstand the assault of a company of Union soldiers. When the Union captures the train, Johnny is not wounded, and he is allowed to drive his wagon to the Union lines where he will be sent to a prisoner-of-war camp in the North. The soldiers who capture the wagon train are black and Johnny is guarded by a young escaped slave, Cush, who has enlisted in the Union Army. All the prejudice of his background makes Johnny react harshly against Cush at first, but as time goes on and a number of circumstances put both of them in peril, they establish an uneasy alliance.

Teaching Considerations ▪ This book is readable, and the adventure in the book will appeal to many upper elementary and middle school readers. It has powerful lessons about prejudice and honor. In a preface to the book, the Collier brothers discuss their use of the word "nigger." This will be a helpful source for explanation and discussion with students.

After Reading: Suggested Student Activities

1. Christopher Collier has said that one of the purposes of historical fiction is to be a vehicle for transmitting the values of a culture. Identify and discuss the values that are presented and developed in this book.

2. Write a brief character portrait of Johnny at the beginning of this book and another one of him at the end. In what ways has he changed? In what ways has he stayed the same? (Teacher's Note: See the guidelines in chapter 1 for this strategy.)

3. Research the educational conditions for young people growing up in the South and in the North.

4. In a persuasive paper, explain why education was essential for blacks to become contributing citizens of a democracy.

5. Using the discussion continuum, indicate the position that best represents your position on the following perspectives:

Johnny's primary responsibility was to serve his country.

Johnny's primary responsibility was to honor the promise to his father.

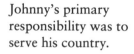

(Teacher's Note: See the guidelines in chapter 1 for this strategy.)

Fleischman, Paul. *The Borning Room*. HarperCollins, 1991. 101 pages.

And behind the kitchen, as in his New Hampshire home, a borning room, set aside for both dying and giving birth—the room my father was born in before the window glass had yet arrived. It's not a room that's seen much use. But the times it has stand up in my memory more than the months and years in between. Most of my life's turnings have taken place here. (p. 4)

At a Glance ▪ This short historical novel demonstrates the strength of family and tradition on an Ohio farm. Much of the book's action takes place during the years of the Civil War. The book is appropriate for upper elementary or junior high/middle school students.

Summary ▪ Georgina Lott's grandfather leaves New Hampshire to settle in Ohio where he builds a family farm. She lives there with her parents, brothers and sisters, and her grandfather. From her experiences on the farm, Georgina Lott learns about life and death. She also learns about doing the right thing when she discovers a runaway slave and hides her in the family's barn. While the actual Civil War battles are fought far from the farm, the family has strong abolitionist sentiments. They are also concerned for relatives fighting in the Civil War. The book truly gives to the reader a sense of continuity and family tradition.

Teaching Considerations ▪ This is a quiet book, with little excitement or adventure. For this reason, some readers might relate better to it than others. Among the awards it has received are the Golden Kite Award Honor Book for Fiction, *The Horn Book* Best Book, and *School Library Journal* Best Book.

After Reading: Suggested Student Activities

1. Identify the major historical events that are alluded to in the book by establishing a timeline.

2. Compare and contrast the family tradition in this book with either your family or a family you know. (Teacher's Note: See the guidelines in chapter 1 for this strategy.)

3. Analyze the impact that war has on even those who remain on the homefront.

Forrester, Sandra. *Sound the Jubilee.*
Lodestar Books, 1995. 184 pages.

"We just got word the government's setting up a permanent community for freed slaves here on the island," the captain told them. "The unoccupied land to the north will be divided into one-acre lots. A lot will be assigned to each family."

"You mean, you're givin' us the land?" somebody in the crowd called out.

"That's what I've been told to do," the captain said. But Maddie thought he didn't sound happy about it. "The land's been confiscated from its owners. The presi-

dent's giving it to you in repayment for your loyalty to
the Union." (p. 121)

At a Glance ▪ Running away from their owners, the Henry family
escapes to Roanoke Island where they become part of a community
of freed slaves until the end of the war. This historical novel tells
the little-known story of the black community that was established
off the coast of North Carolina by the U.S. government during the
Civil War, but then forced off its land after the war. This book
is appropriate for upper elementary and junior high/middle school
students.

Summary ▪ Maddie and her family are slaves on the River Bend
Plantation in North Carolina. Her father, Titus, longs for the blue-
coats to arrive and grant them freedom while her mother, Ella, is
frightened and thinks they should be content with what they have.
Afraid that Union troops will come to the plantation, their mistress
decides to flee to their summer home on the coast at Nags Head,
and she takes the slaves with her. When Union troops capture the
islands off the coast of North Carolina and threaten Nags Head,
their mistress prepares to flee again. Maddie and her family use this
opportunity to run away, and they escape to Roanoke Island. Here
they make a home as part of a settlement established by the U.S.
government. They face many challenges and hardships in making a
new life but learn important skills and contribute to the development of a thriving community of 3,000 former slaves. Unfortunately, they also learn that not all promises are honored and what
the government gives, it can take away. When the war is over, the
land on Roanoke Island is restored to the original owners who have
received pardons, and the blacks are forced to leave.

Teaching Considerations ▪ While the reading level of *Sound the
Jubilee* is not difficult, it does have embedded within the story a
number of complex moral and social issues that students will need
help to understand. The story is engaging and the characters are
interesting, but students may need additional information to place
the events of the book within the context of the times. This book
also provides students with another perspective on what life on the
homefront was like during the Civil War.

After Reading: Suggested Student Activities

1. Discuss with your class why teaching slaves to read and write was forbidden by law and why it was so important to them to become literate.

2. Imagine that you are Maddie. Write a persuasive letter to the president of the United States giving the reasons why you think the former slaves should be allowed to keep the land on Roanoke Island.

3. While some Union soldiers were friendly and helpful to the Henry family and the other former slave families on Roanoke Island, other soldiers were hostile and prejudiced. Discuss why this occurred.

4. Choose a character or event from this story that has special meaning for you. Use a creative medium to express its significance. (Teacher's Note: See the guidelines in chapter 1 for this strategy.)

Holland, Isabelle. *Behind the Lines.* Scholastic Hardcover, 1994. 194 pages.

Katie was feeling almost actively ill. She knew she ought not to have been surprised when Mrs. Lacey, forgetting her presence, as she did so often, spoke of the kind of people now in the streets rioting and her pleasure in the fact that her son was no longer in danger of losing his life on the battlefield. It was obvious to Katie that, with her mission accomplished to get her son excused from the draft, Mrs. Lacey, unlike her mother, was oblivious of Katie's feelings and anxieties. Katie had been in the Lacey household for a while now, but never had she seen so clearly that, for people like her mistress, other people who were different, like her own family, were not even human, did not exist. (p. 160)

At a Glance ▪ The novel deals with serious topics of discrimination against Irish immigrants as well as against African Americans; the struggle between the social classes; and race riots during the Civil

War. The main character, Katie O'Ferrell, faces a number of challenges with courage, making her an appealing character for both male and female readers. This book would be enjoyed by junior high/ middle school students and even able upper elementary aged students. It has a highly romanticized book jacket, however, that is misleading.

Summary ▪ Since her mother's death fourteen-year-old Katie O'Ferrell has worked as a kitchen maid for a wealthy New York family, the Laceys, to help support her younger brothers and sister. She would rather be at home caring for them, but her father says they need her meager salary to put food on the table. Katie is lonely and mistreated by the housekeeper where she works. She finds a stray dog and they adopt each other, but she can't keep Paddy at work and her father has no use for animals. Jimmy, the groom at a neighbor's stable, helps her by keeping Paddy in his room. Jimmy is a free man but the son of a former slave.

Times are difficult for Northerners in 1863 and those difficulties touch Katie and the family for whom she works. The war has lasted longer than they expected and their troops have fought a number of battles in which they incurred high casualties. In need of soldiers, the North has instituted a draft for young men over the age of twenty. Katie's employer has a son who would like to enlist, but his parents want him to finish his education at Harvard. According to the law, drafted men could hire a substitute to go to war for them. For $300 a rich man could avoid military service, but that was a luxury not afforded the poor. The Laceys decide to try to hire Katie's older brother Brian to substitute for their son. Katie is upset by this and tries to convince her family not to let it happen.

In the midst of this personal trial for Katie, New York erupts in deadly draft riots. Many of the rioters are young Irish immigrants who feel that the Civil War has nothing to do with them. As the draft riots gain momentum, they turn into the worst race riots in our history. The poor blame the blacks for the war, believing that slavery is the sole cause for it. Katie's friend Jimmy is endangered by the rioting and she must try to find a way to help him.

Teaching Considerations ▪ Teachers may need to help students to recognize that bigotry can exist anywhere. This novel raises a number of questions that will be powerful springboards for discussion and writing, including the race riots, the treatment of immigrants, and the policy of hiring someone to serve your enlistment.

After Reading: Suggested Student Activities

1. The draft riots of 1863 were among the most serious in our history. As a complement to your reading of this book, find some nonfiction accounts of the riots and compare them with the insight you get from Holland's book.

2. Debate the issue of whether or not people should be able to pay someone else to fulfill their military service. Speculate about what would happen if that policy were enacted today. (Teacher's Note: This activity also could be used with a whole class by implementing it as a discussion continuum. See the guidelines in chapter 1 for this strategy.)

3. Katie is faced with a number of difficult choices in the book. Select one and analyze the choice she made and its alternatives. What would you have done in her place and why?

4. When we think of discrimination during the Civil War period, we think of the treatment of African Americans in the South. Discuss the bigotry and discrimination in New York City during this time.

5. Select a value or ideal that is developed in this book and do a values/ideal map of it. (Teacher's Note: See the guidelines in chapter 1 for this strategy.)

Hunt, Irene. *Across Five Aprils.* Follett, 1965. Berkley, 1986. 190 pages.

Then Ellen spoke. Her voice was no longer tremulous; it carried the authoritative note sharpened by long years of mothering a large family.

"That will be enough, boys. There will be no more talk of war or the troubles leadin' to war at this table tonight. The rest of our meal we will eat as a fam'ly that respects one another and honors our comp'ny." (pp. 32–33)

At a Glance ▪ *Across Five Aprils* is a classic of young adult literature. It is frequently used as required reading in either English or American history classes in junior high/middle school; however, able upper elementary students would enjoy it as would secondary students.

Summary ▪ The Civil War affected families and whole communities, and the Creighton family is no exception. When the war begins, Jethro, who is nine, watches his three older brothers, a cousin, and his teacher enlist and go to war. While his father and two brothers are ardent supporters of the Union, Jethro's favorite brother, Bill, feels that he cannot side with the industrial powers that influence the Union cause. After Bill leaves home, everyone assumes that he has gone to Kentucky to join with his mother's relatives, who are Confederate sympathizers. Some neighbors call the family Copperheads because they refuse to denounce Bill. His father is so enraged by the charge that he suffers a heart attack. From that point on, Jethro has to be the "man of the family" because his father is no longer able to farm. The Creightons suffer more hardship: they are harassed; their barn is burned; and Jethro's brother Tom is killed in the war. Throughout the war, Jethro must learn to cope with many challenges. This book is in the tradition of coming-of-age books.

Teaching Considerations ▪ *Across Five Aprils* presents a number of the issues that confronted those on the homefront. The family loyalties are divided between Union and Confederate when family members fight on both sides. Among the awards this book has received are Newbery Honor Book and Society of Midland Authors Book Award.

After Reading: Suggested Student Activities

1. Analyze the arguments presented in the book for the Union and Confederate positions.

2. Discuss how Jethro grows and changes through his experiences in the book. Use the "Create a Character Portrait" strategy to see his changes. (Teacher's Note: See the guidelines in chapter 1 for this strategy.)

3. While Irene Hunt relates a story based on her grandfather's life in this novel, the book can be seen as representative of the experiences of many families. Identify the elements that make it a universal story.

4. Hunt provides a detailed view of Jethro's life. Imagine that you were living at that time and do the strategy, "What Would It Have Been Like to Live In _____?" (Teacher Note: See chapter 1 for guidelines for doing this literature involvement strategy.)

Josephs, Anna Catherine. Illustrated by Bill Ersland.
Mountain Boy.
Raintree Publishers, 1985. 32 pages.

It was a journey that Tommy would never forget. When he and the small band of men set out, the trees were covered with ice, the ground was slippery, and there was about two feet of snow on the ground. (p. 21)

At a Glance ▪ *Mountain Boy* is a beautifully illustrated picture book written by a remarkable fourth grader who tells the story of her great-grandfather, Tommy Zachary, a fourteen-year-old boy living in the mountains of North Carolina during the Civil War. Tommy helped guide Union soldiers, and escaped from a Confederate prison through the mountains to freedom. This book is appropriate for elementary and junior high/middle school students or could be used as a teacher read-aloud.

Summary ▪ Tommy Zachary is a fourteen-year-old boy who lives with his family in a small log cabin in the dense mountain woods of North Carolina. One winter night a small band of Union soldiers who have escaped from a Confederate prison in South Carolina appears at their cabin seeking help. Because Tommy's dad is ill, the family decides that Tommy will guide the men through the mountains to freedom. It takes Tommy and the men 52 days to make the dangerous 120-mile journey to Sweetwater, Tennessee. For many year thereafter, Tommy receives letters from one of the men and then after his death, from his wife.

Teaching Considerations ▪ Nine-year-old Anna Catherine Josephs wrote this Heritage Story as a class assignment for Raintree's 1985 Publish-A-Book contest. She had heard her grandparents tell the story of her great-grandfather many times and had often visited her grandmother at the mountain homestead in North Carolina. Anna's story won the nationwide contest.

After Reading: Suggested Student Activities

1. Imagine that you are Tommy Zachary guiding the escaped soldiers to freedom. Keep a journal for one week of your dangerous adventures. Base your journal entries upon available historical data about life during the Civil War.

2. Dramatize this story with a small group of your classmates.

3. Interview an older member of your family or a neighbor about any historical event they remember from their lifetimes or those of their ancestors.

Kantor, MacKinlay. *Gettysburg*. Random House, 1952, 1980, 1993. 151 pages.

War is a mix-up of mistakes, delays, neglect, sudden decisions, sudden attacks, sudden defenses. And luck plays a great part. (p. 72)

History is tangled, history is strange. (p. 117)

At a Glance ▪ Kantor provides fascinating glimpses of little-known information about the people of Gettysburg and its surrounding area along with battlefield stories and the response of the civilian population after the bloody three-day battle. Part of the Landmarks in American History series, *Gettysburg* is appropriate for junior high/middle school students and upper elementary students and will appeal to readers of all ages interested in learning more about the human and social aspects of the Civil War.

Summary ▪ Many of the books about Gettysburg and the Civil War primarily describe major military figures and famous battlefield scenes. While Kantor doesn't ignore these aspects of the Battle of Gettysburg, his emphasis is more on the human dimension, describing both little-known people and experiences and some that have become part of our national folklore. The reader learns about John Burns, an elderly civilian determined to fight the Rebels, and twenty-year-old Jenny (Mary Virginia) Wade, killed by a stray bullet behind two doors in her own home while she made biscuits for her sister who had a new baby. Other stories include those about the organization of the young and invalid into emergency militias; the refusal of the storekeepers to fulfill the Confederate demand for supplies; and Father William Corby, a Catholic priest who gave absolution to an entire brigade of Irish troops before they went into battle. Kantor also describes the terrible aftermath of the three days of fierce fighting when tens of thousands of dead, dying, and seriously wounded soldiers lay spread over the countryside with only limited and primitive medical services available. Hundreds of people from the North came to help treat the wounded or to search for missing relatives or friends. Kantor's book gives the reader important insight into living conditions during the 1860s before many of the daily conveniences we take for granted existed. *Gettysburg* concludes with a chapter on the dedication of the National Soldiers Cemetery and Lincoln's Gettysburg Address.

Teaching Considerations ▪ As the quote "History is tangled, history is strange" (p. 117) indicates, Kantor's book can be used to help dispel the notion that history is nothing more than a bunch of boring facts, names of dead people, and obscure dates of long ago battles and wars. This book can be paired effectively with other books that have a stronger military focus to help provide students with a comprehensive view of this significant event in our nation's history.

After Reading: Suggested Student Activities

1. Describe how historical events can get twisted and changed as they become part of the folklore of a nation. Use two examples from *Gettysburg* to illustrate your point.

2. Analyze the effects of the lack of mass communications on both the civilian population and the military forces during this time.

3. Select an incident from this book that demonstrates the effects of the Civil War on the civilian population. Prepare a script with a small group of classmates and then dramatize it for your entire class.

4. After the dramatization, have the class discuss the difference between historical facts and historical interpretations as presented in the drama.

Reit, Seymour. *Behind Rebel Lines.* Harcourt Brace and Company, 1988. 114 pages.

Along with the surgeons and other nurses, Pvt. Franklin Thompson was classed as noncombatant; still, everyone had to go through the same training. In war nothing was certain; there was no telling when medical and service troops might have to help fight off a sudden enemy attack. (p. 11)

At a Glance ▪ This is an account of the true story of Emma Edmonds, one of an estimated more than 400 women who fought on both sides during the Civil War. Disguised as men, these young women took their places on the battle lines; many who fought were never discovered. This is an exciting account of Emma Edmonds's role as one of the most successful spies for the Union Army. *Behind Rebel Lines* is appropriate for junior high/middle school students; some secondary students would enjoy it also.

Summary ▪ Emma Edmonds disguised herself as a man and enlisted in the Union Army. She was accepted as Private Franklin Thompson, 2nd Michigan Volunteers of the United States Army. Frank (Emma) was attached to the medical corps as a nurse where she assisted the doctors. When Thompson heard of the death of an old friend at the hand of snipers, "he" decided to take action. The opportunity arose when General McClellan's spy in Richmond was caught and executed by the Confederates. Thompson volunteered to go behind the Confederate lines as a spy. In this new role, Emma became a master of disguises, from Pvt. Thompson to a young black slave named Cuff to a timid peddler woman named Bridget O'Shea to a black laundry woman to the mysterious Mr. Mayberry. Although Emma experienced injury and illness, she managed to keep her true identity unknown until she became very ill with malaria and needed to hospitalized. But hospitalization meant exposure, so she fled and entered a hospital as Emma Edmonds. Once she recovered, she planned to return to being Private Franklin Thompson, but she found out that Thompson had been reported as a deserter. Emma Edmonds then spent the last two years of the war as a nurse, using her own name.

Teaching Considerations ▪ Reit includes background information at both the beginning and end of this book that will help to answer questions about Emma. Among the awards it has received is IRA-CBC Teachers' Choice. Another book that describes the life and experiences of Emma Edmonds is:

> Stevens, Bryna. *Frank Thompson: Her Civil War Story.* Macmillan, 1992.

This book uses extensive information, quotes, and illustrations from Edmonds's autobiography, *Nurse and Spy,* first published in 1865, and provides still more information about this fascinating and controversial individual.

After Reading: Suggested Student Activities

1. Research the role of spies and the secret service during the Civil War and present your finding to the class in a manner that reflects the kind of life many of them lived.

2. Imagine that you are a spy experiencing the type of challenges that Emma faced. Write about them in either journal form or as a report for the general.

3. Emma Edmonds elected to take unusual actions for a woman of her time. Write a profile of her that focuses on those characteristics that made her unique. (Teacher's Note: See the guidelines in chapter 1 for this strategy.)

4. Select one event from the book and rewrite it as a scene that you and another classmate will act out for the class.

Rinaldi, Ann. *In My Father's House.* **Scholastic, 1993. 323 pages.**

> "Your stepdaddy told you 'bout the shortages in this town? How we don't have coffee, sugar, spices or medicines?"
>
> "He did, yes," I said.
>
> "Y'all got sugar up to your house?"
>
> There it was. Everyone was eyeing us. I held my breath. They *knew* that Will McLean was speculating in sugar.
>
> "We may have a bit we brought down from Charlottesville," I allowed.
>
> He nodded. "Sugar's scarcer than hen's teeth in these parts. The county authorities give salt out on salt days. Bring it up from the southwest part of the state. Each family gets a box. Don't suppose y'all be needin' any, though. Hear tell y'all got everthin' needed up to your place." (pp. 196–97)

At a Glance ▪ Rinaldi's engaging historical fiction tells the story of a Southern family during the Civil War through the eyes of Oscie, stepdaughter of Will McLean. By a strange twist of fate, the first battle of the Civil War, the Battle of Bull Run in Manassas, was fought on McLean property; the surrender agreement ending the Civil War was signed in the drawing room of the house in Appomattox where they had moved to escape the war. *In My Father's House* is appropriate for secondary students and able junior high/middle school students.

Summary ▪ *In My Father's House* spans the thirteen years from 1852 when Oscie is seven, until April 12, 1865. During this time, strong-willed Oscie undergoes enormous changes in her life, beginning with her widowed mother's marriage to Will McLean, which she opposes. Belonging to a wealthy plantation family that owns slaves, Oscie can't imagine that anything will ever change the Southern way of life. Will McLean, however, knows that its days are numbered and is determined to educate his stepdaughters and expose them to other ideas. He brings a Northern teacher, Miss Buttonworth, to the family to tutor the girls. Oscie develops a friendship with the teacher which she maintains even when Miss Buttonworth must return to the North as conditions worsen between the North and South. Even more changes occur when after the fall of Fort Sumter, Virginia regiments camp near the McLean home in Manassas, and Oscie falls in love with a dashing Confederate officer who is married. The McLeans leave their home before the Battle of Bull Run, but life is never the same as they struggle to cope with changing social, economic, and political conditions. Oscie also must face her conflicting attitudes toward black people, especially Mary Ann, a slave she has misjudged and misused.

Teaching Considerations ▪ Rinaldi concludes this novel with an author's note that provides fascinating information about her research on the McLean family. She also discusses the differences among historical facts, fiction, and unanswered questions, citing examples from the novel. Readers should note that her use of the term "nigra" is in accord with the common usage of the times.

After Reading: Suggested Student Activities

1. Describe and analyze the major ways in which daily life in the South changed during the Civil War. Create a visual representation of those changes.

2. Develop a list of arguments for and against the way in which Will McLean provided for his family during the Civil War. Then write a paper describing and supporting your position on the issue or present your arguments orally to your class. (Teacher's Note: This activity also could be used with a whole class by implementing it as a discussion continuum. See the guidelines in chapter 1 for this strategy.)

3. Oscie is a strong-willed, independent-minded character who faces the challenges of life head-on. Select three events that occurred in her life because of the Civil War and analyze how these affected her and what changes she had to make as a result of them.

4. Discuss the Southern perspective on the war as it is presented in this book. How does this information support or conflict with your prior knowledge of the period?

5. Discuss what you think the book's title means.

Rinaldi, Ann. *The Last Silk Dress*. Holiday House, 1988. 331 pages.

> "Susan, did you ever think it would turn out this
> way? When we collected the dresses for the balloon, I
> mean. I thought it was a lark. I never dreamed it was all
> about . . . killing." (p. 248)

At a Glance ▪ Set in Richmond during the first years of the Civil
War, Rinaldi tells the engrossing and adventurous story of Susan
Chilmark and her family with its terrible secrets. In the beginning,
Susan is in love with "the Cause," with its festive parties, thrilling
parades, and stirring music. But as the horrible realities of war
touch her and she learns the truth about her family, Susan must
rethink her life and how to live it. *The Last Silk Dress* is appropriate for secondary students and able junior high/middle school
students.

Summary ▪ Susan Chilmark is an impetuous and high-spirited
young woman who wants to do something important to aid the
Southern Cause. She and her best friend, Connie, decide to collect
silk dresses to make an observational balloon for spying on the
Yankees. During this time, she seeks out her handsome and dashing
older brother, Lucien, who is estranged from the family and considered to be immoral and scandalous by the high society of Richmond. Through him, Susan meets a Yankee, Timothy Tobias
Collier. Collier is in the South to draw sketches of the war for *Harper's*, and eventually plays an important part in changing how
Susan views the Southern way of life and the war. As the civilian
population of Richmond begins to feel the terrible effects of the
war, Susan also experiences its consequences and begins to question
what she has done. When her father is killed and her mother cruelly
tells her the family's secrets, Susan's world crumbles, and she must
make some life-altering choices.

Teaching Considerations ▪ In addition to being a compelling story,
The Last Silk Dress addresses difficult moral issues and questions
and can help students to better understand some of the complexities
of the social structure of the South during the 1800s. These issues
and questions can be used to help students view events and actions

through several different perspectives. Among the awards it has received is ALA Best Book for Young Adults.

After Reading: Suggested Student Activities

1. Describe and analyze the significant changes Susan makes in what she believes and thinks is important. Create a visual representation of these changes.

2. Select one of the underlying moral issues in this book and state the arguments for and against it as seen through the eyes of two characters with differing perspectives. Then develop your own position on it.

3. New technology played an important role in the Civil War. Describe and analyze the ways in which it has an impact on the characters and events in this novel.

4. Through the increased use of photographs and sketches in newspapers and magazines, the Civil War became our first media war. Discuss the role of journalism and its consequences.

5. This book presents a number of moral and ethical dilemmas involving issues of race, sex, fidelity, money, social status, and secret actions and behaviors. Identify and discuss how these themes contribute to the book.

Shura, Mary Francis. *Gentle Annie: The True Story of a Civil War Nurse.* Scholastic, 1991. 184 pages.

Over and again she had been thrown into circumstances that were outside of her control—her father's business failure, the move to Wisconsin, and the loss of both her father and husband. For once she was really taking control—doing what she wanted to do on her own. Joy combined with a tingling of fear to quicken her steps. (pp. 46–47)

At a Glance ▪ This fictionalized biography is the story of Annie Etheridge, who volunteered to serve with the 2nd Michigan Volunteer Regiment. Appropriate for upper elementary or junior high/

middle school students, this book presents one of the roles played by women during the Civil War. While the protagonist is a woman, her courage and the adventures she undertakes make her an appealing subject for all readers.

Summary ▪ The Union Army called for volunteers. Annie Etheridge answered that call. She was sure that hundreds of women would sign up for the twenty openings to cook, do laundry, and nurse the wounded for the regiment. Shortly before her seventeenth birthday, Annie was accepted as a volunteer with the 2nd Michigan Volunteer Regiment. She continued to serve throughout the war and was on the front lines in every battle that the Army of the Potomac was involved in, from 1861 to 1865.

Teaching Considerations ▪ This book is readable and the adventure in the book will appeal to many upper elementary and middle school readers. The book tells a story of battlefield nurses that most students will not be familiar with. Based on facts and describing the events in a real person's life, the narrative includes details and encounters that are invented by the author to flesh out the book.

After Reading: Suggested Student Activities

1. Research the other nontraditional roles women played in the Civil War.

2. Imagine that you are Annie. Keep a journal for three days describing your experiences.

3. Find out more about Annie's friend, Franklin Flint Thompson (Emma Edmonds). Write a story about Thompson's experiences.

Smith, Carter, editor. *Behind the Lines: A Sourcebook on the Civil War.* Millbrook Press, 1993. 96 pages.

The Civil War changed the way Americans lived. In the North, the drive to manufacture vast quantities of war materials spurred industrialization. In the South, a rural economy based on slave labor was destroyed, plunging

a once-prosperous region into decades of poverty. . . .
On both sides of the Mason-Dixon line, women began
leaving their homes to work in munitions factories, in
hospitals, and on farms. (p. 19)

At a Glance ▪ This book is one of the American Albums from the
Collections of the Library of Congress. Its subtitle, "A Sourcebook
on the Civil War," accurately identifies this book's value to teachers
and students alike. It provides a good overview of many of the fac-
ets of the period between April 1861 and April 1865. Each section
of this book is brief and could easily be read by many elementary
students as well as junior high/middle school students. Secondary
school students looking for a succinct introduction to numerous
topics related to the Civil War might also find this book useful.

Summary ▪ This book, replete with photographs, drawings, and
paintings, begins with introductory material and a map that shows
the United States in 1861. This is followed by a timeline beginning
with the events in April 1861 and continuing until the end of the
war. The timeline is divided into two parallel strands: one describing "Behind the Lines," the other describing "Military Events."
These strands provide readers with a chronology of the major
events that occurred both militarily and socio/politically. These two
strands are then reflected in the remainder of the book. Part I, entitled "Politics and Civilian Life," examines the conditions on both
sides of the Mason-Dixon Line during the war. Among the topics
presented are leadership (both South and North), economic conditions on both sides, the role of African Americans in the war, slavery, the role of women on both sides, and life under occupation.
Part II, entitled "Life in the Army," presents such topics as recruitment of soldiers for both the North and South, camp life on both
sides, the role of African Americans in the military, medicine, prisoners, and more aspects of military life. Each section of the book
is accompanied by actual photographs, sketches, or paintings. Of
particular interest are photographs of documents and announcements from the times.

Teaching Considerations ▪ While this book provides an excellent
overview of the times, it is an overview rather than an in-depth

examination. Students may need additional information as context to understand some of the events. The concise sections of this book could be read aloud as introductory information.

After Reading: Suggested Student Activities

1. Select a topic from "Politics and Civilian Life" and prepare a report to present to the class

2. Imagine that you are a civilian living during the Civil War. Describe what a typical day would be like for you on the homefront. Write two entries: one from the perspective of a person living in the South; and the other from the perspective of a person living in the North. Use the following perspectives to frame your response:

   - race
   - gender
   - age
   - political beliefs
   - economic status
   - regional loyalty
   - social class

3. Select one of the photographs or illustrations from the book and write a story about the people and events portrayed in it.

4. One of the major misconceptions about the Civil War is that blacks played a relatively minor role. Describe the various contributions that African Americans made during this time.

More Books

Currie, Stephen. *Music in the Civil War*, Betterway Books, 1992. 111 pages.

This is a wonderful, captivating account of the importance of music to both the North and South in the Civil War. The book provides background information about composers and their music as they reflect the times. Additionally, there are a number of vintage photographs as well as photographs of the covers of sheet music from the Civil War era, sheet music and lyrics, reproductions of posters, and sketches. This account is readable and could be used with junior high school/middle school or secondary school students.

Denenberg, Barry. *When Will This Cruel War Be Over? The Civil War Diary of Emma Simpson*. Scholastic, 1996. 144 pages.

One of the books in the Dear America series, this novel is written in the form of diary entries by Emma Simpson for the year 1864 in Gordonsville, Virginia. The year begins with Emma mourning the death of her brother, a Confederate soldier; worrying about her father, a Confederate officer; and musing about her first love, who has recently joined General Lee's Army of Northern Virginia. During the year in which she turns fifteen, Emma experiences a number of personal tragedies as conditions in the South steadily worsen. This book is appropriate for upper elementary and junior high/middle school students and provides readers with a view of the Southern perspective and way of life during the Civil War.

Forman, James D. *Becca's Story*. Charles Scribner's Sons, 1992. 180 pages.

Based upon family letters, diaries, and stories, Foreman's moving novel provides the reader with perspectives from both the homefront and the battlefield during the Civil War. Rebecca Case (Becca) has two beaux, Alex and Charlie, and all three of them are best friends in a small town in southern Michigan. Caught up in the patriotic fever of 1861, the young men join the 7th Michigan Regiment where they discover that war is not the romantic adventure they imagined. Becca must grow up and change her own romantic notions about life when one of her friends is seriously injured and the other is missing in action. *Becca's Story* is a lovely story of friendship and love set against the backdrop of the loss of innocence brought on by the Civil War. It is appropriate for secondary students and able junior high/middle school students.

Garrison, Webb. *A Treasury of Civil War Tales*. Ballantine Books, 1988. 261 pages.

As the title states, this collection is a treasure. This nonfiction collection of short, readable selections covers the period leading up to the Civil War through its aftermath. The author draws upon a wealth of sources to provide a rich and comprehensive portrait of both well-known people and events and lesser-known aspects of the Civil War experience. *A Treasury of Civil War Tales* is a valuable resource and a useful accompaniment to any study of the Civil War period. Appropriate for secondary students and able junior high/middle school students; teachers could also use excerpts from it for read-alouds.

Houston, Gloria. *Mountain Valor.* The Putnam & Grosset Group, 1994. 239 pages.

Set in a remote region of the Appalachian Mountains and based on the experiences of one of the author's ancestors, this historical novel spans the years from 1861 to the end of the Civil War. Valor McAimee and her family experience the terribly divisive nature of this conflict because some of the men from the area are away fighting for the Confederacy and others for the Union. Life becomes increasingly difficult as renegades from both armies roam the countryside, terrorizing people and stealing their crops and livestock. Valor chaffs at the restrictions placed on young women and longs for the freedom to take action like a man. After renegades commit murder and plunder their farm, Valor dresses like a boy and enters the war to recover their livestock and avenge her family. Appropriate for upper elementary and junior high/middle school students, this book tells a dramatic story of life on the homefront during the Civil War.

Kassem, Lou. *Listen for Rachel.* Avon Books, 1986. 165 pages.

When her parents die fighting a fire at their store in Nashville, Rachel, age fifteen, is taken to live with grandparents she has never met in an isolated mountain area of Tennessee. A city girl and an "outlander," Rachel feels lonely and out of place with her mountain kin. Gradually she learns mountain ways and grows to understand and love the people and the mountains. But when Tennessee secedes from the Union, the Civil War touches even their remote area as family and neighboring loyalties are divided and many of the men go off to fight. When Ben, a wounded Yankee soldier from Philadelphia, stumbles upon their cabin, Rachel nurses him back to health using the herbal and naturalistic doctoring taught her by old Granny Sharp. They fall in love, but Rachel, now seventeen and increasingly needed for her doctoring skills, is torn between her love for Ben and her desire to stay and help the mountain people. This historical novel is appropriate for secondary school students and able junior high/middle school students.

Lunn, Janet. *The Root Cellar.* Puffin Books, 1981. 247 pages.

Winner of numerous awards, this time travel fantasy takes the reader back to the time of the Civil War. In the present, Rose, an orphan, is sent to live with her aunt and family in Canada after her grandmother dies. Unhappy with her relatives and the new surroundings, she wanders down the stairs to the old root cellar, but when she climbs up she is back in time in the 1860s. Rose makes friends with Susan and Will, and for awhile shifts back and forth between the present and the past. But when Will doesn't return home from the Civil War, she and Susan embark upon a journey to find him that takes them to New York City and Washington D.C. *The Root Cellar* is appropriate for junior high/middle school students or anyone who enjoys learning about the Civil War through a time travel adventure.

Lyon, George Ella. Paintings by Peter Catalanotto. *Cecil's Story.* Orchard Books, 1991. 28 pages, unnumbered.

Beautifully illustrated, this simple picture book could be read by early elementary students. When young Cecil's father is wounded in the Civil War, his mother must go away to bring him home. Cecil waits at home, wondering about whether his father will ever return. This book can be used effectively as a teacher read-aloud with students at any level.

Moore, Kay. Illustrated by Anni Matsick. . . . *If You Lived at the Time of the Civil War.* Scholastic, 1994. 64 pages.

One in a series for elementary students, . . . *If You Lived at the Time of the Civil War* provides basic information in a question-and-answer format. Written in a simple style, it tells what life was like from 1861 to 1865 in both the Union and the Confederacy. Each page of text is accompanied by illustrations.

Nixon, Joan Lowry. *Keeping Secrets.* Bantam Doubleday Dell, 1995. 163 pages.

Living in Missouri in 1863, eleven-year-old Peg Kelly and her fifteen-year-old brother, Danny, are caught up in a dangerous episode with Civil War spies. Through their heroic actions, important information reaches the Union troops in time, but Danny pays a terrible price. *Keeping Secrets* is part of the popular Orphan Train Adventures series written by Joan Lowry Nixon and inspired by true stories of children sent by train from the slums of New York City to find new homes in the Midwest and West between 1854 and 1929. Appropriate for upper elementary and junior high/middle school students, it is an exciting book that describes yet another aspect of the Civil War.

Reynolds, Arlene. *The Civil War Memories of Elizabeth Bacon Custer.* University of Texas Press, 1994. 181 pages

This account is reconstructed from the diaries of Libbie Custer, the wife of George Armstrong Custer. As the wife of the youngest general in the Union Army, she witnessed the war firsthand. She tells of her experiences in Washington and in the camps. This book would best be used with secondary school students.

Straubing, Harold Elk. *In Hospital and Camp: The Civil War through the Eyes of Its Doctors and Nurses.* Stackpole Books, 1993. 166 pages.

Far more of the fatalities on both sides during the Civil War were the result of disease than of wounds inflicted by the enemy. This book is a collection of the personal accounts of ten physicians and nurses of their experiences dealing with the sick and injured during the war. Most notably there is a selection from Louisa May Alcott's *Hospital Sketches* and one from *Specimen Days: The Complete Prose Works of Walt Whitman.* Secondary school students would find this an interesting account.

Whitman, Walt. *Civil War Poetry and Prose.* Dover Publications, 1995. 90 pages.

This collection of Whitman's work, edited by Candace Ward, includes the poetry that he wrote during the Civil War, selections from *Memoranda During the War*, and some of the letters that he wrote while in Washington, D.C. during the war. Although Whitman was a strong supporter of the Union, he helped both Union and Confederate soldiers who were wounded and sent to Washington. He recorded his impressions of the war and its grim realities in notebooks that he later collected and published as *Memoranda During the War*. Some of the letters and poems in this volume reflect Whitman's feelings for President Lincoln. "O Captain! My Captain!," "This Dust Was Once the Man," "When Lilacs Last in the Dooryard Bloom'd," among others, are tributes to the fallen president. Whitman's work is appropriate for secondary students and able junior high/middle school students.

7

Rebuilding the Nation

For so many on both sides of the war, the impact continued long after Lee surrendered. In the South defeat only added to the already immense suffering that many of its inhabitants experienced because so much of the fight took place on its soil. The armies of both sides had plundered farms, plantations, factories, and towns in support of their cause. The South was largely in ruins. But it was the human casualties of war that made Reconstruction as difficult as it was. The Union lost 260,000 soldiers in the Civil War; one of every five adult, white males in the South died in the war or in war-related circumstances. It is estimated that over one million men on both sides were seriously injured. A generation of young Union and Confederate men had been affected by the war: many died, many others were wounded, and virtually all the survivors were changed by what they had experienced and witnessed.

The last major casualty of the war was Abraham Lincoln, and perhaps his assassination did more to hinder the smooth transition from war to peace than any single event. As the president who led the Union throughout the war, Lincoln's goal was peace and the re-establishment of the Union. He was eager to facilitate the reentrance of the Confederate states back into the Union. The process of healing became more difficult with Lincoln's death. President Andrew Johnson tried to facilitate the reunification of the nation by pardoning Confederate soldiers who were technically traitors. Only the highest ranking officials were tried for treason.

The defeat of the South was both painful and humiliating. The aristocratic, plantation structure of the Old South was based upon certain assumptions about white superiority and the innate inferiority of black people. The social structure was shattered during the war, but many Southerners retained the assumptions. The bitterness of their defeat was frequently projected as anger and bigotry against blacks. Within a year of Lee's surrender, many Confederate veterans formed secret societies that united to become the Ku Klux Klan, a vicious white supremacist group. The Klan sought to frighten and control blacks by trying to deny their rights, frequently in violent ways.

Shortly before the war ended, the federal government had founded the Bureau of Refugees, Freedmen, and Abandoned Lands, most frequently known as the "Freedmen's Bureau." The Bureau was created to assist and protect the newly freed slaves and white refugees. The Bureau's workers played a significant role in helping the freed slaves to learn to read and write. The government, however, responded primarily to the problems in the South through legislation. In April, the Civil Rights Bill of 1866 was passed by Congress. Although this bill said that no one could be discriminated against based on his or her race, blacks were still denied the right to vote throughout the South. Two months later Congress passed the Fourteenth Amendment to the Constitution, stating that all people born in the United States were entitled to full rights as citizens. Among those rights was the right to vote; however, in most of the old Confederate states, blacks were still denied this right. There was some resistance to the Fourteenth Amendment in the South, and Congress responded by imposing military rule in place of the elected state governments. In 1867 this led to Congress passing the Reconstruction Act, which mandated military governments for the former Confederate states. Later in 1867, Congress extended the military governmental power by passing the second Reconstruction Act, thus allowing the military governments to determine who could vote. The Fourteenth Amendment was ratified in 1868.

Congress then responded to the difficulties that blacks had in being allowed to vote by passing the Fifteenth Amendment in 1869.

Learning About the Civil War

This amendment, ratified the following year, assured that black men were able to vote. While these legal provisions were being established, racial violence continued. In a pattern that continues even today, the government failed to realize that it could pass any number of laws, and even enforce them, but it could not legislate changes in beliefs and attitudes. The government kept federal troops in the South until 1877.

In this chapter we present books that address the conditions of life following the war. Families, now reunited, had to look to the future and reconstruct their lives. Most of the books in this chapter are novels that tell of young people caught in this difficult time.

Prior to Reading: Think About . . .

Young people need to do some preliminary thinking and talking to prepare them to understand what they read or what is read to them about the period after the Civil War. They need opportunities to ask questions and to raise issues and concerns. The following questions and activities can be used to prompt this discussion:

- What do you already know about conditions in this country immediately after the Civil War? Make a list.

- Do you know why the time period from after the war to 1877 is now called Reconstruction?

- What events are you familiar with that occurred during this period? Do you know what ended Reconstruction?

- What things are you interested in learning about from the time period known as the Reconstruction ? Make a list.

- What do you think life was like for ordinary people during Reconstruction? How do you think it differed in the North and South?

- What do you think life was like for former slaves after the Civil War?

- Choose a quotation taken from one of the books described in this chapter. What do you think it means? What does it make you curious about in the book?

Focus Books

**Beatty, Patricia. *Be Ever Hopeful, Hannalee.*
Troll Company, 1988. 216 pages.**

I shivered in the hot weather, thinking of the news that had drifted back to Roswell of Sherman's march through our state to Savannah. Folks claimed he left a fifty-mile-wide swath through Georgia as bare as an apple tree after a November windstorm.

"Don't look so down in the mouth, Hannalee," Davy said. "It ain't as if Atlanta's goin' to look all busted up the way it was when Sherman left. It's risin' truly fast to be a city again. It ain't a town that can be kept down long—not Atlanta." (pp. 22–23)

At a Glance ▪ In this novel, a sequel to *Turn Homeward, Hannalee* (see entry in chapter 6), the family is reunited in their rural Georgia community after the war. Hannalee's older brother decides that they should move to Atlanta and make a new start. The book is appropriate for upper elementary or junior high/middle school students.

Summary ▪ After the Civil War ended, many Southerners continued to experience difficult times. In *Be Ever Hopeful, Hannalee*, Hannalee and her family struggle to make a home in Atlanta, which is still occupied by federal soldiers. Hannalee, her mother, and two brothers all try to find work to support the family. Her brother, Davy, who lost an arm when he served in the Confederate Army, must find a new profession because he can't return to work as a carpenter. He goes into training to become a Western Union telegraph operator. Their mother finds work as a housekeeper. Even Jem, her younger brother, is hired to sell newspaper ads. Hannalee works in a shop owned by a Yankee carpetbagger and his daughter. At first, she is suspicious of them, but later she realizes that they are not her enemies. Life in Atlanta has numerous hazards, and Davy falls victim to one of the most serious ones. He is accused of murdering a federal army officer and is scheduled to be tried. Hannalee must find a way to help her brother.

Teaching Considerations ▪ *Be Ever Hopeful, Hannalee* presents a serious view of the hardships that many Southerners experienced during Reconstruction. In its characterization of an emerging society, it captures the new roles of poor whites and blacks in an area where only the landed gentry had held power prior to the war. As with any good historical novel, many of the events in this novel mirror those of the time. The book can be read independently of *Turn Homeward, Hannalee* (see entry in chapter 6); however, readers will benefit from reading the books in sequence because a number of events from the first book are alluded to in the sequel.

After Reading: Suggested Student Activities

1. Imagine that you are living in Atlanta as Hannalee did and write a letter attempting to persuade the federal army officials to do something about the living conditions. Include some suggestions in your letter.

2. Discuss whether or not you believe that the title of chapter 11, "Worse Than War," is an accurate description of the family's life in Atlanta.

3. Research the conditions under which the Confederate states were readmitted to the Union.

4. Discuss the relationship between Hannalee and Delie. How does it reflect the state of race relations during Reconstruction? How does Delie view white people in general?

Calvert, Patricia. *Bigger.* Troll Medallion, 1994. 137 pages

Size don't make a man a hero; it's his heart that accounts for that. Tyler folded the letter, feeling braver already. Papa said it didn't matter if a person was thin and small (he himself was only twelve to boot) if he had a big heart. (p. 26)

At a Glance ▪ This novel introduces readers to information about those Confederate soldiers who fled to Mexico rather than surrendering to the Union. This book is appropriate for upper elementary or junior high/middle school students.

Summary ▪ When his father left to fight for the Confederacy, Tyler was expected to be the man of the family and help his mother care for their farm and his younger brother and sister. The Civil War has ended, but Tyler is still waiting for his father to come home. The family doesn't even know if "Black Jack" Bohannon is even alive. When a stranger, on his way home from the war, tells the family that General Joseph O. Shelby refused to surrender to the Union and is leading a group of his followers to regroup in Mexico, Tyler knows where his father is. Tyler decides to go in search of his father, by walking 800 miles from their home in Missouri to Texas where Shelby and his followers will cross the Rio Grande into Mexico. His arduous journey is made easier by a traveling companion, a large dog whom he names Bigger. Bigger provides Tyler with support and friendship as he tries to find his father. In the literary tradition of a journey that takes on symbolic significance, Tyler learns about himself and his values.

Teaching Considerations ▪ The story of General Joseph O. Shelby and his followers is an interesting chapter of the Civil War. It can be used to help students recognize the ongoing impact of the Civil War, especially for many supporters of the Confederacy. Among the awards *Bigger* has received are Bank Street Book of the Year, New York Public Library "Books for the Teen Age" list, candidate for Texas Blue Bonnet Award, and candidate for Rhode Island Children's Book Award.

After Reading: Suggested Student Activities

1. Imagine that Tyler's father returns in 1867 with Shelby and write a description of the homecoming, especially focusing on Tyler's reaction to seeing his father again.

2. Research the role in the Confederacy that General Joseph O. Shelby played. Find out more about him and the time he spent in Mexico. Share your responses with the class.

3. Imagine that you are Tyler. Write a journal entry for one day of his journey.

4. Discuss the choices that Tyler freely makes and those he is forced to make along his journey. What do they reveal about his character? Which choices, if any, would you have done differently?

Hansen, Joyce. *I Thought My Soul Would Rise and Fly: The Diary of Patsy, a Freed Girl.* Scholastic, 1997. 194 pages.

He said we should not be ashamed because we had once been enslaved. He said there were black people who had done great things. (p. 68)

At a Glance ▪ As the Civil War ends, former slaves are confronted with difficult decisions about their future. Told in the form of diary entries of a newly freed girl on a South Carolina plantation, this historical novel spans the period from April 21, 1865 to January 2, 1866. It is appropriate for upper elementary and junior high/middle school students.

Summary ▪ Patsy's story is one of freedom discovered for the slaves who lived their whole lives on a South Carolina plantation. When they learn that the Civil War has ended and that they may go anywhere they wish, Patsy and her friends are faced with difficult decisions. Should they leave or should they stay on the plantation as paid employees under contract? If they stay, their former owner has promised improved conditions, wages, and a school where everyone could learn to read and write. (Literacy was a significant issue for former slaves because it was one key to a better future.)

When the promises are not kept, Patsy takes action. Although she is young, lame, shy, and stammers when she is pressed to talk, her intelligence allows her to overcome physical disabilities. Hers is the story of triumph, the triumph of her spirit and her mind. She had taught herself to read and write while listening to the lessons that were given to the niece and nephew of the plantation owner.

Since slaves were forbidden by law to learn to read and write, Patsy kept her skills a secret. In this trying situation, Patsy emerges as a remarkable, if unlikely, source of strength and direction for the former slaves who choose to stay for a time on the plantation.

Teaching Considerations ▪ Award-winning author Joyce Hansen has written a highly readable story based on the tumultuous time immediately after the Civil War. Part of the Dear America series, this is a Coretta Scott King Honor Book. It could be used in units studying the Reconstruction Period in social studies, as well as in English classes. Female readers will particularly respond to Patsy and her courage.

After Reading: Suggested Student Activities

1. Identify a value that is important to Patsy. Then create a Values map with evidence from the book to support the importance of this value for her. (Teacher's Note: See guidelines in chapter 1 for this strategy.)

2. The book ends on January 2, 1866 when Patsy makes the significant decision to leave the plantation. Write a series of diary entries that reveal what her life is like after that.

3. Patsy experiences many changes during her life. Develop a character portrait that demonstrates some of these changes. (Teacher's Note: See guidelines in chapter 1 for this strategy.)

4. Choose an event from this book to dramatize. Prepare it with some of your classmates and then present it to your entire class.

Hansen, Joyce. *Out from This Place.*
Avon Camelot Books, 1988. 135 pages.

"And Easter, you run the school until the new teacher comes. You can do it."

"I can't. I don't know too much my ownself."

"You can. You know how to teach those little ones their letters and numbers."

Learning About the Civil War

"But what about the geography and the arithmetic and the history and . . ."

Miss Grantley smiled slightly. "Just teach what you know, and that's plenty. One day you'll come to the school in Philadelphia. Promise, Easter." Before Easter could say anything, however, Miss Grantley said, "No. That's not fair, to make you promise such a thing now. Think about coming to the school. Will you promise to do that?' The teacher took off her glasses and wiped her eyes again.

Easter nodded, having to force back tears herself. "I promise," she barely whispered. (pp. 87–88)

At a Glance ▪ This novel, a sequel to *Which Way Freedom?*, is Easter's story as she seeks to make a life after slavery. This book can be used appropriately with junior high/middle school students. It also can be read independently of *Which Way Freedom?* (see entry in chapter 3); however, together they present a vivid picture of conditions for African Americans during the waning days of slavery and the early days of freedom.

Summary ▪ With freedom in sight, Easter plans to return to the plantation where she grew up. The plantation is the only "home" she has ever known. When she and Obi left, they were unable to take their friend, Jason, the remaining slave on the plantation, with them. Obi, Easter, and Jason are "family" to one another although they are not related by blood. Obi is fighting with the Union forces, but Easter wants to go back to find Jason. For Jason, she is willing to risk capture.

Once Easter rescues Jason from his owner, they join with other slaves to escape to territory held by the Yankees. There the soldiers hire them to work on a plantation with other escaped slaves. For Easter, her mission is only partially successful. While she and Jason are reunited, the family is incomplete without Obi. She is convinced that she must wait until the war is over to search for Obi. One inducement to staying is that she is promised that she can learn to read and write. When a school is started for the former slaves, Easter becomes a prize student and is asked to be the acting teacher when the regular one leaves. Living in an all-black community until the end of the war, the members work hard and plan for the future in which they are led to believe that the land will be theirs. Promises are not always kept and the community has to make decisions about the future as the war ends.

Teaching Considerations ▪ This book is fiction, but it is grounded in actual events from the Civil War and the early days of Reconstruction. While the major part of this book takes place during the war, the escape to the Williams plantation begins a new life for the former slaves. Rayford's willingness to teach Easter to read during that time gives her the tools to free her mind and to be ready for a positive role in the postwar black society. An overview of the major events in *Which Way Freedom?* are in the prologue and provide background for readers unfamiliar with that book.

After Reading: Suggested Student Activities

1. Discuss the role of the family as it is presented in this book.

2. Select one character from this book and do a character portrait. (Teacher's Note: See guidelines in chapter 1 for this strategy.)

3. Discuss the characteristics and actions of Easter that make her such a powerful and significant survivor.

4. Research the all-black communities that developed after the war. Present your findings to the members of your class.

Mettger, Zak. *Reconstruction: America After the Civil War.* Lodestar, 1994. 122 pages.

Sidney Andrew, a white journalist from the North, traveled through South Carolina, North Carolina, and Georgia for several months after the end of the war, talking with hundreds of former slaves and Confederates. He observed that "The whites seem wholly unable to comprehend that freedom for the Negro means the same thing as freedom for them . . . they appear to believe that they still have the right to exercise over him the old control." (p. 34)

At a Glance ▪ Mettger provides a comprehensive view of the turbulent period following the Civil War, accompanied by vintage photographs, drawings, and personal vignettes. *Reconstruction: America After the Civil War* is part of the Young Readers' History of the Civil War series and is appropriate for junior high/middle school students and able elementary students.

Summary ▪ Mettger describes the major social, economic, and political changes in the South from the end of the Civil War in 1865 through the disputed national presidential election of 1877. Some information is also provided about changes in the North during this same time period, and the last chapter of the book briefly describes significant events until the end of the century. Some of the many topics covered include the quest for land, education, and suffrage by blacks; the rise of black churches; the dire economic straits of virtually everyone in the South; the work of the Freedmen's Bureau; the infamous Black Codes; and the "night riders." Mettger aptly summarizes this period of history following the Civil War: "Reconstruction was a period of great hope and crushing disappointment. Freedom did not bring former slaves the equality they had hoped for. And peace did not return the former Confederate states to their cherished way of life. But important progress *was* made during Reconstruction, progress that helped lay the groundwork for momentous changes in American life" (p.110).

Teaching Considerations ▪ The political conditions during the Reconstruction were complex, and they are frequently confusing, even to adults. Students will need help to sort it out and understand what occurred and why. Also, the photographs and descriptions of the terrible, senseless violence perpetuated by racists and groups such as the Ku Klux Klan can be disturbing and upsetting to readers of all ages. Students may need opportunities to ask further questions and express their feelings. In several instances, Mettger uses mild profanity and the word "nigger" when quoting speakers from the era. While "nigger' is used in a derogatory manner, the quotations are essential to understanding the attitudes during this period, i.e., "There is no law against killing niggers & I will kill every d———d one I have if they do not obey me and work just as they did before the war" (p. 62). While this terminology should not act as a deterrent to using this fine book, care must be taken to help students understand the times and context in which it was spoken.

After Reading: Suggested Student Activities

1. As you read this book, keep a chart that compares and contrasts the changes black and white people in the South experienced after the Civil War. (Teacher's Note: See guidelines in chapter 1 for this strategy.)

2. Analyze the importance of education, church, and owning their own land to African Americans in the South during Reconstruction.

3. Construct a timeline that shows the attitudes of the people in the North toward the former Confederacy between 1865 and 1877.

4. When the Civil War ended, there were some cases of social and economic gains for the newly freed blacks; however, many still lived in poverty and fear. The success of a few fueled the fires of bigotry and created new social and economic problems. Trace how the problems that were allowed to fester during Reconstruction led to the Civil Rights movement of the 1960s.

Paulsen, Gary. *Sarny: A Life Remembered.* Delacorte, 1997. 180 pages.

"Here," he said. "You're free now—on your own."

"Thank you." He meant free of the chain but I took it for the long road, free now, free. We were all free. Could walk where we wanted to walk, be where we wanted to be.

Free.

I didn't stand long. There were those who stood, looking, wondering. I saw them later. Those who had used the chains for bracing, leaned against slavery to give them strength. Suddenly the brace was gone and some stood, wondering where to turn, how to live. (p. 25)

At a Glance ▪ This novel is a continuation of Sarny's story, which was begun in *Nightjohn* (see entry in chapter 3). The story begins with the waning days of slavery and plantation life. Sarny has grown into a young woman, widowed with two young children. When her children are sold, just before the end of the Civil War, finding them becomes the focus for Sarny's life. The story traces her search for the children and continues through the remainder of her life until 1930, when she is "writing her memoir," this book. While the book is at a fairly easy reading level, the social conditions demand relatively sophisticated junior high/middle school readers.

Summary ▪ As a ninety-four-year-old woman, Sarny looks back at her life and the impact that two remarkable people had on her by opening doors for her to learn and grow. These people were Nightjohn, her fellow slave, who defied the law and taught her to read when she was just a girl on the plantation, and Miss Laura, her friend, employer, and benefactor.

A week before the Union troops liberate Sarny and the others on her plantation, her owner sold her two young children. When freedom came, her only interest is to find them. She found their records which said they had been sold to a man in New Orleans. She has no idea where New Orleans is but she and Lucy, one of the others from the plantation, begin the 350-mile trip on foot, asking directions as they go along. Later they find a wheelbarrow to carry the supplies they forage along the way. They also rescue a young white boy whose family had been slaughtered on their plantation. New Orleans is still held by the Confederates when their journey begins, and as they travel further South, they encounter more and more soldiers. At one point they are caught in a skirmish between the Union and Confederate forces. Sarny and Lucy stay with four of the Union soldiers who are fatally wounded to comfort them in their last hours.

Their journey becomes easier when a carriage comes along driven by a black man. Its passenger is the "prettiest white woman" Sarny has ever seen. The woman, Miss Laura, has connections with powerful men in the military and in politics. She knows the man who had bought Sarny's children and develops a plan to help get them back. Miss Laura gives Sarny the run of her library, and she also finds more books to help her learn. Sarny even runs a school when she isn't working for Miss Laura. Teaching is a calling that Sarny follows for the rest of her life.

Teaching Considerations ▪ This novel is the sequel to *Nightjohn*, Paulsen's award-winning story, but it can be read independently. Three scenes in this novel are graphic: the battlefield scene; the scene where Sarny and Lucy find the slaughtered bodies at the plantation; and the scene when Sarny's husband is taken by members of the Ku Klux Klan. Additionally, the allusions to Miss Laura's means of support will need to be addressed.

After Reading: Suggested Student Activities

1. Discuss why reading and writing was so important to former slaves.

2. Throughout her life, Sarny had lots of experiences and met lots of people. In your journal, describe why she credited Nightjohn and Miss Laura with having the greatest impact on her.

3. What were conditions like for blacks in New Orleans during Reconstruction? Was this typical, according to your research about the period? Why or why not?

4. From the earliest days of her childhood when she learned to read, Sarny showed courage and determination. What do you believe was her major accomplishment? Why?

Reeder, Carolyn. *Shades of Gray.* Avon Books, 1989. 165 pages.

"I don't want to hear any more about traitors, either. Your uncle wasn't a traitor. He didn't help the Yankees, he just didn't fight them. I don't approve of that any more than you do, Will, but the war's over. It's time to forget the bitterness." (p. 2)

At a Glance ▪ Will Page, son of a Confederate cavalry officer, is left an orphan by the Civil War. Angry and bitter, he is sent to live with his uncle, who refused to fight in the war. Eventually he comes to understand his uncle's courage and in the process, learns some important lessons about life. *Shades of Gray* is appropriate for junior high/middle school students and upper elementary students who are given help to understand the complexity of the moral issues in the book.

Summary ▪ The Civil War is over, but life does not easily or readily return to normal for many families. For Will Page, age twelve, the losses are especially devastating. In a family devoted to the Confederate cause, his brother and father were killed by Yankees, and his sisters and mother died of disease and grief. Will is sent to live with relatives in Virginia who were estranged from his family because, although they were Southerners, they chose not to fight. Will considers his Uncle Jed a coward and traitor, and is determined not to like him or understand his position about the war. He is shocked, therefore, when he learns how much his Uncle Jed's family also suffered during the war and how difficult life continues to be even though the war is over. As time goes by, Will begins to respect and admire his uncle, until the family lets a wounded Yankee soldier, Jim, stay with them until he is well enough to travel. Will is furious because he hates all Yankees; but eventually, through his association with Jim and other personal experiences, he comes to question his belief that all Yankee soldiers were wicked and all Rebel soldiers acted honorably. Will must wrestle with complex and painful feelings while he learns that there are many different kinds of courage and there is no one simple way of understanding how people acted during the Civil War.

Teaching Considerations ▪ Reeder's historical novel is excellent for helping students to understand the complexities of the multiple perspectives surrounding the Civil War, the divided loyalties within families and communities, and the heavy social and economic costs of the war. Some of its underlying themes have to do with making difficult choices and learning to accept loss. Among the awards it has received are ALA Notable Book, Scott O'Dell Award for Historical Fiction, Jefferson Cup award, and Bank Street College award.

After Reading: Suggested Student Activities

1. Create a visual representation that illustrates how Will Page changed during this story. Then write a summary explaining how and why he changed.

2. One of the themes in this book is about making difficult choices. Select three examples and explain each choice and its consequences.

3. Some people do not realize how difficult life was for many families after the Civil War. Using examples from this book, write a letter to a friend or relative describing what life was like as if you were living during that time.

4. This book presents an excellent example of illusion versus reality. Will is willing and even eager to see things on a superficial level of "us and them." How does his perspective change throughout the book? What does this tell us about his character?

5. Identify and discuss the different points of view about the war and how those perspectives were disruptive to Will's immediate and extended families.

Robinet, Harriette. *Children of the Fire.* Atheneum, 1991. 134 pages.

The well-dressed mother took one glance at Hallelujah and snatched her child away. She scolded, "Don't you know what she is? She's a nigger. You shouldn't talk to niggers!" (p. 42)

At a Glance ▪ In a story set in Chicago six years after the Civil War, during the Great Chicago Fire, eleven-year-old Hallelujah struggles to understand who she is and how to make a life for herself. This book is appropriate for upper elementary and some junior high/middle school students.

Summary ▪ An orphan, Hallelujah lives in Chicago with the LaSalles. Before she died, Hallelujah's mother escaped on the Underground Railroad with her children. It is now 1871 and Chicago is a melting pot of races and nationalities, including a large number of new immigrants from Europe and former slaves from the South. Fires are almost a daily occurrence, economic conditions are difficult for many immigrants, and black and white struggle to learn how to live together in the post-Civil War era. Hallelujah is an implusive, self-centered young girl who is ashamed of being an orphan. During the three days of the Great Fire, she has a number of dangerous adventures that help her to grow up and to come to accept herself and value others.

Teaching Considerations ▪ This book can be used to help students learn about both living conditions after the Civil War and the Great Chicago Fire. Chicago was a bustling city filled with people of many nationalities and races when on October 8, 1871, the fateful fire broke out that almost destroyed the city. It raged for three days, killing over 300 people, and leaving 100,000 homeless. "In sad clusters, fathers, mothers, and children stood knee-deep in the lake facing the burning city. Rich families. Colored families. Poor families. Working people families. Business people families. Immigrant families. Danger threatened all equally (p. 56)." The word "nigger" is used within the context of the time period in which the story is set. Among the awards *Children of the Fire* has received are Friends of American Writers Award and Notable Children's Trade Book in the Field of Social Studies.

After Reading: Suggested Student Activities

1. Create a class mural that depicts the experiences that Hallelujah had during the three days of the Great Chicago Fire.

2. Develop a "before and after" poster of Hallelujah that describes what she was like before the fire and how she changed.

3. Hallelujah had many dangerous and exciting experiences during the fire. Select one of them and dramatize with some of your classmates.

4. Hallelujah and some of the other children were very resourceful after the fire. Write the next chapter in their lives.

Smith, Carter, editor. *One Nation Again: A Sourcebook on the Civil War*. Millbrook Press, 1993. 96 pages.

Another troubling legacy of the war was drug dependency. Union surgeons used morphine and other opiates as painkillers, not fully understanding the dangers of chemical addiction. As a result, many men left the service with drug habits. Morphine use among veterans was so common in parts of the North that it was labeled the "soldier's disease." Addiction was less of a problem in the South: Ill-equipped Confederate hospitals rarely offered more than ether or a slug of raw whiskey to wounded soldiers. (p. 36)

At a Glance ▪ This book, part of the American Albums from the Collections of the Library of Congress, covers the years from 1865 to 1877. The series could be read by many elementary students as well as junior high/middle school students. Secondary school students looking for a succinct overview would also find these books useful.

Summary ▪ This book, replete with photographs, drawings, and paintings, begins with introductory material and a map that shows the United States during this time period. A timeline of major events follows, divided into three parallel strands: World History, American History and Culture, and Reconstruction. The primary portion of the book is divided into two sections. The first, "With Malice Toward None," describes Washington, D.C. in 1865; Lincoln's assassination and the aftermath; the return home of the soldiers in both the North and South; and the initial attempts to help those freed from slavery. The second part, "Reconstruction," describes the political events and social turmoil until the election of Hayes and the withdrawal of troops from the South.

Teaching Considerations ▪ The subtitle, "A Sourcebook on the Civil War," accurately identifies this book's value to teachers and students alike. While none of the subjects are treated in-depth, their brevity and conciseness can be used to provide an overview, introduce a specific topic, or create interest and arouse curiosity about a topic.

After Reading: Suggested Student Activities

1. Make a list of ideas that you had about the Reconstruction prior to reading this book. Then next to each item on the list record the new information that you have learned. What have you learned about this period that surprises you?

2. Select a key political or social decision that was made during this period. Illustrate the short-term and long-term effects and implications through a series of drawings or cartoons that specifically reflect the decision's impact.

3. Discuss with your class the various factors that contributed to the social and political problems and failures during the Reconstruction.

4. In cooperative learning groups, select an event from the book as the basis for an in-depth study. Building on the information that the group has developed, formulate a debate question on the issue and have members of the group take either a pro or con position. Present your debate before the rest of the class.

More Books

Armstrong, Jennifer M. *Mary Mehan Awake*. Knopf, 1997. 119 pages.

In this sequel to *The Dreams of Mairhe Mehan,* the war has ended and Mary must make a life for herself. She is suffering from her brother's death in battle and her father's return to Ireland. Mary is also numbed by the suffering she witnessed helping the wounded. Her friend and mentor, Walt Whitman, helps her to find a position assisting a naturalist in his work. It is through this new life that Mary's awakening begins.

Armstrong, Jennifer M. *Steal Away*. Orchard Books, 1992. 207 pages.

After hearing from her old friend, Bethlehem, Susannah and her granddaughter Mary travel to Toronto for a farewell meeting with her old friend in 1896. The story of their reunion and the circumstances of their forty-year friendship frames the story which focuses on the introspective reflections of two old friends as they meet for the last time. Bethlehem, a teacher, is ill and being cared for by Free, one of her students, but she and Susannah want their story to be told. The story within the story tells of Susannah, orphaned at thirteen, who is forced to leave New England and live with relatives in Virginia. Although she is opposed to slavery, her relatives "give" her Bethlehem. Susannah is upset about the gift and never accepts her role as the mistress of another person. Life in the South is intolerable for her and she devises a plot to escape and return to Vermont. She decides to take Bethlehem with her to freedom. The story they tell is of their escape and the evolution of their friendship, and it is recorded by Mary and Free. The story of the old friends is juxtaposed with the growing relationship between the two young girls. Their friendship reflects the uneasy racial conditions in the late nineteenth century.

The audience for this book may be limited primarily to middle school girls. While the adventure the girls undertake and the courage they display might appeal to males, the story is primarily about a growing sense of friendship. The shift in time periods and in narrators may be troublesome for unsophisticated readers who will need some pre-reading assistance.

Duey, Kathleen. *American Diary: Emma Eileen Grove, Mississippi, 1865.* Aladdin Paperbacks, 1996. 142 pages.

The Civil War has ended, their mother has died, and their father is still missing, and Emma, her older brother, and younger sister must travel up the Mississippi River to a new home. They board a paddle-wheel steamboat, the *Sultana,* headed for their uncle's home in St. Louis. The steamer is dangerously overloaded with Union soldiers who have been released from Confederate prisons and are headed home. Emma is angry with the Yankees and resents that they are on the boat. Her brother even gets into a fight with one of them. When they dock in Memphis, her brother Randall gets off the boat to see the town and misses it when it departs. Emma and Claire are then left on their own when the boat is ripped by an explosion and catches fire.

Gaines, Ernest J. *The Autobiography of Miss Jane Pittman*. Bantam Books, 1971. 246 pages.

This novel, considered by many to be a contemporary classic, tells the courageous and inspiring story of the legendary Miss Jane Pittman. While actually fiction, it is written as the tape-recorded recollections of a black woman, born a slave, who lived 110 years. During those years she experienced the Civil War, the Reconstruction and its bitter aftermath, and the twentieth century through the black militancy movement of the 1960s. Divided into four parts, the book puts a human face on the tumultuous changes former slaves encountered in the ensuing decades after the Civil War and is appropriate for secondary students.

Hakim, Joy. *Reconstruction and Reform*. Oxford University Press, 1994. 192 pages.

This book, part of the ten-volume A History of US series intended for upper elementary and junior high/middle school students, will also be useful for some high school students. Writing in a conversational, almost chatty style, Hakim presents a wealth of information about the post-Civil War era in our nation's history. Every page of text is accompanied by some form of visual aid, such as vintage photographs, cartoons, and posters. The author describes the people and the social, economic, and political events and conditions of this period in a simple manner with key words defined throughout the text and a chronology of key events from 1865 to 1896 at the end of the book.

Myers, Walter Dean. *The Glory Field*. Scholastic, 1994. 375 pages.

In this novel, Walter Dean Myers presents a family saga through four generations, with an acknowledgment to Muhammad Bilal, their African ancestor taken in slavery from his home and brought to South Carolina. The story tells of life on the Live Oak Plantation on Curry Island, South Carolina, where Moses and Saran are slaves. The owners are anxious because it is 1864 and many slaves have run away from their plantations to the protection of the Union Army. Moses's son, Lem, and his Uncle Joshua both run off, but Lem is caught. Young Lizzy helps Lem to escape, and Joshua comes back for him; then all three run away. Hunted by men with whips and tracking dogs, and separated from Joshua again, young Lem and Lizzie are almost captured, but they arrive in a Union camp where they are safe. Reunited with Joshua, Lem accepts the chance to fight for the Union Army in a new colored regiment. After the Civil War, it is Muhammad Bilal's descendants who are given a parcel of eight acres of land on Curry Island by the Union troops. This was land that the family worked as slaves. When it becomes theirs, all Moses can say is "Glory," and so the land becomes the Glory Field. It is their love of the land and their sense of ownership that sustain the family through numerous hardships and difficulties down through the generations. The Glory Field was the family's heritage. This book is appropriate for junior high/middle school and secondary students.

Wright, Courtni C. Illustrated by Gershom Griffith. *Wagon Train: A Family Goes West in 1865*. Holiday House, 1997. 30 pages, unnumbered.

This picture book tells the story of a former slave family traveling from their old plantation home in Virginia to a new life in California as part of a caravan of twelve covered wagons. The journey is long and filled with hardships and dangers, but the family, including a small baby and elderly grandparents, endures. This book could be used to introduce elementary students to one of the ways African Americans sought to make new lives when the war ended.

8

Resources

There are many ways to help young people learn about the Civil War. While literature is the primary focus of this book, this chapter provides a sampling of information about other resources that can be used effectively in conjunction with the literature described in the preceding chapters. Indeed, we believe that learning is most effective when young people are given a variety of approaches and multiple opportunities to experience content. This chapter is organized into four major categories: media; web sites; selected museums and historical sites; and lesson plans, posters, photographs, and other teaching aids. Because of the overwhelming number of available resources, we have selected only a few to feature within each category.

Media

Audio Recordings

- *American History Through Narration and Song.* Boxed set of "Civil War Songs" includes historical narration and notes on songs; upper elementary through secondary school.

- *General Robert E. Lee at the Battle of Gettysburg.* A review and analysis of the battle by Civil War battlefield study leader Ed Bearss; secondary school.

- *Legacies: An Audio Cassette on the History of Women and the Family in America.* Provides information about women in different periods of our history, including the Civil War; includes stories, diary excerpts, and songs; junior high/middle school and secondary school.

- *Lincoln Live.* Portrayal of Lincoln including his humor and Gettysburg Address; upper elementary and junior high/middle school.

- *Rebel in the Woods: Civil War Songs from the Western Border.* Presents traditional music and songs, including those from the homefront and those from the battlefields; upper elementary through secondary school.

- *Two Strategies for Victory: Sherman and the Civil War.* Discussion and description by noted historian James McPherson; secondary school.

- *Why Married Soldiers Fought in the Civil War.* Historian James McPherson analyzes motivation of Civil War soldiers based on their letters and private diaries; secondary school.

Films, Laserdiscs, and Video

- *Abraham Lincoln.* Provides a description of this complex president narrated by prominent historian James McPherson; includes period music, photographs, and paintings. Color; 35 minutes; junior high/middle school and secondary school.

- *Abraham Lincoln: The Great Emancipator.* A survey of Lincoln's life, including quotations and photographs. Color and black-and-white; 15 minutes; junior high/middle school and secondary school.

- *America Divided: The Civil War and Reconstruction.* Overview of this historical time period with an emphasis on political and economic issues that divided the nation. Color; 60 minutes; upper elementary through junior high/middle school.

- *Andersonville Trial.* Award-winning drama directed by George C. Scott raises significant political and moral questions related to this infamous Civil War P.O.W. camp. Color; 150 minutes; secondary school.

- *Antietam Visit.* Reenactment of this battle framed by a historical perspective of the Civil War. Color; 27 minutes; junior high/middle school and secondary school.

- *Black Fugitive.* Provides a succinct history of slavery in the U.S. followed by a dramatization of runaway slaves and the Underground Railroad; information is also provided about free slaves who settled in Canada. Color; upper elementary through secondary school.

- *Ken Burns's Civil War* (PBS). Honored as the most comprehensive accounting of the Civil War period based on diaries, archive stills, and artifacts from the period. Color and black-and-white; 11 hours; junior high/middle school and secondary school.

- *The Civil War.* Well-researched overview narrated by Bruce Catton. 35 minutes; secondary school.

- *Civil War Diary.* Based on Irene Hunt's award-winning novel *Across Five Aprils.* Color; 82 minutes; upper elementary and junior high/middle school.

- *Civil War: The Fiery Trail.* Documentary overview, including ample use of maps, photographs, and period music. Color and black-and-white; 35 minutes; junior high/middle school and secondary school.

- *The Civil War General Series.* Chronicles the lives of Robert E. Lee, Stonewall Jackson, and Ulysses S. Grant. Color; 30 minutes each; secondary school.

- *The Civil War: National Park and Monument Series.* Overview of this era beginning with a short introduction to slavery and ending with Lincoln's assassination. Black-and-white; 30 minutes; upper elementary through junior high/middle school.

- *The Civil War: Two Views.* Multimedia kit helping students to understand the impact of the war on both the North and the South. Color; junior high/middle school and secondary school.

- *The Divided Union: The Story of the American Civil War, 1861–1865.* Comprehensive examination of the period combines reenactments, excerpts from diaries and letters, archival photographs, paintings and analyses by Civil War scholars. Laserdisc set; 6 hours; secondary school.

- *The Events Which Led to the Emancipation Proclamation.* Overview of the issues and events leading to Lincoln issuing the Emancipation Proclamation. Color and black-and-white; 15 minutes; junior high/middle school and secondary school.

- *Harriet Tubman and the Underground Railroad.* Part of the Walter Cronkite CBS "You Are There" series, this features an escape led by Tubman and focuses on the Fugitive Slave Law and the attempts to enforce or circumvent it. Color; 22 minutes; upper elementary and junior high/middle school.

- *Firebell in the Night.* Documentary created, written, and narrated by Alistair Cooke explores the roots of the Civil War and the still unresolved racial conflicts in our society. Color; 52 minutes; secondary school.

- *Freedom Road.* Tells the story of a former slave during Reconstruction who educates himself and is finally elected to the U.S. Senate; based on the novel by Howard Fast. Color; 186 minutes; secondary school.

- *From These Honored Dead.* A reading of the Gettysburg Address framed by background of both the battle and the speech. Color; 13 minutes; upper elementary through secondary school.

- *Gettysburg: The Turning Point.* Describes and examines this historic battle and its consequences. Color and black-and-white; 15 minutes; junior high/middle school and secondary school.

Learning About the Civil War

- *Gettysburg: The Video History of the Civil War.* Combines reenactment with archival photographs, paintings, and drawings to create a sense of being there for the viewer. Color; 40 minutes; junior high/ middle school and secondary school.

- *Gettysburg.* This film, starring Jeff Daniels as Joshua Chamberlain, covers the events leading to the Battle of Gettysburg, but its focus is on the three-day battle. Color; 254 minutes; secondary school.

- *Glory.* This film traces the experiences of the first black company based on letters of Col. Robert G. Shaw, the commander. Color; 122 minutes; junior high/middle school and secondary school.

- *Ironclads: The Monitor and the Merrimac.* Retells the historic battle and provides the story behind the design and construction of these battleships; also provides underwater footage of the *Monitor.* Color; 30 minutes; secondary school.

- *Lincoln* (PBS). Four-part series on Lincoln and the Civil War; includes educational resource packet. Junior high/middle school and secondary school.

- *Lincoln's Assassination: The Reconstruction of a Conspiracy.* Presents the people involved in and the events of Lincoln's assassination; video enhanced by still photographs and illustrations from the period. Color and black-and-white; 20 minutes; junior high/middle school and secondary school.

- *Lincoln's Gettysburg Address.* Broad background of the events and conditions that led up to the Battle of Gettysburg and Lincoln's Address. Concludes with a reading of the Address by Charleton Heston. Black-and-white and color; 15 minutes; junior high/ middle school and secondary school.

- *The Nomination of Abraham Lincoln.* One of the Walter Cronkite CBS "You Are There" series, this presents the May 1860 Republican party nominating convention. Color; 22 minutes; upper elementary and junior high/middle school.

- *Reconstruction.* Portrays and examines the issues, events, and people of this time; draws upon folk songs, drawings, political cartoons, and photographs from the period. Black-and-white; 35 minutes; secondary school.

- *The Reconstruction of the South: Where Historians Disagree.* Provides several interpretations of the impact and importance of Reconstruction, as well as its significance and implications. Color; secondary school.

- *The Red Badge of Courage.* Realistic film of a young soldier's experiences in the Civil War based on Stephen Crane's novel. Black-and-white; 70 minutes; secondary school.

- *Uncle Tom's Cabin.* A condensed version from the 1852 dramatization of Beecher's historic novel. Color; 55 minutes; secondary school.

- *War Between the States.* Two-part program tracing the events and issues leading up to the Civil War, and then an overview of the war, Lincoln's presidency, and the decision to issue the Emancipation Proclamation. Color; 60 minutes; junior high/middle school and secondary school.

Simulations and Computer Software

- *Civil War.* Educational strategy game with battlefield tactics and political intrigue; secondary school.
  http://www.entrex.org

- *Civil War II: Unconditional Surrender.* Recreates events of the war from several different perspectives; encourages independent thinking and strategic planning; secondary school.
  http://www.entrex.org

- *Civil War Encyclopedia.* Provides wealth of information on the issues, people, and battles; secondary school.
  http://www.entrex.org

- *Civil War Keyword.* Apple simulation using Civil War clues to guess mystery words; secondary school.

- *Battle of Gettysburg.* The movie of the Battle of Gettysburg can be viewed on the most frequently used Web browsers, including Netscape Navigator. SHOCKWAVE Movies. www.icorps.com/shockex.htm

- *Lincoln's Decisions: Simulation.* Students gain an in-depth understanding of the problems of the Civil War period as they are challenged to view the major decisions that confronted Abraham Lincoln and to put themselves in his place by making decisions that he faced; junior high/middle school.

- *United States Civil War.* Interactive Living History Adventure; secondary school. http://www.uscivilwar.com/uscwhp2.cfm

Web Sites

Listed below are web site addresses that were available at the time of publication. Please be aware that the state of the technology is such that web addresses change frequently. The new addresses, however, usually are made available at the previous site for a limited period of time.

- American Civil War Home Page http://cobweb.utcc.utk.edu/~hoemann/cwarhp.html

- Causes of the Civil War This site provides a number of useful documents to give a background understanding of the Civil War. It has many links to political documents, secession documents, speeches, and correspondence, among other documents from and about the period. http://members.aol.com/jfepperson/causes.html

- Civil War Sites http://repository.gmu.edu

- Duke University: Civil War Women This site provides the papers of women such as Rose O'Neal Greenhow, Alice Williamson, and Sarah E. Thompson and attests

to the role of women both as observers of an participants in the war.
http://scriptorium.lib.duke.edu/collections/civil-war-women.html

- Duke University Special Collections Library on Slavery
  Online resources included in "Slave Voices" cover slave trade, plantation life, impact of freedom, among other implications of slavery.
  http://scriptorium.lib.duke.edu/slavery/

- Gettysburg Address
  http://lcweb.loc.gov/exhibits/G.Address/ga.html

- Gopher
  For primary sources, book reviews, reference tools, and conference announcements.
  gopher://gopher.uic.edu/11/research/history/hnexx/40227000

- Lincoln Links
  Many sites about Abraham Lincoln are listed here.
  http://www.netins.net/showcase/creative/lincoln/links.htm

- Museum of African Slavery
  http://www3.la.psu.edu/~plarson/smuseum/

- Slave Narratives
  These excerpts of forty-six narratives edited by Steven Mintz of the University of Houston are organized as follows to reflect life in slavery: enslavement, the Middle Passage, arrival, conditions of life, childhood, family, religion, punishment, resistance, flight, and emancipation.
  http://vi.uh.edu/pages/mintz/primary.htm

- United States Civil War Center
  This is the one of the most comprehensive sites on the internet. It includes links to over 2,100 sites about the Civil War.
  http://www.cwc.lsu.edu

- University of Virginia Valley of the Shadow
  http://jefferson.village.virginia.edu/vshadow2/

Selected Museums and Historical Sites

- Abraham Lincoln Birthplace National Historic Site
  Route 31E
  Hodgenville, KY 42748
  (502) 358-3137
  http://www.nationalparks.org/guide/parks/abraham-linc-1776.htm

- African-American Civil War Memorial
  10th and U St., N.W.
  Washington, D.C.
  (888) 648-USCT
  http://www.itd.nps.gov/cwss/dcmem.html

- Antietam National Battlefield
  P.O. Box 158
  Sharpsburg, MD 21782
  (301) 432-5124
  http://www.nps.gov.anti

- Andersonville National Historic Site
  Route 49, Box 800
  Andersonville, GA 31711
  (912) 924-0343
  http://www.nps.gov/ande

- Appomattox Court House National Historical Park
  P.O. Box 218
  Appomattox, VA 24522
  (804) 352-8987
  http://www.nps.gov/apco

- Arlington House, The Robert E. Lee Memorial
  c/o George Washington Memorial Parkway
  Turkey Run Park
  McLean, VA 22101
  (703) 557-0613
  http://www.nps.gov/arho

- Boston African-American National Historic Site
  46 Joy Street
  Boston, MA 02114
  (617) 742-5415
  http://www.nps.gov/boaf

- Frederick Douglass National Historical Site
  1411 W Street, S.E.
  Washington, D.C. 20020-4813
  (202) 426-5961
  http://www.nps.gov/ncro/naces/freddoug.html

- Chickamauga & Chattanooga National Military Park
  P.O. Box 2128
  3370 Lafayette Road
  Fort Oglethorpe, GA 36742
  (706) 866-9241
  http://ngeorgia.com/site/chickamauganmp.shtm/

- Ford's Theatre National Historic Site
  511 10th Street, N.W.
  Washington, D.C. 20004
  (202) 426-6924
  http://www.nps.gov/foth

- Fort Sumter National Monument
  1214 Middle Street
  Sullivan's Island, SC 29482
  (803) 883-3123
  http://www.nps.gov/fosu

- Fredericksburg & Spotsylvania County
  Battlefield Memorial National Military Park
  1013 Lafayette Boulevard
  Fredericksburg, VA
  (703) 373-6122
  http://www.nps.gov/frsp

- General Grant National Memorial
  Riverside Drive and 122nd Street
  New York City, NY 10003

(212) 666-1640
http://www.nps.gov/gegr

- Gettysburg National Military Park
Gettysburg, PA
(717) 334-1124
http://www.nps.gov/gett

- Harpers Ferry National Historical Park
P.O. Box 65
Harpers Ferry, WV 25425
(304) 535-6298
http://www.nps.gov/hafe

- Lincoln Boyhood National Memorial
(and Lincoln State Park)
P.O. Box 1816
Lincoln City, IN
(812) 937-4757
http://www.nps.gov/libo

- Lincoln Home National Historic Site
413 South 8th Street
Springfield, IL 62701-1905
(217) 492-4241
http://www.nps.gov/liho

- Lincoln Memorial
900 Ohio Drive, S.W.
Washington, D.C.
(202) 426-6841
http://www.nps.gov/linc

- Manassas National Battlefield Park
12521 Lee Highway
Manassas, VA 20109-2005
(703) 754-1861
http://www.nps.govmana

- National Museum of Civil War Medicine
48 E. Patrick Street

Frederick, MD 21705
(301) 695-1864
http://www.nps.gov/med.org

- Shiloh National Military Park
  Route 1, Box 9
  Shiloh, TN 38376
  (901) 689-5275
  http://www.nps.gov/shil

- Vicksburg National Military Park
  3201 Clay Street
  Vicksburg, MS 39180
  (601) 636-0583
  http://www.nps.gov/vick

- Wilson's Creek National Battlefield
  424 W. Farm Road 182
  Republic, MO 65738
  (417) 732-2662
  http://www.nps.gov/wicr

Lesson Plans, Posters, Photographs, and Other Teaching Aids

American Civilization Lesson Plans and Units
Civil War lesson plans are available for grades 2 and 5.
http://www.trinity.edu/departments/education/core/lessons
/amerplans.htm

Amistad Site
This site combines information from the National Archives and
adds curricular connections and teaching activities.
http://www.nara.gov/education/teaching/amistad
/teach.html

Civil War for Buffs
Cyber course for secondary school students and adults.
http://cyberschool.4j.lane.edu/CivilWar/CWFB.html

Civil War Generals

Posters of fifteen Union Army generals and fifteen Confederate generals with accompanying booklet that provides background information about their careers. Perfection Form.

The Civil War News

Monthly paper with information about events, national parks, reenactments, and other areas of interest.
(800) 222-1861

Civil War Times Illustrated

Magazine for Civil War aficionados with largest circulation.
Cowles Magazines
2245 Kohn Rd., P.O. Box 8200
Harrisburg, PA 17105-8200
www.thehistorynet.com/CivilWarTimes/

Civil War Poster

Double-sided poster with a chronology of the major events of the Civil War on one side and sites of major battles and campaigns on the other.
Educational Materials Associates.

Crossroads K-16 Curriculum:
"Now We Are Engaged in a Great Civil War: 1848–1880"

Includes objectives and description of lessons/activities for students grade 4. Topics are organized in three lessons: "Slavery and the Underground Railroad"; "The People of the Civil War"; and "After the Civil War: Segregation."
http://ericir.syr.edu/Virtual/Lessons/crossroads

Lesson Plan—5th grade

Includes a letter-writing experience about the Civil War.
http://www.d46.k12.ilus/lesplans/civwar.html

National Archives teaching kits

These boxed teaching units cover many aspects of American history, including "The Civil War: Soldiers and Civilians." Each

unit, recommended for grades 7–12, includes objectives, lessons, activities, and an annotated bibliography.
SIRS, Inc. Publishers.

Selected Civil War Photographs Collection
Library of Congess Civil War Homepage
1,118 images from the Civil War, many
from Mathew Brady's works.
http://rs6.loc.gov/cwphome.html

Small Planet Communications Lesson Plan: The Civil War
This is a literature-based unit which includes period background, activities, and links to other Civil War sites.
http://www.smplanet.com/civilwar/civilwar.html

Social Studies Lesson Plans and Resources
This site includes one of the most comprehensive sites of links for teaching many topics and aspects in social studies.
http://www.csun.edu/~hcedu013/

Stratford Hall Plantation Seminar on Slavery for Secondary School Teachers of History and Social Studies
Jeanne A. Calhoun, Director of Research and Education
Stratford Hall Plantation, Stratford, VA 22558
FAX: (804) 493-8006
e-mail: shpedu@nnn.edgeinc.com

Teaching with Documents: Using Primary Sources from the National Archives
Washington, D.C.: National Archives

Teaching with Historic Places
The National Register of Historic Places has a number of sites of interest including "Aboard the Underground Railroad." It also has a set of fifty-five lesson plans, nine of which are related to the Civil War:
Chatham Plantation: Witness to the Civil War
Choices and Commitment: The Soldiers at Gettysburg
The Battle of Stones River: The Soldiers' Story

Fort Pickens and the Outbreak of the Civil War
Clara Barton's House: Home of the American Red Cross
First Battle of Manassas: An End to Innocence
Andersonville: Prisoner of War Camp
The Old Courthouse in St. Louis: Yesterday and Today
When Rice Was King

Facsimilies of original documents of the Civil War era
Jackdaw Publications
PO Box 503
Amawalk, NY 10501
(914) 962-6911
http://www.cr.nps.gov.nr/nrhome.html

Appendix

National Standards for United States History

We have included the national standards for the period that led up to the Civil War, the Civil War, and Reconstruction. For chapters 2 through 7, we have included all of the focus books in charts indicating which of the standards are addressed in the content of the books.

ERA 4 • Expansion and Reform (1801–1861)

Standard 1: United States territorial expansion between 1801 and 1861, and how it affected relations with external powers and Native Americans

Standard 2: How the industrial revolution, the rapid expansion of slavery, and the westward movement changed the lives of Americans and led toward regional tensions

    2A: Demonstrate understanding of how the factory system and the transportation and market revolutions shaped regional patterns of economic development.

    2B: Demonstrate understanding of the first era of American industrialization.

    2C: Demonstrate understanding of the rapid growth of slavery after 1800 and how African Americans coped with the "peculiar institution."

2D: Demonstrate understanding of the settlement of the West.

Standard 3: The extension, restriction, and reorganization of political democracy after 1800

> **3A:** Demonstrate understanding of the changing character of American political life in "the age of common man."

> **3B:** Demonstrate understanding of how the debates over slavery influenced politics and sectionalism.

Standard 4: The sources and character of reform movements in the antebellum period and what the reforms accomplished or failed to accomplish.

> **4A:** Demonstrate understanding of the abolitionist movement.

> **4B:** Demonstrate understanding of how the Second Great Awakening, transcendentalism, and utopianism affected reform.

> **4C:** Demonstrate understanding of changing gender roles and the roles of different groups of women.

ERA 5 ▪ Civil War and Reconstruction (1850–1877)

Standard 1: The causes of the Civil War

> **1A:** Demonstrate understanding of how the North and South differed and how politics and ideologies led to the Civil War.

Standard 2: The course and character of the Civil War and its effects on the American people

> **2A:** Demonstrate understanding of how the resources of the Union and Confederacy affected the course of the war.

> **2B:** Demonstrate understanding of the social experience of the war on the battlefield and homefront.

Standard 3: How various reconstruction plans succeeded or failed

3A: Demonstrate understanding of the political controversy over Reconstruction.

3B: Demonstrate understanding of the Reconstruction programs to transform social relations in the South.

3C: Demonstrate understanding of the successes and failures of Reconstruction in the South, North, and West.

Chapter 2
A Troubled Land

ERA 4 Standards

Author	2A	2B	2C	3B	4A
Catton	■		■		■
Frank			■		
Hansen			■	■	■
Haskins	■			■	
Myers	■		■	■	■
Robertson	■		■	■	■
Ruby		■		■	■
Sandler	■		■		■
Smith	■	■	■	■	■
Turner			■		■
Walter			■	■	■
Zeinert			■	■	■

ERA 5 Standards

Author	IA	2A	2B	3A	3B	3C
Catton	■	■	■	■	■	■
Frank						
Hansen	■	■	■			
Haskins	■	■			■	

Chapter 2
A Troubled Land

ERA 5 Standards

Author	1A	2A	2B	3A	3B	3C
Myers	■	■	■	■	■	■
Robertson	■	■	■			
Ruby						
Sandler	■	■	■	■	■	■
Smith	■	■				
Turner						
Walter						
Zeinert						

Chapter 3
Struggling to Be Free

ERA 4

Author	2A	2B	2C	3B	4A	4C
Feelings						
Freedman	■	■	■	■	■	■
Hamilton			■	■		
Hansen	■	■	■	■	■	■
Haskins			■	■		
Hooks			■			
Hopkinson			■			
Johnson	■	■	■	■	■	■
Lasky			■	■	■	■
Lester			■			
Lyons			■			■
McKissack	■	■	■	■	■	■
McPherson	■	■	■	■	■	■
Meriwether			■			

Chapter 3
Struggling to Be Free

ERA 4

Author	2A	2B	2C	3B	4A	4C
Paulsen	■	■	■	■	■	
Ringgold	■	■	■	■	■	■
Winter	■	■	■	■	■	

ERA 5

Author	1A	2A	2B	3A	3B	3C
Feelings						
Freedman			■			
Hamilton						
Hansen			■			
Haskins						
Hooks						
Hopkinson						
Johnson	■	■				
Lasky						
Lester			■		■	■
Lyons	■		■			
McKissack	■	■				
McPherson			■			
Meriwether	■	■	■	■	■	■
Paulsen	■					
Ringgold	■					
Winter	■					

Chapter 4
Those Who Made a Difference

ERA 4

Author	2A	2B	2C	3A	4A	4B	4C
Archer							
Brown					■		
Douglass			■				
Ferris			■				
Freedman	■	■	■		■		■
Fritz					■	■	■
Hamilton			■	■	■		
Hargrove	■	■	■		■		■
Lincoln							
Marrin							
McKissack (*Rebels*)			■		■		
McKissack (*Sojourner*)	■		■		■		
Miller	■	■	■		■		
Petry			■		■		■
Quackenbush	■	■	■		■		■
Schroeder	■	■	■		■		■
Stepto			■		■		
Whittier							

ERA 5

Author	1A	2A	2B	3A	3B	3C
Archer	■	■		■		
Brown	■	■	■		■	
Douglass	■				■	
Ferris			■			■
Freedman	■	■	■			
Fritz						

Chapter 4
Those Who Made a Difference

ERA 5

Author	1A	2A	2B	3A	3B	3C
Hamilton						
Hargrove	■	■				
Lincoln	■	■	■			
Marrin	■	■	■			
McKissack (*Rebels*)						
McKissack (*Sojourner*)				■		
Miller	■	■	■			
Petry			■			
Quackenbush	■	■	■			
Schroeder	■	■				
Stepto	■				■	
Whittier			■			

Chapter 5
War Experiences

ERA 4

Author	2A	2B	2C	3B	4A
Beatty (*Charley*)					
Beatty (*Jayhawker*)	■	■	■	■	■
Bolotin					
Bunting					
Cox	■	■	■	■	■
Crane					
Fleishman					

Chapter 5
War Experiences

ERA 4

Author	2A	2B	2C	3B	4A
Kent *(all)*					
Mettger	■	■	■	■	■
Murphy *(Boy's War)*					
Murphy *(Gettysburg)*					
Nixon					
Phillips					
Polacco					
Ray					
Shaara					
Wisler					

ERA 5

Author	1A	2A	2B
Beatty *(Charley)*		■	■
Beatty *(Jayhawker)*	■		
Bolotin	■	■	■
Bunting			■
Cox		■	■
Crane	■	■	■
Fleischman	■	■	■
Kent *(all)*	■	■	■
Mettger			■
Murphy *(Boy's War)*	■	■	■

Chapter 5
War Experiences

ERA 5

Author	1A	2A	2B
Murphy *(Gettysburg)*		■	■
Nixon	■	■	■
Phillips		■	■
Polacco			■
Ray		■	■
Shaara		■	■
Wisler	■	■	■

Chapter 6
On the Homefront

ERA 4

Author	2A	2B	2C	3B	4A	4C
Armstrong						
Beatty						
Chang						■
Collier & Collier						
Fleischman			■	■	■	■
Forrester						
Holland	■	■		■	■	■
Hunt			■	■		
Josephs			■			
Kantor						
Reit			■	■		■
Rinaldi *(House)*	■					■
Rinaldi *(Dress)*	■					

Chapter 6
On the Homefront

ERA 4

Author	2A	2B	2C	3B	4A	4C
Shura				■		■
Smith	■	■	■	■	■	■

ERA 5

Author	IA	2A	2B
Armstrong			■
Beatty	■	■	■
Chang			■
Collier & Collier		■	■
Fleischman			■
Forrester			■
Holland			■
Hunt			■
Josephs			■
Kantor		■	■
Reit			■
Rinaldi *(House)*	■		■
Rinaldi *(Dress)*	■	■	■
Shura			■
Smith	■	■	■

Chapter 7
Rebuilding the Nation

ERA 5

Author	IA	2B	3A	3B	3C
Beatty			■	■	
Calvert		■	■		
Hansen	■			■	■
Hansen	■			■	■
Mettger			■	■	■
Paulsen	■		■	■	
Reeder			■	■	
Robinet			■	■	
Smith		■		■	■

Index of Authors and Titles

Chapter 2: A Troubled Land

Focus Books

More Books

Chapter 3: Struggling to Be Free

Focus Books

More Books

Chapter 4: Those Who Made a Difference

Focus Books

More Books

Chapter 5: War Experiences

Focus Books

More Books

Chapter 6: On the Homefront

Focus Books

Chapter 7: Rebuilding the Nation

Focus Books

STONEHAM PUBLIC LIBRARY

3 1509 00543 9149

016.9737 Stephens, Elaine C.
STEP
            Learning about-- the
            Civil War

	DATE DUE		

STONEHAM PUBLIC LIBRARY
431 MAIN STREET
STONEHAM, MA 02180